# JOURNAL FOR THE STUDY OF THE OLD TESTAMENT
## SUPPLEMENT SERIES
# 224

*Editors*
David J.A. Clines
Philip R. Davies

*Executive Editor*
John Jarick

*Editorial Board*
Robert P. Carroll, Richard J. Coggins, Alan Cooper, J. Cheryl Exum,
John Goldingay, Robert P. Gordon, Norman K. Gottwald,
Andrew D.H. Mayes, Carol Meyers, Patrick D. Miller

Sheffield Academic Press

# Reliable Characters in the Primary History

## Profiles of Moses, Joshua, Elijah and Elisha

### Paul J. Kissling

Journal for the Study of the Old Testament
Supplement Series 224

Copyright © 1996 Sheffield Academic Press

Published by Sheffield Academic Press Ltd
Mansion House
19 Kingfield Road
Sheffield S11 9AS
England

Printed on acid-free paper in Great Britain
by Bookcraft Ltd
Midsomer Norton, Bath

British Library Cataloguing in Publication Data

A catalogue record for this book is available
from the British Library

ISBN 1-85075-617-1

# CONTENTS

ACKNOWLEDGMENTS

The following work is a revised version of my doctoral dissertation, written under the supervision of Professor David J.A. Clines at the Department of Biblical Studies at Sheffield. Professor Clines's constructive criticism and encouragement kept me from many errors and his creative questioning was a real inspiration to me. I am grateful. My thanks go also to the Department of Biblical Studies at Sheffield for helping to create such a stimulating environment in which to study and write. I would like to thank the Warden and staff of St Deinol's Residential Library, Hawarden, Clwyd, where most of the thesis was actually written. Finally, and most importantly, to my wife Cathy and our sons, Joshua and Jeremy, who believed in me, and encouraged me and helped me in more ways than I can remember much less repay, all my thanks and love.

# ABBREVIATIONS

| AB | Anchor Bible |
|---|---|
| *AJT* | *American Journal of Theology* |
| AnBib | Analecta Biblica |
| ATANT | Abhandlungen zur Theologie des Alten und Neuen Testaments |
| ATD | Das Alte Testament Deutsch |
| AV | Authorized Version |
| BAT | Die Botschaft des AT, Stuttgart |
| BDB | F. Brown, S.R. Driver and C.A. Briggs, *Hebrew and English Lexicon of the Old Testament* |
| *BHS* | *Biblia hebraica stuttgartensia* |
| *Bib* | *Biblica* |
| BZAW | Beihefte zur *ZAW* |
| CBC | Cambridge Bible Commentary |
| *CBQ* | *Catholic Biblical Quarterly* |
| DJD | Discoveries in the Judaean Desert |
| DSB(OT) | Daily Study Bible (Old Testament) |
| *EncJud* | *Encyclopaedia Judaica* |
| GNB | Good News Bible |
| HKAT | Handkommentar zum Alten Testament |
| *IB* | *Interpreter's Bible* |
| ICC | International Critical Commentary |
| *IDB* | G.A. Buttrick (ed.), *Interpreter's Dictionary of the Bible* |
| *IDBSup* | *IDB*, Supplementary Volume |
| *Int* | *Interpretation* |
| IntBC | Interpretation, A Bible Commentary for Teaching and Preaching |
| *ISBE* | G.W. Bromiley (ed.), *International Standard Bible Encylopedia*, rev. edn |
| ISBL | Indiana Studies in Bible and Literature |
| ITC | International Theological Commentary |
| JB | Jerusalem Bible |
| *JBL* | *Journal of Biblical Literature* |
| *JSOT* | *Journal for the Study of the Old Testament* |
| JSOTSup | *Journal for the Study of the Old Testament*, Supplement Series |
| KHAT | Kurzer Handkommentar zum AT, Tübingen |
| NAB | New American Bible |
| NCBC | New Century Bible Commentary |
| NEB | New English Bible |
| NICOT | New International Commentary on the Old Testament |

| | |
|---|---|
| NIV | New International Version |
| NJPSV | New Jewish Publication Society Version |
| NRSV | New Revised Standard Version |
| OTL | Old Testament Library |
| REB | Revised English Bible |
| *RGG* | *Religion in Geschichte und Gegenwart* |
| RSV | Revised Standard Version |
| *RSR* | *Recherches de science religieuse* |
| SBLDS | SBL Dissertation Series |
| SBT | Studies in Biblical Theology |
| *TTod* | *Theology Today* |
| *TDOT* | G.J. Botterweck and H. Ringgren (eds.), *Theological Dictionary of the Old Testament* |
| TOTC | Tyndale Old Testament Commentaries |
| *VT* | *Vetus Testamentum* |
| VTSup | *Vetus Testamentum*, Supplements |
| WBC | Word Biblical Commentary |
| *ZAW* | *Zeitschrift für die alttestamentliche Wissenschaft* |

INTRODUCTION

The aim of this work is to investigate the reliability of Moses (within Deuteronomy), Joshua, Elijah, and Elisha, as these characters are presented in the final form of the Primary History.[1]

## 1. *Final Form Analysis*

I have chosen to do final form analysis, not out of some desire to return to a naive, pre-critical reading of the Bible (which in any case tended to oversimplify the portrayals of biblical characters even more than historical-critical scholarship), nor from a cavalier dismissal of the aims and procedures of traditional scholarship, but out of adesire to expose the subtlety of narrative portrayal in the texts as we have them. While it is not one of my purposes to address the complex questions of sources and the process of redaction, the sort of analysis which I am doing can make a real contribution to forming the foundation upon which the question of sources and redaction can be re-examined. This is especially important in the current climate in which the hypothetical sources and history of redaction of biblical narratives are once again the subject of intense debate.[2]

My work is not an attempt to deny the rather obvious fact that the biblical books in the Primary History have a long and complex pre-history.[3] Rather it constitutes an argument that these texts must be read with great sensitivity as the absolute prerequisite for any investigation of

1. For the term 'Primary History' see Freedman 1976: 226.
2. The debate on the pentateuchal sources can be seen by comparing the views of Rendtorff 1990; Van Seters 1975; 1983; and Whybray 1987.
3. Tigay (1982) has attempted to demonstrate the likelihood of such a complex pre-history by analogy with analysis of the various extant forms of the Gilgamesh Epic. While I would still emphasize that for the Primary History the sources are hypothetical, and Tigay's work only argues for *some* complex development, and does not support a particular hypothesis such as the Documentary Hypothesis or Noth's Deuteronomistic History, his essential point remains a convincing one.

sources or redactional history. My work is one small part of the necessary groundwork for such investigation.

One of the notable features of the Hebrew Bible narratives is the vividness with which major characters are portrayed. Although generally lacking in the detailed physical description and in-depth psychological analysis by which characters in the modern novel are given literary life, they nevertheless create in the reader a sense of their lifelikeness. As Robert Alter has written, 'from these laconic texts emerge characters who...have been etched as indelibly vivid individuals in the imagination of a hundred generations' (Alter 1981: 27). In my view it is regrettable that the atomistic tendency (Clines 1978: 7-9) which has sometimes dominated traditional biblical scholarship's approach to biblical stories has unintentionally resulted in the loss, as legitimate objects of scholarly inquiry, of the complex unified portraits of the characters which those stories present. Not that interest in major characters has ceased in historical-critical scholarship. On the contrary, we continue to see a steady stream of books and articles written from this perspective about Moses, for example.[4] But the picture of major characters that emerges from such analysis is often reductive, lacking the subtlety and depth which the texts as we have them display.

There is also a marked tendency, at least in terms of characters who are regarded as heroes—the deuteronomic Moses, Joshua, Elijah, and Elisha are prime examples—to idealize the characters by emphasizing the positive aspects of their portrayals, and minimizing or ignoring the evidence for negative aspects. In some cases source- or tradition-criticism has facilitated this process of idealization. For example, by removing Deut. 32.48-52 as a P insertion, the obvious conflict between Moses' and Yahweh's points of view over Moses' exclusion from the promised land (1.37; 3.26; 4.21) is lost, and a vital clue to the discontinuity in viewpoint between the narrator, whose point of view is apparently given expression through Yahweh, and Moses is overlooked. Other evidence of this conflict is dismissed or explained away, and Moses as a character consequently emerges either as an innocent suffering mediator (von Rad 1966b: 45) or as a deeply tragic figure (Barzel 1974). As I will attempt to show in the chapter on the deuteronomic Moses, such a reading of the portrayal of Moses is somewhat simplistic and idealizing.

4.   Some representative studies are Gunkel 1930; Buber 1958; von Rad 1960; Auerbach 1975; and Coats 1988.

## 2. *The Primary History as the Narrative Context for the Present Work*

The narrative context for the analysis of Moses (within Deuteronomy), Joshua, Elijah, and Elisha in this work is the Primary History or 'Enneateuch',[5] that is, the books of Genesis to 2 Kings, excluding Ruth. No doubt there are other narrative contexts which could be chosen. One could easily take Polzin's approach (1980) and treat the entirety of the Deuteronomic History or alternatively treat each character within the context of their respective books, Deuteronomy for Moses, Joshua for Joshua, Kings for Elijah and Elisha.

My reasons for selecting the Primary History as the context are several. First, the Primary History has a unified story-line which begins with creation and ends with Israel's exile. To use only part of that story as the broader narrative context from which our characters are to be analyzed tends to separate the portrayal of characters from the plot in which the characters are enmeshed in an artificial way. Examples of the intertwining of plot and narrative portrayal in the Primary History abound. Joshua's oath against the rebuilder of Jericho (Josh. 6.26) finds its fulfilment immediately prior, textually speaking, to the introduction of Elijah (1 Kgs 16.34). Part of the portrayal of Joshua is tied up with the later plot in which his oath is fulfilled. Similarly, the fact that immediately following the report of the fulfilment of Joshua's oath, Elijah makes a similar sort of oath, which also is fulfilled (1 Kgs 17.1, 7) links Elijah to the antecedent plot and Joshua to the subsequent plot. Elijah and Elisha are inseparably intertwined in the present form of the narrative and Elijah is often portrayed as parallel to Moses, both in Deuteronomy and in Exodus to Numbers. Moses is repeatedly portrayed in Deuteronomy as referring back to and interpreting the events recorded in the earlier narratives in Genesis to Numbers. While other examples of the intertwining of plot and narrative portrayal will arise in the course of the discussion, the above are sufficient to show the fruitfulness of analyzing character in the light of both the subsequent and antecedent plot within the Primary History as well as the artificiality of separating them. The overall coherence (Clines 1990: 85-105) of the plot of the Primary History makes it a natural, that is, non-artificial, starting point for a final form analysis of the portrayal of our figures.

A second reason for choosing the Primary History is the fact that the

---

5.   For the term see Eissfeldt 1965: 136, 156.

division of the Primary History into 'books' is rather artificial. While we do not know with certainty when or even if the Primary History was ever conceived of as a narrative block, the existence of the story-line is *prima facie* evidence that the narrative block is older than the division into books. The artificiality of the division between Samuel and Kings has often been noted (Eissfeldt 1965: 134-36, 241-43). Joshua follows directly upon the end of Deuteronomy, and Deuteronomy itself is tied to the earlier books both by story-line and by the many references which Moses is portrayed as making to previous events in Israel's history. As von Rad has noted (1966a), a series of prophecies and their fulfillments tie some major portion of the 'former prophets' together. Undoubtedly the text as we have it has been stitched together, but it is by no means any longer to be assumed that we have a scholarly consensus about when and how this was done. What we do have is a series of books which, in some sense, hang together. It is the stance of this work that it is best to start from what we know and this stance has influenced the decision to use the Primary History as the broader narrative context in which the specific narratives in view are studied. While an interpreter may legitimately choose to read a story within any of a variety of literary contexts, the Primary History is, I would argue, the least artificial context for final form analysis.

A third consideration is the fruitfulness of this choice for examining the question of the reliability of characters. Let me give two examples of the interesting results which arise from reading within the context of the Primary History. First, a close comparison of the version of events in the life of Moses recounted by the narrator in Exodus to Numbers with Moses' version of those same events in Deuteronomy brings to light in a clearer way the fact that the narrator's main character, Moses, is not always portrayed as representing the narrator's point of view. Polzin rightly sees divergence in point of view between the narrator and Moses within Deuteronomy itself (1980: 25-72) but treats this divergence as an internal dialogue designed to bolster what he sees as the Deuteronomist's implicit claim to be the prophet Moses had predicted in 18.15-20 (1980: 35, 61). He fails in my view to take sufficient notice of the narrator's denial in 34.10 that anyone, which must include the narrator, had even arisen in Israel who was a prophet like Moses. By contrasting the narrator's version of events with the interpretation of those events which Moses is portrayed as making, the fact that the narrator does not present Moses in a simplistically positive fashion and that he is not always a conveyor of the narrator's viewpoint is brought into sharper focus.

A second example is the problem which prophets and prophecy pose for the narrator in Kings and the way this could influence the reader's evaluation of the reliability of Moses, the founder of prophecy. In my analysis of the narrative portrayal of Elijah and Elisha within Kings I argue that the narrator has a complex, as opposed to a simplistically positive, attitude towards prophets and prophecy. For example, preceding or enmeshed within the Elijah narratives are three passages in which the narrator leads the reader to hesitate about prophecy. In the first a genuine prophet lies to a 'man of God' in order to convince him to disobey a clear command which the man of God had personally received from Yahweh even though disobedience to the command carried the death penalty (1 Kgs 13.1-32). How, the reader is led to ask, was the man of God to know that the prophet was lying the first time when he convinced the man of God to disobey Yahweh's command, and telling the truth the second time when he delivered an oracle of judgment against the man of God? The second passage (1 Kgs 20.35, 36) sees a prophet attacked and killed by a lion for refusing to strike another prophet when the latter demands he do so. Again, the reader asks, 'How could the first prophet have known that disobeying such an unusual request would result in being eaten by a lion?' In the third (1 Kgs 22.19-23), Micaiah ben Imlah claims that Yahweh sent a lying spirit to deceive the 400 prophets whom Ahab and Jehoshaphat had previously consulted. If Micaiah is to be believed, the reader is led to ask, 'How can anyone ever trust a prophet's word since it may be a lie sent from Yahweh to harm you?' If Micaiah is lying, why do his words related to the lying spirit which predicted Israel's defeat and Ahab's death come true? When prophecy is portrayed as such a complicated phenomenon, the reader re-evaluates Moses and asks, 'Why should the founder of prophecy in Israel, the pre-eminent prophet (Deut. 34.10), be unquestioningly trusted?'

By first presenting events as they 'really happened' (in Exodus to Numbers), and then reporting Moses' reinterpretation of those events in a self-justifying way in Deuteronomy, the narrator leads the reader to question other aspects of Moses' activity. 'If Moses is self-serving in the way he retells the past', the reader asks, 'is he also self-serving in other aspects of his activity?' One such aspect is his prophetic activity. When coupled with the subsequent context in Kings, which leads the reader to hesitate about prophets and prophecy in general, this narrator-inspired questioning of Moses' prophetic activity yields surprising results. When Moses is portrayed as altering the word which Yahweh gives him, which can only be discovered by comparing Yahweh's version in Exodus and Leviticus,[6] how is the reader to evaluate what Moses has done? Is he to be trusted in his prophetic activity completely or with some reservations? If Moses, in delivering Yahweh's word—in this case the Torah—changes it, do other prophets change it? Are they to be trusted? When no word of Yahweh is explicitly said by the narrator to be given to Elijah, is Elijah to be trusted when he claims he has a word from Yahweh? These interesting questions arise from treating the Primary History as the wider narrative context for our analysis.

In traditional exegesis, heroes such as Moses and Elijah are unquestioningly deemed to be the vehicle for communicating the narratorial point of view. One of the results of the present work is to problematize this assumption. Using the final form of the Primary History, as opposed to the Deuteronomic History, the Pentateuch, or the individual books, as the narrative context makes the distinction in point of view between the narrator and the points of view attributed to characters more striking.

## 3. *The Selection of Major Characters*

The choice of characters studied in this work is based on a desire to avoid duplicating the work of others (Gunn 1978; 1980; Fokkelman 1981; Miscall 1986), the necessary constraints on length, and to a degree on the personal interests and circumstances of the author. The term 'major' requires some comment. I use the term to identify characters who appear in several scenes and who are complex characters in the literary sense. It is to be regretted that contemporary literary theory has done less to advance our understanding of character portrayal than any other major component of narrative analysis.[7] Theory has not advanced much beyond E.M. Forster's distinction between 'flat' and 'round' characters (1963: 73-77). According to Forster, flat characters are those constructed around a single idea or quality which they always display, that is, they do not develop. Round characters by contrast do develop and are multifaceted. Forster himself recognizes that these two categories are too

6.    In the final form we have no record of Moses ever actually delivering many of the laws in Leviticus.

7.    Rimmon-Kenan 1983: 29. One reason for this is the tendency in structuralist thought to reduce character to a series of functions (Culler 1975: 230-38).

neat, for he states of flat characters, 'When there is more than one factor in them, we get the beginning of the curve towards the round' (p. 73). Additionally, as Rimmon-Kenan (1983: 40-41) notes, within his apparently simple categories Forster 'seems to confuse two criteria which do not always overlap'. Characters can be complex and unchanging or simple and developing.

The four major characters under analysis in this work are multi-faceted, complex characters. Whether it is helpful to speak of character development depends upon the specific individual in view. For example, does Moses develop as a character in Deuteronomy? The virtual absence of narrative in the book makes it inappropriate to speak of development, but by any reasonable criterion Moses is a complex character deserving of Berlin's description, 'full-fledged character in the modern sense' (1983: 31). About such full-fledged characters she explains:

> They are realistically portrayed—their emotions and motivations are either made explicit or are left to be discerned by the reader from hints provided in the narrative... [They have] a broader range of traits (not all belonging to the same class of people) and about [them] we know more than is necessary for the plot (Berlin 1983: 31-32).

About each of our four characters we are told more than is strictly necessary for the story-line to proceed and each has a mixture of traits which are not ordinarily confined to one select class of people.

### 4. *The Means of Narrative Portrayal*

Literary critics, both inside and outside of biblical scholarship, have identified a variety of narratorial techniques for portraying characters. While our specific texts have not received thorough analysis by such literary critics, and we must therefore rely mainly on our own independent analysis, the way in which narrators in general lead their readers to construct a portrait of a text's characters, and the way in which other biblical narrators do so, can serve as a useful guide for what to look for in our analysis. We may be surprised to find that our narrator uses completely different means of narrative portrayal from other narrators. While we must always be open to this possibility, an analysis of how other narrators portray characters will serve as a useful starting point.

Shlomith Rimmon-Kenan helpfully observes,

> In principle, *any element* in the text may serve as an indicator of character... [b]ut there are elements which are most frequently, though not exclusively, associated with characterization...' (1983: 59, my emphasis).

It is important to remember this when we recognize that plot and character are inextricably interwoven[8] and that biblical narratives are generally 'plot-dominated' rather than 'character-dominated'.[9] Given this cautionary note, we may concur with Adele Berlin's general statement:

> The reader reconstructs a character from the information provided him in the discourse: he is told by the statements and evaluations of the narrator and other characters, and he infers from the speech and action of the character himself (Berlin 1963: 34).

More specifically, Rimmon-Kenan divides the means of character portrayal into direct definition, indirect presentation, and reinforcement by analogy (1983: 59-70). By 'direct definition' she means those statements, by the most authoritative voice in the text, in which a trait of a character is mentioned directly, for example the narrator's statement in 1 Kgs 18.3, 'Obadiah greatly feared Yahweh'.

Indirect presentation entails the narrator's having the character display and exemplify a trait rather than mentioning it explicitly. This is done by means of the actions, speech, external appearance, and environment of a character. The portrayal of a character's actions are one way of revealing the nature of a person. In plot-centered narratives such as the Bible's, a character's actions are, as Bar-Efrat (1989: 77) notes, 'the foremost means of characterization'. A single action may not be evidence for an enduring trait, but a repetition of such action or of other actions indicative of the same trait would be. Even a unique action, however, tells us something about a character. Ahab habitually crumbles into submission before strong characters, whether the character be Naboth, Elijah, or Jezebel. Elijah, on the other hand, only once runs away in fear (1 Kgs 19.3), but it is an action that occurs at a crucial point in the story and so tells us something about Elijah. Action may sometimes be described by the lack of action (Ahab takes no action to stop Jezebel from plotting against Naboth) or even the contemplation of an action.

---

8.    Note Henry James's proverbial remark, 'What is character but the determination of incident? What is incident but the illustration of character?' (1963: 88).

9.    Cf. Berlin's comment (1983: 34) 'character tends to be subordinate to plot'. Todorov, in challenging Henry James's ideal of character as psychology, writes of an entire tendency in literature in which the actions of figures are not there to 'illustrate' character. On the contrary the characters are 'subservient to the action...[M]oreover the word "character" signifies something altogether different from psychological coherence or the description of idiosyncrasy' (1977: 66). While not specifically mentioning it, Todorov's remark surely applies to the Hebrew Bible.

A character's speech is also an important indirect means of portrayal. When Samuel chastises Saul in 1 Sam. 13.13, 14 for no apparent reason, since Saul had waited the time set by Samuel (v. 8), his words display the harshness of Samuel's attitude toward Saul more than they inform us of the narrator's evaluation of what Saul had done in taking a priest's prerogative by offering the burnt offering (Gunn 1978: 33-40). When Obadiah greets Elijah with the words, 'Is it you, *my lord* Elijah?', Elijah's response, 'It is I. Go, tell *your lord*, "Behold, Elijah is here"', tells us something about Elijah (1 Kgs 18.7, 8). His rejection of Obadiah's professed loyalty to him is part of a pattern in the portrayal of Elijah as one who has difficulty in accepting the loyalty of others to Yahweh. A prominent feature of recorded speech in the Hebrew Bible is the importance given to the way in which the narrators and other speakers refer to other people, a phenomenon helpfully analysed by Berlin (1983: 18, 59-61) under the term 'naming'.

While the physical appearance of characters is given great prominence in modern stories, the biblical narratives are rather sparse in this regard.[10] When we are given such information, however, it usually serves to further the plot and is of special significance. It is not just to give the reader a memorable visual image that we are told that Elijah was 'hairy' (2 Kgs 1.8), nor that Elisha was 'bald' (2 Kgs 2.23). The contrast in their physical appearances leads the reader to contrast them and compare them in the ensuing narrative.

The physical surroundings and human environment of characters are often trait-connoting. The social class of Elisha, for example, can perhaps be roughly reconstructed from seemingly incidental facts learned from the narrative. He stays periodically with a well-to-do woman (2 Kgs 8.3). He and his band of prophets live together and are able to build a larger place of residence, albeit with a borrowed axe (2 Kgs 6.1-7). He is economically secure enough to refuse Naaman's offer of a gift (2 Kgs 5.16-24), yet during a famine, as well as during a financial crisis, he resorts to miraculous means of provision (2 Kgs 4.1-7, 38-44). While none of these pieces of information helps the reader to locate Elisha in a specific social class, they do contribute to his portrayal as someone who is not in abject poverty but who nevertheless rejects the unnecessary accumulation of wealth.

Rimmon-Kenan's third means of narrative portrayal, reinforcement

---

10. 'There is no precise detailed description of the physical appearance of characters in biblical narratives' (Bar-Efrat 1989: 48).

by analogy, is for her only a means of reaffirming and underlining what has already been accomplished by other means. She cites the example of Laura in Katherine Anne Porter's *Flowering Judas* whose 'rigidity of dress parallel[s] that of her personality' (1983: 67-68). She cites 'analogous names and landscapes' and 'analogy between characters' as techniques used in analogical reinforcement. In the Bible the widespread use of etymologically significant names is striking. For example, the name of Obadiah, 'Yahweh's servant', reinforces the narrator's portrayal of his piety. The use of 'the wilderness' as the place where Elijah goes when feeling self-defeated (1 Kgs 19.4) is an example of analogous landscape. Of particular importance in the texts under analysis here is the analogy between characters. The allusions and parallels to, and contrasts with, Moses are a prominent feature of the portraits of Joshua and Elijah. The similarities, and particularly the contrasts, between Elijah and Elisha are absolutely crucial in the portrayal of the latter.

## 5. *The Reliability of Characters*

One rather obvious notion, drawn from literary theory in a broad sense, which plays a significant part in this work is the distinction in point of view between the narrator and the narrator's characters. The words which a narrator puts in the mouths of characters may or may not represent the point of view of the narrator. Further, a character's speech and/or actions may or may not have the narrator's approval, morally or ideologically. When a character's speech and/or actions always represent the narrator's point of view and always have the narrator's moral and ideological approval, that character is said to be a thoroughly reliable character. When a character's speech and/or actions do not convey the narrator's point of view and therefore do not have the narrator's moral or ideological approval, the character is said to be unreliable in that particular instance.

While the convention that a distinction must be made between the point of view of the narrator and the narrator's characters in a work has guided reading from ancient times, it is often applied to the reading of the Bible in a rather simplistic fashion. It is often tacitly assumed that prominent characters in the biblical stories are either good or bad in some simplistic sense and that the moral ambiguity that is so much a part of contemporary literary characterization is not found in the Bible. We are led to believe that Moses, in deuteronomistic contexts at least, is beyond reproach (Miller 1988, 1989), and yet the portrayals of characters such as Saul, Samuel, David and Jehu, not to mention Elijah and Elisha, make it clear that in texts usually assumed to be influenced by deuteronomistic thinking, if not actually written by one or more deuteronomists, complex, morally or ideologically ambiguous characters are quite prominent. The assumption that certain characters' speech and/or actions meet with the approval of the narrator unless such approval is explicitly denied is the most prominent effect of this simplistic approach to the biblical narratives. This assumption is challenged in this work several times.

Eslinger makes a similar point. In referring to how many contemporary biblical scholars assume the great speeches of certain characters in the Deuteronomistic History coincide with the narrator's point of view, he writes:

> This canonized reading of the narrative is accepted by scholars and believers alike, an accord that seems more expressive of the common place of contrition and guilt in the Judeo-Christian psyche than of the perspective of the narrative. Unfortunately the collective religious psyche of biblical readers has refused to allow the Dtr's representation to have its own say about the way of God with man. Readers have failed to hear the narrator's subtle insurgent voice because they are so attuned to hear and accept the clamorous pieties of the human characters of the Bible, with whose existential predicament and religious sentiments they can so easily identify. With regard to the great orations in the Dtr narrative, this means that readers have been disposed to hear the narrative in the light of [*sic*] the orations rather than to read the orations in the light of their existing narrative context. Contemporary scholarly readers see one, undifferentiated plane of utterance in the narrative; if there are discrepancies in the views expressed they are to be comprehended in terms of literary history and the multiplicity of writers who have had a hand in creating the narrative (1989: 228-29).

## 6. *Reader-Response Criticism*

The present work uses a form of reader-response criticism[11] where the focus of analysis is on the response of real or imaginary readers to a

---

11. I use this rather catch-all phrase in the broad sense in which Tompkins (1980: ix) does:

> Reader-response criticism is not a conceptually unified critical position, but a term that has come to be associated with the work of critics who use the words *reader, the reading process*, and *response* to mark out an area for investigation.

text, rather than the real author's intent, as in traditional literary criticism, or upon the meaning which a text supposedly 'has', as in New Criticism. Reader-response criticism recognizes the essential role which the reader plays within the reading process in the creation of meaning and seeks to foreground that role by asking what the reader's response to a text is or is likely to be. In this work I have chosen to construct an imaginary ancient reader of the Primary History and attempted to analyze what that reader's likely response would be to the question of the reliability of our four major characters.

It is now common in literary criticism, especially reader-response criticism, to conceptualize the reading process in terms of communication between three pairs of persons as shown in the chart below.[12]

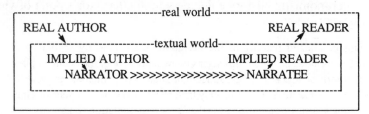

### a. *Real Authors and Readers*

The first pair of participants in the reading process are the real author and the real reader who are extra-textual. Real flesh and blood authors write literary works which real flesh and blood readers read. The real authors and readers may or may not communicate effectively. Authors may not get their intention across clearly or they may be vague or ambivalent about intending any meaning at all. Readers may not share the same language or culture, may have a bad memory, be morally deficient, or their own prejudice or situation may cause them to misread the text or read it in a way which its author would deem unfair. Any of these or many other factors may prevent effective communication taking place between the real author and the real reader.

### b. *Ideal Authors and Readers*

The other two pairs of participants in the reading process, the implied author and reader, and the narrator and narratee, are intra-textual, that is, they have no existence outside of the reading process but are idealized theoretical constructs. Such ideal authors and readers communicate

12. The chart is adapted from Chatman 1978: 151.

perfectly. The reader-response critic who is interested in analyzing a work in terms of these theoretical personae, as I am, seeks to present to the scholarly community an analysis of the effect of a work on an ideal reader which is convincing to that community in terms of its stated or implied canons of acceptability. Obviously a critic cannot perfectly determine the intention of an ideal, perfect author nor its effect on an ideal, perfect reader. The critic can only approximate it in a way which the community of which one is a part finds acceptable.[13]

*Narrators and narratees.* In narrative texts there is always implied a person, the narrator, who tells the story to another implied person, the narratee. The narrator, as an idealized construct, communicates perfectly with the narratee, who as another idealized construct, understands the narrator perfectly and accepts the narrator's point of view in every particular.

*Implied authors and readers.* In some narratives competent readers intuitively feel that the narrator does not represent the norms of the work as a whole, but is being used, in much the same way as a narrator uses unreliable characters, to give voice to a point of view that is not identical with the norms of the work (Rimmon-Kenan 1983: 87). When the norms of a work are referred to in personal terms the phrase 'the implied author' is used. The implied author's communication partner in the reading process is 'the implied reader'. The implied reader understands the implied author completely and knows when the narrator is representing the implied author's point of view and when not.

### c. *Unreliable Narrators*
While the implied author of a work can always be conceptually distinguished from the narrator, it is especially in narratives with an unreliable narrator that the distinction between the implied author and the narrator is of practical importance. It is also in works with unreliable narrators that the distinction between the implied reader and the narratee is important since in such narratives the implied reader, in contrast to the narratee,

13. Culler (1975: 124) says,

> The meaning of a poem within the institution of literature is not, one might say, the immediate and spontaneous reaction of individual readers but the meanings which they are willing to accept as both plausible and justifiable when they are explained.

does not always believe the narrator's words or accept the narrator's perspectives.

An example of an unreliable narrator from modern fiction is Holden Caulfield, the mentally confused, adolescent, first-person narrator of Salinger's *The Catcher in the Rye*. Holden is a compulsive liar who frequently contradicts himself. He has an obviously jaundiced view of others and the reader eventually discovers that he is writing from a mental institution about the events surrounding his breakdown. The reader senses, however, that Holden is only the tool of some other voice or norm. This voice calls upon the reader not to believe Holden's lies, nor even necessarily to figure out from Holden's biased statements what really happened, but to empathize with him as a person who is not fundamentally bad, but as one who just does not fit in with modern society's norms and expectations of behavior.

It is often assumed that unreliable narrators are a modern convention and that, therefore, in ancient works such as the Bible, narrators are always reliable. Alter refers to the biblical narratives as 'reliable third person narratives' (1981: 116) and Bar-Efrat observes, 'Biblical narrators' objectivity and lack of tendentiousness in representing characters and events has often been noted' (1989: 32). Similarly, Sternberg (1987: 51) asserts:

> [T]he Bible always tells the truth in that its narrator is *absolutely* and *straightforwardly* reliable. Historians may quarrel with his facts and others call them fiction; but in context his remain accounts of the truth communicated on the highest authority. In terms of the internal premises established by the discourse—and these alone determine reliability in interpretation—the reader cannot go far wrong even if he does little more than follow the statements made and the incidents enacted on the narrative surface. For the narrator who conveys them to him cannot go wrong himself, unlike so many of the *misguided* tellers in modern literature, errant in knowledge and evaluation alike [my emphasis].

But such generalizing statements may be somewhat too hasty.

While it may be typically modern to use unreliable narrators, we should not *assume* that 'primitive' literature cannot display an unreliable narrator. Todorov (1977: 53-65) argues against the very concept of primitive literature, particularly as it involves the imposition of a naive, simplistic aesthetic upon ancient literature. Using the *Odyssey* as his example, Todorov demonstrates how imposing purist ideas of what a good narrative is causes many modern readers to misread the *Odyssey*. This false aesthetic has led to the hypothesizing of redactors and later scribal additions in a fashion reminiscent of traditional biblical scholarship. Such notions as psychological verisimilitude, stylistic unity, non-contradiction and repetition and anti-digression do not apply to the *Odyssey* any better than they apply to Sterne's *Tristram Shandy* or Joyce's *Ulysses*. There is no inherent implausibility in suggesting that an ancient author might use an unreliable narrator in order to convey another message from the implied author to the implied reader, both of whom are created by the literary work.[14]

Within biblical studies, Berlin (1983: 52-53) addresses this issue in a tangential way when she urges caution in always assuming a convergence in point of view between the narrator and the reader, when in fact there may be more than one narrative voice. The fact that Berlin's work predates the use of reader-response criticism by biblical scholarship in a nuanced way meant that she did not have the necessary methodological concepts to do other than suggest Polzin's work as a future possibility. She writes:

> The foregoing analysis becomes even more complicated in light of Robert Polzin's study of the deuteronomic history *Moses and the Deuteronomist* in which he has detected two different narrative voices, one reinterpreting the other. This suggests that both the perceptual and the conceptual points of view of the narrator(s) and the narratee(s) are much more complex than has hitherto been acknowledged. It seems best, then, to leave for future studies the question of whether we should separate the point of view of the narrator from that of the narratee/reader (1983: 53).

Because of this possible complexity it seems best to leave open the possibility of unreliable narrators in the biblical narratives and answer the question of whether they exist inductively.[15] Although I take the possibility

---

14. Staley (1988: 27) says,

> The rhetorical investigations of Perelman [1969: 17-40] and Ong [1982: 78-116] make it clear that implied authors were invented by neither modern novelists nor by modern narratologists.

I have read Ong's work and find no discussion of implied authors. Perelman discusses only the fact that among the Greeks the rhetoricians were conscious of the distinction in audiences to which an ironic speaker addressed himself, i.e. a naive and a subtle audience. This is not exactly the notion of the implied author although it is similar.

15. Nelson's article (1988) treats this subject briefly, concluding that the narrator of Kings is not reliable. It is difficult to determine whether he intends this in the strict literary sense of narratorial unreliability or whether he, as a modern reader, cannot

of an unreliable narrator seriously[16] the scope of the present work prevents a detailed consideration of the possibility of narratorial unreliability. I will, however, refer to the potential fruitfulness of such an analysis at various points. I have, therefore, chosen to ignore the question of narratorial reliability methodologically by working with the *assumption* that the narrator of the Primary History is reliable. A rigorous analysis of narratorial reliability must await future research. I have also assumed the complete reliability of Yahweh as a character.

In this work, since I have assumed a reliable narrator, I use the terms 'reader' and 'implied reader' interchangeably to refer to the intra-textual recipient of the reading process, rather than the term 'narratee'. When the narrator is deemed to be reliable, as here, there is no real difference between the message the implied reader receives and what the narratee receives, and thus making a distinction between the narratee and the implied reader is unnecessary.

### d. *Our Reader*

There are five characteristics of our imaginary reader which underpin this work. First, our imaginary reader is a post-exilic, but pre-Christian, Jew who is fluent in Hebrew and believes that Yahweh is the one true God.

Secondly, our reader is a 'causally minded' reader. That is, our reader is able accurately to infer causes that are not explicitly mentioned in the narrative. In defining plot, Forster (1963: 87) distinguishes between a story and a plot thus: '"The king died and then the queen died" is a story. "The king died and then the queen died of grief" is a plot'. But surely, as has been often noted (Rimmon-Kenan 1983: 17) even what Forster terms a 'story' is a plot for the causally-minded reader. While

---

trust the narrator. In any case he assumes, rather than establishes, that the narrator's point of view is always presented by prophetic figures. Since these prophets turn out to be unreliable, he concludes that the narrator is therefore also unreliable since on his assumption they are the vehicle of the narrator's point of view. This is the very thing that I repeatedly question in this thesis. Gunn (1990), rightly in my view, questions Sternberg's assumption of narratorial reliability in the stories of the Hebrew Bible. McConville's citation of Sternberg against Nelson fails to account for Gunn's arguments (1989: 33).

16. In Josh. 21.43-45, for example, the concept of an unreliable narrator is one way of accounting for this text which appears to be radically discontinuous with the frequent notes of the failure of Israel to take control of all of the promised land (Josh. 11.22; 13.13; 15.63; 16.10; 17.12, 13, 14-18).

the 'story' does not explicitly tell us the cause of the queen's death or its specific relation to the king's death, their mere juxtaposition in the narrative leads the causally-minded reader to infer an implicit plot. The reader's inferring of causes that are not explicit in a story is an essential part of the reading process. Readers often make such inferences, usually unconsciously. For example, in Josh. 7.7 Joshua complains to Yahweh about Israel's defeat at Ai. The reader infers that the cause of Joshua's distress is his expectation that it was Yahweh's responsibility to ensure Israel's victory.

Thirdly, our reader does not share the skepticism of modern Western readers towards reports of miracles, but accepts the supernatural in what many modern readers might consider to be a very naive fashion. It seems to me that the Primary History is going to be seriously misread if our modern skepticism toward the miraculous is anachronistically imputed to its implied reader. While it is perfectly legitimate to use an imaginary reader who shares the skepticism toward the miraculous of many modern readers in analyzing a piece of literature—a critic can invent any sort of imaginary reader desired—I will not pursue such a line of inquiry here. One of my interpretative interests is in what a post-exilic Jew, who reads the Primary History as a unified whole, would be likely to conclude about the reliability of Moses, Joshua, Elijah, and Elisha. It seems to me to be highly unlikely that such a person would share the modern reader's skepticism towards the miraculous.

Fourthly, our reader, as a post-exilic Jew, does not share the difficulties which many modern readers have with religiously condoned violence. Once again, it seems unlikely and anachronistic to impute our modern attitudes towards the sort of violence in which the perpetrators of it claim divine sanction to a post-exilic Jew. For example, it seems to me to be a complete misreading of Elijah's contest with the prophets of Baal to assume that in killing the prophets of Baal the reader should infer that Elijah had done some horrendous evil for which he should receive the reader's condemnation.

Finally, our reader is a second-time reader. While an analysis of a first-time reader's response is an entirely legitimate and potentially very interesting line of scholarly investigation (Turner 1990), our interest is in what the reader who knows how the story turns out is likely to conclude about the reliability of our four human figures. In some instances, however, especially in the Elijah chapter, I have found it helpful to distinguish between the likely responses of the first-time reader and the

second-time reader and have therefore included some analysis of the
first-time reader's response.

### 7. *Polzin's* Moses and the Deuteronomist

Robert Polzin's book, *Moses and the Deuteronomist*, is the first of a
series of volumes in which he attempts to give a synchronic, literary
reading of the Deuteronomic History. In it he argues forcefully for the
methodological priority of literary to historical-critical analysis, and uses
the final form of the Deuteronomic History (including, oddly enough,
Deut. 32.48-52) as his starting point. His work therefore shares with
mine a similar methodology and point of departure for reading the books
of Deuteronomy and Joshua, and yet comes to very different results.

Some of this divergence is admittedly due to the differing narrative
contexts from which we read: Deuteronomy to 2 Kings for him; Genesis
to 2 Kings for me. Polzin claims that his use of the Deuteronomic
History as his point of reference, rather than say, the Pentateuch or the
Primary History, is not based 'upon previous historical critical analysis'
(1980: 18). While I do not doubt his sincerity in making such a statement, it is a curious choice from a purely literary point of view.[17]

Polzin's choice to use the Deuteronomic History has enormous implications for the way he reads Deuteronomy in particular. For example,
Polzin lays great stress on Moses' claim, in Deut. 5.22-31, that the ten
words (Deut. 5.6-21) are different from the later legislation (in chs. 12–
26) in that his audience had heard the ten words directly, while the later
legislation was conveyed indirectly through Moses. From this distinction
he draws an analogy to Deuteronomy where God's words are heard
'directly' through Moses (whom Polzin assumes to be a basically reliable
vehicle of Yahweh's words) and Joshua to 2 Kings where his words are
interpreted (heard indirectly) through the narrator. But a close comparison of the two accounts of the giving of the ten words (Exod. 20.2-17;
Deut. 5.6-21) shows that even though Moses claims that his words in
5.6-21 are a quotation of words spoken by Yahweh, those words cannot
be Yahweh's exact words since they differ from the narrator's earlier
account of Yahweh's words. Moses is portrayed as altering the ten
words when he delivers them to Israel in 5.6-21. When this part of
Moses' portrayal is coupled with the fact that the generation who heard
the words directly had all died (with three exceptions) and thus could

17. Cf. my reasons for choosing the Primary History given above.

not verify Yahweh's words orally, Moses' *absolute* reliability as a conveyor of Yahweh's word is placed in doubt. This doubt is intensified when the narrator's version of Yahweh's further law in Exodus and Leviticus is compared with Moses' interpretation of it in Deuteronomy 12–26. In fact, when the earlier narratives, that is Exodus 21–40 and Leviticus, are taken into account, the interaction between two voices which Polzin finds in Deuteronomy can be viewed as an outright conflict between the point of view of the narrator and that of Moses.

Polzin tends to minimize this conflict, and part of the reason for him doing so is his choice of the Deuteronomic History as his point of departure. This minimizing of the conflict in point of view between the narrator and Moses has, however, more fundamental causes than the relatively arbitrary choice of narrative context.

By minimizing the conflict, while simultaneously affirming its presence, Polzin is able to suggest that the Deuteronomist (our narrator) uses the authority of Moses to establish his or her own authority. He writes (Polzin 1980: 10-11):

> The principal role of Moses, as seen in the Book of Deuteronomy, is hermeneutic: he is the book's primary declarer (*maggîd*) and teacher (*mĕlammed*) of God's word. He not only declares what God has said, he teaches or interprets what the divine words mean for Israel. And he is pictured as doing so in an authoritative manner that was consonant with the status he is pictured as enjoying within the Israelite community... Even if we confine our illustrative remarks to the book of Deuteronomy, it is still obvious here at the beginning of the history that by the end of the book the narrator has also established *his* authoritative role as *maggîd* and *mĕlammed* of Moses' words. And the narrator accomplishes the establishment of his authority amazingly enough while remaining mostly in the background of his narrative: the reporting speech of the narrator comprises only about fifty-six verses of the book. He will, of course, come to the foreground with the preponderantly reporting narrative of Joshua–2 Kings. Indeed, what is obvious, even on a first reading of the history, is that in the narrator's reporting words, comprising the bulk of Joshua–2 Kings, we have some kind of authoritative interpretation of the words of Moses insofar as they affect the subsequent history of Israel.

Polzin uses what he sees as a biblical precedent for continuing re-interpretation of God's word by Moses and the narrator of Deuteronomy to kings to argue for a similar sort of continual re-interpretation (à la Gadamer) in *contemporary* biblical interpretation. (1980: 205-12). But his argument has validity only if it is *assumed* that the narrator is unequivocally in favor of Moses' interpretative activity.

Despite the literary sensitivity and the many helpful insights of Polzin's book, he is guilty of the same heroic idealization of the Deuteronomic Moses which is so pervasive in the scholarly literature on Deuteronomy. Thus Polzin writes:

> What is immediately obvious here is the absolutely authoritarian, or at least authoritative, nature of Moses' interpretive function.
>
> The immediate hero of the book is Moses as the spokesman of God.
>
> ...the narrator seems at great pains to impress upon his reader that it is Moses, and Moses alone, who possessed the type of reliable authority to convey accurately and authoritatively the direct words of God that form most of the book.
>
> ...we find not even a hint concerning the possibility that Moses might presume 'to utter in my name what I have not commanded him'. That there is no consideration of such a situation is entirely appropriate since the book of Deuteronomy presents its hero's authority as *already* established (Polzin 1980: 9, 26, 27, 62).

Polzin identifies *some* of the evidence for a partially negative portrayal of Moses in Deuteronomy, but only to interpret that evidence as the means which the deuteronomist uses to establish his or her simultaneous authority. The deuteronomist does not, in Polzin's view, permanently diminish the status of Moses, on whom the deuteronomist, as the authoritative interpreter of Moses' words, depends for his or her own status. But this conclusion arises from the text only if Moses' status is assumed to be 'already established'. My analysis of the portrayal of Moses questions this assumption.

Polzin not only explains away and ignores some of the evidence for conflict between the narrator and Moses, but he also posits conflict where none is present. While this could be demonstrated in a number of places, only two are of such import as to distinguish my approach from his. The first is the fashion in which Polzin separates two voices within Deuteronomy. One voice emphasizes sin, its consequent judgment, and the non-uniqueness of both Israel and Moses. The other emphasizes the mercy and blessing of God and the uniqueness of Israel and Moses. These voices are remarkably similar to the covenant of law–covenant of grace dichotomy in Protestant theology.[18] While Polzin argues that

---

18. Polzin sometimes even explicitly uses theological terms from this tradition, e.g. 'election' (1980: 37, 42); 'grace' (p. 42); 'covenant of law' (p. 50); 'covenant of mercy' (p. 50); and 'unconditional covenant with the fathers' (pp. 53, 55).

eventually some sort of merger of the two voices takes place, in which the immutable covenant of grace has an element of conditionality added to it while the conditional covenant of law has an element of unconditionality added to it (Polzin 1980: 68) it is less than clear that such a dichotomy ever existed except in the mind of a very Protestant-thinking exegete.

Polzin hypothesizes the two voices by, among other things, interpreting the sentence 'not with our fathers did the Lord make this covenant' (Deut. 5.3 RSV) as referring to a supposedly unconditional patriarchal covenant as opposed to a conditional covenant rooted in the law given at Horeb. This enables him to see a conflict between two different sorts of covenants. But it seems much more natural (and Gadamerian!) to understand 'our fathers' as referring to the previous generation and understand Moses to be 'actualizing' the Horeb covenant for the new generation (Groves 1987). One wonders whether a reading such as Polzin gives could arise without the background of the tension in Protestant theology.

The second conflict which Polzin reads into the text is the supposed conflict between Deuteronomy 13.1-6, representing the voice of 'authoritarian dogmatism' which prohibits the revision of the law in any way, and 18.15-22, representing the voice of 'critical traditionalism' which allows for such revision (Polzin 1980: 59, 67-68). But, as the text stands, 13.1-6 does not prohibit new prophetic revelation *except* when such revelation counsels apostasy from Yahweh to the 'other gods' of Canaan (v. 2). One wonders from this and from his choice of the Deuteronomic History as his narrative unit, whether Polzin has been completely successful in his aim of giving priority to a literary reading over a reading at least partly based on previous theological and historical-critical discussion.

## Chapter 1

## THE RELIABILITY OF MOSES IN DEUTERONOMY

### 1. *Introduction*

This chapter is an analysis of the reliability of the character Moses within
the book of Deuteronomy which in turn is viewed as a part of the
Primary History. It is the implicit assumption, if not the explicit assertion,
of much traditional Hebrew Bible scholarship that the deuteronomic
portrayal of Moses is an unqualifiedly idealistic one. Those passages which
appear to conflict with such an idealistic picture are typically dismissed
on source-critical grounds as later interpolations. By contrast, Polzin has
recently argued for a fairly radical disjunction in point of view between
the Deuteronomist as implied author on the one hand, and the character
Moses, on the other (Polzin 1980: 71-72). My analysis, based on a
different textual context, leads to a conclusion that is somewhere between
these two extremes. It is the thesis of this chapter that the deuteronomic
Moses is portrayed as an essentially reliable character, who for the most
part *is* the mouthpiece for the narrator's point of view, but who nevertheless is sometimes unreliable and occasionally speaks only for himself
and not for the narrator.

When Moses speaks, his primary activity in Deuteronomy, he is
usually being used as a mouthpiece for the narrator. When he acts without speaking, the reader is usually led to infer that his actions have the
narrator's tacit approval. There are, however, exceptions. My approach
will be first to establish the fundamental convergence in point of view
between Moses and the narrator and then to analyze the evidence for
some limited divergence in point of view.

### 2. *Evidence for Convergence in Point of View*

Perhaps the strongest evidence for the basic convergence in point of
view between the narrator and Moses is the fact that the vast majority of

the book is comprised of the narrator's quotation of Moses in direct speech. Of the 959 verses in Deuteronomy Moses is quoted in direct speech in at least some portion of about 900 of them.[1] Very little space is left for the narrator's commentary and evaluation or for the quotation of other characters. Yahweh, for instance, the only other character who is quoted as an individual, is quoted by the narrator in only thirteen verses.[2] Further, with the important exception of 32.48-52, all of the narrator's own words and all of the words which are put into the mouth of Yahweh lead the reader to evaluate Moses in a positive light.

If the narrator intended the reader to take a one-sided negative view of Moses with such a dearth of commentary the only strategy available would be to have Moses condemn himself out of his own mouth. But, as we will see, Moses' own words demonstrate that he usually either speaks for the narrator or expresses a point of view that is virtually indistinguishable from the narrator's. The evidence for the basic convergence in the points of view, therefore, comes from the narrator's own voice, from the words of Yahweh and Moses' response to them, and from the words of Moses himself.

a. *The Narrator's Own Voice*
*Deuteronomy 1.3.* In 1.3 the narrator informs us that when Moses spoke the words which are recorded for us in Deuteronomy he spoke 'in accordance with all that Yahweh had commanded him concerning them'. In other words, the narrator would have the reader believe that there was some genuine correspondence between what Moses said and what Yahweh had previously commanded him to say. In its present context within the Primary History this verse seems to refer back to those words given by Yahweh to Moses which are recorded in Exodus to Numbers.[3] As we shall see, Deut. 1.5 makes it clear that the correspondence between what Yahweh commanded Moses to say and what Moses actually says is not expected to be exact. Moses is no dictationist. He explains or even reinterprets Yahweh's word for the new generation. But even when Moses does reinterpret Yahweh's word, 1.3 assures the

---

1.  The 59 verses which clearly contain no direct speech of Moses are: 1.1-5; 2.10-12, 23; 3.9, 11, 14; 4.41-49; 10.6, 7; 27.11; 28.69; 31.1, 9, 14-25, 30; 32.44, 48-52; 33.1; 34.1-12.

2.  Deut. 31.14, 16-21, 23; 32.49-52; 34.4.

3.  Mayes (1979: 115) recognizes that this is the point of this verse in the final form.

reader that there is still genuine correspondence between what Moses says and what Yahweh had previously commanded him to say. If the narrator and Yahweh are to be trusted, and here I have assumed that this is so, there can be no radical discontinuity in point of view between what Moses says and what Yahweh and the narrator say since Moses is portrayed as merely explaining or reinterpreting what he has received from Yahweh. If there were no other evidence for convergence in point of view, 1.3 contains a very strong argument for it.

*Deuteronomy 1.5.* In this verse the narrator informs the reader that Moses, 'undertook to explain (באר) this law' (RSV). The use of the rare verb באר in Deut. 27.8 and Hab. 2.2 allows for the sense of either 'write clearly' or 'make clear'. Certainly the use of לאמר implies the latter sense here. Thus Moses is not being portrayed as physically writing the Torah or mechanically dictating it, but as expounding it (NRSV), or explaining it (RSV), or even applying it afresh to the new generation. The 'Torah' in this verse refers back to the instructions which are mentioned in v. 3, which in turn refer back to the earlier pentateuchal instructions in Exodus to Numbers. Moses is thus portrayed both as being faithful to the instructions which Yahweh had given him (v. 3), and yet also as reapplying those instructions (v. 5), which implies altering them in some fashion.

When Moses finally turns from exhortation to the actual delivery of the laws in 12.1–26.19 it is clear from even a superficial comparison with the laws in Exodus to Numbers that Moses changes the laws slightly when he delivers them to the new generation. Deut. 1.3, 5 make it clear that in the narrator's view this is a perfectly appropriate thing for Moses to do since even in reapplying the Torah (v. 5) he still speaks in accordance with what Yahweh commanded him to speak (v. 3). Moses should not, therefore, receive the reader's opprobrium for altering the Torah. The importance of this point will become clear in our later discussion of the reader's evaluation of the interpretative activity of Moses.

*Deuteronomy 34.* The book of Deuteronomy ends with the story of the death of Moses and the narrator's final evaluation of his life. Moses receives the unparalleled honor of being buried by Yahweh (vv. 5, 6). The narrator informs us that Moses was unique as a prophet both in the intimacy of his relationship with Yahweh (v. 10) and in the awesomeness, scope and power of the miracles which he performed (vv. 11, 12).

The magnitude of his greatness is given emphasis by the six-fold use of the word 'all' in vv. 11 and 12. The narrator's final evaluation of Moses is thus very positive, even heroic. It is therefore difficult to envisage how a radical disjunction in point of view between the narrator and Moses can be posited after such a glowing obituary. If the narrator is consistent (a part of being reliable) any deficiencies which the narrator might lead the reader to see in Moses can only be relatively minor in view of this passage.

*The narrator's parenthetical insertions into Moses' first address*. In 2.2–3.22 Moses narrates Israel's journey from the time when Yahweh announced the end of the period of wandering until their arrival in Transjordan. Moses explains why Israel bypassed Edom, Moab, and Ammon, but conquered Sihon and Og. In this section of the first address five parenthetical comments in the narrator's own voice are inserted into the speech of Moses (2.10-12; 2.20-23; 3.9; 3.11; 3.13b, 14).

Polzin (1980: 31-32) has observed that these narrative interruptions create psychological as well as temporal distance between Moses and the narrator. They make it clear that Moses is only a character and as such is subject to the same sort of evaluation as any other character in a narrative. While I am not happy with the way Polzin uses this observation to hypothesize a radical distinction in point of view between the narrator and Moses[4] the observation stands.

But these insertions not only serve to make it clear to the reader that Moses does not necessarily always express the narrator's point of view when he speaks. The insertions also function to confirm Moses' ideology about which nations are legitimate objects of conquest and which are not. In 2.2–3.22 Moses recalls how Yahweh had directed him to stop the wandering and begin the long-awaited journey to the promised land by way of Transjordan. In a rather structured fashion[5] Moses recalls how Israel passed by Edom, Moab and Ammon and then conquered Sihon and Og,[6] all Transjordanian kingdoms. Moses arranges his speech so that

---

4.    Coats (1988: 202) rightly argues that Polzin's central thrust in Deuteronomy lacks coherence. The Deuteronomist cannot increase his own authority by diminishing Moses' authority when in fact the Deuteronomist's own authority is dependent on Moses' authority.

5.    While he uses the evidence of structure for very different purposes see Sumner 1968.

6.    Sumner (1968: 217) notes that Ammon is placed third ahead of Sihon even though geographically we might expect the opposite.

it is clear exactly when Israel changes from a wandering to a conquering nation. Moses' narratives of Israel's dealing with the first three of the kingdoms have a common structure:

i.      Divine command forbidding contention with the specified nation (2.5a, 9a, 19a).

ii.     Statement that Yahweh will not give any of the specified nation's land to Israel (2.5a, 9b, 19b).

iii.    Divine rationale for not giving the land to Israel in terms of Yahweh's previous gift of the land to the specified nation's ancestors (2.5b, 9b, 19b).

iv.     Report that Israel was commanded by Yahweh to turn away from the specified nation and/or that they did so (2.8, 13, 24).

Moses adds weight to this structure by noting that when Israel was about to meet the third and last of the protected nations, Ammon (2.17-19), the forty years of punishment for the spy episode had ended with the death of the last of that generation's 'men of war' (2.14-16).

In the cases of Sihon and Og Moses tells of Yahweh's assurance that he would give their kings and land into the hand of Moses (2.24; 3.2).[7] While Yahweh had suggested to Moses that Israel purchase food and water from Edom (2.6), Moses, through his messengers, asked for the same treatment from Sihon, claiming that Moab and Edom had previously consented to this.[8] Instead of consenting, Sihon's heart was hardened by Yahweh in order to provide an opportunity for Israel to defeat his nation militarily (2.30); which Israel then thoroughly did (2.31-36). The defeat of Og is related in similar fashion (3.1-8, 10). In short, according to Moses, the defeat of Sihon and Og was based on Yahweh's encouragement (2.24, 25; 3.2), Yahweh's direct intervention against the psychological attitude of the enemies,[9] and the help of Yahweh in the actual battles (2.33; 3.3). Moses is thus portrayed as giving the encouraging message to Israel that victory over their enemies in the promised land is assured on the basis of Yahweh's decision to give Canaan to Israel, just as he had given Edom to the descendants of Esau, and Moab and Ammon to the descendants of Lot, and especially on the basis of

---

7.   The 'you' in both passages is singular.

8.   According to Num. 20.18-21, Edom had not consented.

9.   Thus Sihon fought against Israel even though the messengers were sent with words of peace (2.26). This was due to Yahweh's direct action (2.30). Note also Yahweh promises to put the 'fear and dread of' Israel on all enemy peoples (2.25).

their past victories over Sihon and Og—kings who had no divine right to their lands.

The narrator demonstrates his full sympathy with Moses at this point by adding parenthetical comments which, in addition to confirming Moses' point, perform several other functions in the narrative.[10] First, the divine right, from the narrator's point of view, of Moab and Edom to their lands as promised by Yahweh in Moses' speech is confirmed, at least partially, by the narrator's note in 2.10-12 that in fact both nations had defeated and dispossessed the original occupants of their respective lands—the Enim (also known as Rephaim) and the Horites. Secondly, the right of the Ammonites to their land is confirmed similarly in 2.20, 21. Thirdly, by making Rephaim a people who could be conquered by Moab and Ammon (2.11, 20) the narrator confirms Moses' statement in 3.2, 3 about Israel's divine right to conquer Og, king of Bashan, by making Og the last of the Rephaim and therefore a legitimate object of conquest (3.11). Fourthly, by not giving a parenthetical comment confirming Sihon's divine right to his land the narrator by implication confirms Moses' words in 2.24, 30. Fifthly, in 2.12b the narrator affirms that Israel's past (from the narrator's point of view) conquest of the land was based on the same divine right that Moab and Edom originally had to their lands. In 2.22 the *present* (from the narrator's point of view) right of Edom to their land is also affirmed. Sixthly, by not giving explicit right to the Caphtorim (the Philistines) to have dispossessed the Avvim (2.23), the narrator may be giving weight to Israel's present (to the narrator) claim of the right to the Philistines' land.

All of these observations show that the narrator affirms the divine right of Israel and its near relations Edom, Moab and Ammon to the lands which they have conquered by dispossessing other peoples who lack this divine right. At this point the narrator is at one with Moses the character and even in a sense uses the principle laid down by Moses of divine right to certain lands and divine denial to others to extend by implication to another people (the Canaanites) not yet conquered by the Israel of Moses' day.

Far from these notes being of merely antiquarian or historical interest they demonstrate that on the question of Israel's right to the land of Canaan, both Transjordan and Cisjordan, the narrator is in complete agreement with Moses.

10. Contra von Rad (1966b: 42) who calls them 'antiquarian notes' and completely misses their function in the narrative.

*The narrator's framework for Moses' first two addresses—Deuteronomy
1.1-5; 4.41–5.1a.* One of the initially perplexing things that the first-
time reader notices about Deuteronomy is the seemingly purposeless
repetition of introductory material in 4.44–5.1a. The narrator has already
provided the setting for Moses' speech in 1.1-5. The need for a second,
mainly repetitive, introduction is difficult to comprehend. Equally confusing is why Moses stops his speech in order to designate the three
Transjordanian cities of refuge (4.41-43). This double introduction is
usually explained either in terms of the influence of Near Eastern
suzerainty treaties on the form of Deuteronomy, whether Hittite (Kline
1963) or Assyrian (Weinfeld 1972), or in terms of the literary formation
of Deuteronomy as an introduction to the Deuteronomistic History
(Noth 1981). But there is a possible explanation for 4.41–5.1a in terms
of the final form of Deuteronomy.

In 4.41-43 the narrator informs us that at the end of the so-called
'first address' Moses fulfilled the command of Yahweh in Num. 35.13,
14, which up until that time had not been fulfilled, by designating three
cities as the Transjordanian cities of refuge. The narrator thus gives an
example of Moses' obedience to Yahweh's commands. Why Moses
waited to obey this command is unclear, but the ambiguous status of the
Transjordanian tribes within Israel may at least partly explain the delay.
The issue of the legitimacy of Transjordan as part of Israel is also one
possible explanation for the double introduction.

In 1.1-5 the reader is informed of Moses' Transjordanian location twice
(vv. 1, 5). Moses is also said to be 'in the land of Moab'. Similarly, in
4.44–5.1a Moses is located in Transjordan three times (4.46, 47, 49), but
this time he is said to be 'in the land of Sihon', not Moab (4.46). There
is no reason to infer that Moses has moved locations, so the reader's
question becomes, 'Why is he said to be in the land of Moab the first
time and in the land of Sihon the second?'

According to the narrator the land of Sihon had originally belonged to
Moab (Num. 21.26-30). When the two and one-half tribes claimed the land
of Sihon and Og as their inheritance (Num. 32), an anomaly occurred.
Israel had no authorization to take land which belonged to Moab (Deut.
2.9) and yet they did have authorization to conquer Sihon's kingdom.
But Sihon's kingdom included part of what was originally Moab's
territory. The legitimacy of the Transjordanian inheritance is thus questionable on two grounds. First, the inheritance was not in Cisjordan,
the promised land as it was originally conceived. Second, part of the

inheritance became Israel's only by right of their having conquered Sihon, but not by divine gift, unlike Cisjordan. Part of the Transjordanian land originally belonged to Moab by divine gift. The ambiguity of this situation may be responsible for the repetition of 'Transjordan' or its equivalent in both 1.1-15 and 4.44–5.1a and for the fact that the narrator simultaneously locates Moses in the land of Moab (1.5) and in the land of Sihon (4.46). The narrator may be implicitly expressing the viewpoint that the legitimacy of the Transjordanian inheritance is questionable. If this view of the narrator's intentions is correct, the narrator and Moses concur in their view of the anomaly which the Transjordanian tribes had created (Jobling 1986: 88-134).

Moses is prohibited from crossing over the Jordan into what he, Yahweh, and the narrator all agree was the real promised land (Deut. 3.25; 4.21, 22). He dies outside of the promised land and yet he dies within the inheritance of the Transjordanian tribes. By obeying Yahweh's command to designate three Transjordanian cities of refuge (4.41-43) Moses in effect legitimizes Transjordan as part of the promised land. Yet for Moses personally Yahweh's refusal to allow him to cross the Jordan means that he is denied the right to lead Israel into the real promised land. The Transjordanian inheritance is for Moses only a part of the promised land in a greatly diminished sense.

Deut. 1.1-5 and 4.41–5.1a show that this ambiguity over the legitimacy of Transjordan which Moses displays is shared by the narrator. The narrator's point of view on Transjordan converges with Moses' point of view. One possible explanation for the presence of the double introduction is the narrator's desire to stress this convergence of viewpoint with Moses.

*The narrator's pessimism over Israel's future faithfulness.* The evidence that Moses takes a pessimistic view of the likelihood of Israel remaining faithful to Yahweh after his death will be gathered in detail below. Here his statement to that effect in 31.27 must suffice.

> For I know how rebellious and stubborn you are; behold, while I am yet alive with you, today you have been rebellious against the LORD; how much more after my death! (RSV).

The narrator's story in the rest of the Primary History, that is Joshua to 2 Kings, makes it obvious that Moses was right to take a pessimistic view of Israel's future obedience (e.g. 2 Kgs 17.7-23; 24.2-4).

*The merging of the narrator's voice with the voice of Moses—Deuteronomy 10.6-9.* Polzin (1980: 35) has observed that in 10.6-9 it is not made clear to the reader exactly what is Moses' speech and what is the narrator's parenthetical comment.

> In 10.6-9 the normal signals that up to now have so clearly separated reported from reporting speech in the book are so muted that it is not possible to say for sure whether vv. 8 and 9 are the reporting utterance of the narrator or the reported word of Moses. The effect of this compositionally is to reinforce in yet another way what has been accomplished by the previous frame-breaks. Once again brought back by 10.6-9 to a brief focal awareness that it is the narrator who is transmitting the words of Moses, not Moses speaking directly, the reader of 10.8-9 now experiences the narrator's utterance and the hero's word as indistinguishable in tone, style, and content; the voice of the Deuteronomic narrator merges for a brief moment with Moses'.

This merger of the narrator's words with the words of Moses, so that the narrator's words and Moses' words are 'indistinguishable in tone, style, and content' is another piece of evidence for the basic convergence in point of view for which I have been arguing.

*Summary and conclusions.* Perhaps the strongest evidence for the convergence in the perspective of the narrator and Moses is the narrator's statement in 1.3 that Moses spoke 'in accordance with all that Yahweh gave him concerning [Israel]'. Moses' speech, his primary activity in Deuteronomy, cannot be in radical opposition with the narrator's point of view if we believe the narrator's statement in 1.3 and also assume that Yahweh's point of view converges with the narrator's. The few actions of Moses which are recorded in Deuteronomy depict Moses as an obedient servant of Yahweh (e.g. 4.41-43). The glowing obituary which the narrator gives Moses (Deut. 34) argues strongly for the inference that in the narrator's view Moses was an exemplary person.

We have also seen that on three important issues, the issue of which Transjordanian kingdoms were legitimate targets for conquest, the ambiguous status of the Transjordanian tribes within a Cisjordanian Israel, and the likelihood of Israel remaining faithful to Yahweh in the future, Moses is portrayed as being in agreement with the narrator. In addition, in 10.6-9, we have noted an example of the narrator using a literary technique to imply a convergence in point of view between the narrator and Moses. In short, the evidence for convergence from the narrator's own voice is strong.

b. *The Words of Yahweh*

As noted above, I am operating with the working assumption that both the narrator and Yahweh are reliable. The assumption that Yahweh is a reliable character who always represents the narrator's perspective means that the reader can safely use evidence about Moses from Yahweh's words and deeds as indicative of the narrator's perspective. In two particular areas Yahweh's perspective gives the reader reason to infer a basic convergence of point of view between Moses and the narrator. Although Yahweh does not speak or act a great deal in Deuteronomy, what little evidence there is points in this direction.

*Yahweh's pessimism over Israel's future faithfulness—Deuteronomy 31.16-21.* We have already noted above that both the narrator and Moses share the view that Israel is unlikely to remain faithful to Yahweh for very much longer. Deut. 31.16-21 makes it evident that Yahweh also shares this view. Indeed, in Yahweh's view Israel was already making plans to forsake Yahweh before he even led them into the land (v. 21).

*Moses obeys Yahweh's commands.* We have already seen in 4.41-43 Moses' obedience to Yahweh's command to designate Transjordanian cities of refuge. There are three other examples in Deuteronomy of Moses' obedience to Yahweh's commands and no examples of disobedience. Since by our working assumption Yahweh is completely reliable, for Moses to obey Yahweh's commands is, in the narrator's view, commendable and further evidence of convergence in the points of view of Moses and the narrator. In 31.14a Yahweh commands Moses:

> Behold the days approach when you must die; call Joshua, and present
> yourselves in the tent of meeting that I may commission him (RSV).

From Moses' own statement in 3.23-29 it is clear that Moses desperately wanted to lead Israel into Canaan. Yet, when Yahweh has denied him his plea, and Moses is instructed to bring Joshua to the tent of meeting to be commissioned to replace him, there is no indication of resistance on Moses' part, no final plea. He simply obeys (31.14b).

In 31.19 Yahweh commands Moses to write down a song and teach it to the people of Israel. In 31.22 Moses' obedience to this directive is noted. A written copy of the song is given in Deuteronomy 32 which gives further confirmation that Moses obeyed Yahweh's command.

In 32.49, 50 Yahweh commands Moses to ascend Mt Nebo and then die there after viewing the promised land from afar. While it is not clear how one obeys a command to die, 34.1 records Moses' obedience to the first part of this command. In 34.5 Moses is said to have died, 'according to the word of Yahweh'. The suggestion seems to be that even in the very act of dying Moses obeyed Yahweh.

c. *Moses' Own Words*
*Moses' pessimism over Israel's future faithfulness—Deuteronomy 6.1–11.32*. Having established the legitimacy of his own role as mediator of Yahweh's law, and his right to expect that law to be obeyed because both Yahweh and the people have chosen him to be the mediator (5.22-33), Moses announces the giving of that law (6.1) only to spend five more chapters: a) imploring Israel to obey the law (6.3, 17, 25; 7.11; 8.1; 10.12, 13; 11.1); b) preparing them for the temptations they will face that might lead them to disobey the law (6.10-12; 7.4; 8.11-14); c) promising them blessing for obedience (6.18, 24, 25; 7.9, 13-16; 8.6-10; 11.8-15); d) warning them of judgment for disobedience (6.15; 7.10; 8.19; 11.16, 17); and e) chastening them for their own stubborn tendency to disobey the law (9.6, 13, 23, 24; 10.16). It is difficult for the first-time reader to know what to make of this digression in Moses' speech. It becomes clear to the second-time reader, however, that Moses' digression is part of a pattern in Deuteronomy of repeated warnings to Israel against falling away from loyalty to Yahweh alone before it happens. In this section of Deuteronomy Moses repeatedly warns Israel of their tendency to lapse into idolatry (6.14; 8.19; 9.6-21; 11.16-17) and of Yahweh's fierce anger should they lapse (6.15; 7.4; 9.7, 8, 18, 19, 22; 11.17). His pleas for them to be careful to obey his word (6.3, 25; 8.1; 11.22, 32) are said to be motivated by his desire to see Israel take the land and prosper in it (6.3, 18, 24; 7.12-15; 8.1; 11.8-10, 13-15, 27). Moses' warnings turn out to be only too relevant to Israel and the reader comes to see that it was quite appropriate to warn the nation in such strong terms because the danger of lapsing was very real. This digression of Moses shows that he understood how likely it was for Israel to lapse. In 9.24, having catalogued a series of examples of Israel's tendency to rebel against Yahweh, Moses concludes, 'you have been rebellious against Yahweh from the day I knew you'. Moses takes a pessimistic view of the likelihood of Israel remaining faithful.

*Deuteronomy 27.11–28.68*. Having finished the giving of the law proper Moses turns to a ceremony which Israel is to perform at Mt Ebal and

Mt Gerizim when they have arrived in the land of Canaan. The note-worthy fact about this ceremony is the predominant emphasis curse has in it as opposed to blessing. While it is clear from 27.12, 13 that the ceremony which Moses commands is one in which both the blessings of obedience to the conditions of the covenant and the judgment and curses on disobedience to the conditions of the covenant are recalled, Moses seems to take such a dim view of the chances of Israel obeying the conditions and thus receiving blessing that the curses threaten to overwhelm the ceremony as Moses describes it.

In 27.1-8 Moses commands the performing of the ceremony. The plastered altar which Israel is to build and on which 'all the words of this law' are to be written plainly (a very big altar indeed) is located, not in the valley that we presume runs between the two mountains, but on the mountain of curse, Mt Ebal (27.4). After a moment of silence to recall that that very day in Moab Israel had become the people of God (vv. 9, 10) Moses delineates the locations the various tribes are to take during the ceremony (vv. 11-13). Moses then commands that the Levites shall begin by speaking the curses (27.14). The ceremonial form of the twelve curses, followed in each case by Israel's 'Amen' (27.15-26), is not followed in enumerating the blessings (28.1-14). After the long diatribe on the consequences of disobedience in 28.15-69 one wonders whether the lack of ceremonial form in the blessings implies that Israel will have no need of being reminded ceremonially of the blessings. The predomi-nance Moses gives to judgment, which will include a wide variety of illnesses as well as military defeats, foreign oppressors, famines and exile shows his pessimism over the likelihood of Israel remaining faithful. For Moses they are not a people who need a carrot unless it is so toughened that it can be used as a stick. Moses even warns that Yahweh would cause Israel to return to Egypt as slaves—in contradiction of his own promise (v. 68).

*Deuteronomy 29.1–30.20*. Having given the law in 12.1–26.19 and prescribed a covenant renewal ceremony in 27.1–28.69, Moses then addresses Israel concerning the making of the covenant that very day, not its future renewal in the promised land. Their assembly is for the purpose of Israel, both present and future generations, entering into the covenant (29.10-15). Moses recalls Yahweh's action in bringing them out of Egypt and caring for them in the wilderness (29.1-7). He calls on them to be 'careful to do the words of this covenant' (29.9) and discusses at length the possibility of covenant renewal even after exile (29.15–30.10). He ends by placing before Israel two alternatives—life and death, blessing and curse—and pleads for Israel to obey and receive life and blessing (30.15-20). The length of the section on the possibility of return after exile leaves the reader with the expectation that Israel will in fact disobey by plunging into idolatry and receive exile as the judgment for their disobedience. Even though Moses sets before Israel two alternatives, his own expectation seems to be that they will choose the bad alternative. While it is encouraging from Israel's point of view to note that even after exile Yahweh will not give up on them, once again we see Moses' view of Israel's chances of obeying the law and as a consequence receiving Yahweh's blessing as slim. In Moses' view this is not because it is just too hard to obey the law (30.11-14), nor because Israel has no choice (30.19) but rather because there are those in Israel who 'walk in the stubbornness of [their] hearts' (29.19).

*Moses' final words to Israel—Deuteronomy 33.* While much of Moses' speech in Deuteronomy is directed to the task of warning Israel against future disloyalty to Yahweh, this passage makes it clear that in doing so Moses was genuinely concerned for the welfare of the nation and genuinely wanted Israel to heed his warnings and receive the ensuing blessings of Yahweh. The song which Yahweh commanded Moses to teach to Israel (ch. 32) is largely negative in tone and its stated purpose is to serve as a future witness against Israel when the nation does in fact fall away from loyalty to Yahweh alone (31.19b). By contrast the blessing of Moses, which comes from Moses without Yahweh's authorization, has a more positive purpose, that is to encourage the various tribes to take their allotted inheritances and prosper there. The message is Moses' personal last word to Israel and it contains words of encouragement and blessing, not warning and curses. It shows Moses' concern for the welfare of the people and demonstrates that though he personally blamed Israel for his own fate (1.37; 3.26; 4.21) he did not allow this to prevent him from wanting the nation to succeed in taking the promised land and enjoying its blessings. Moses is thus depicted as having a generous spirit which enabled him to see beyond his own personal disappointment and genuinely to desire the best for his people.

### d. *Summary and Conclusions*

The evidence for fundamental convergence in point of view between Moses and the narrator is strong. The voices of the narrator, Yahweh, and Moses concur on fundamental issues. Moses is portrayed as an obedient servant of Yahweh and his words are, in the main, to be trusted as representing the narrator's views. In his actions and his words Moses is usually portrayed as an exemplary figure and therefore a reliable guide to the narrator's perspective.

### 3. *Evidence for Divergence in Point of View*

a. *Introduction*
The conclusion that 'Moses is a reliable character' must be qualified by the addition of the word 'usually'. I will discuss four aspects of the portrayal of Moses where the reader should or could question whether Moses really reflects the narrator's point of view. First, in the final form of Deuteronomy there is an obvious conflict between Yahweh's reason for excluding Moses from Canaan (32.51) and the reason that Moses gives to Israel three times in the first address (1.37; 3.26; 4.21). Secondly, there is also some reason for the reader to infer that when Moses retells events from Israel's recent past in which he was personally involved he sometimes makes Israel look slightly worse and himself slightly better than in the narrator's version of those same events. Thirdly, Moses' role as interpreter of Yahweh's Torah also could occasionally raise questions in the reader's mind over the freedom with which Moses sometimes handles Yahweh's words. Finally, it is also possible to accuse Moses of sometimes taking over roles that the reader would ordinarily assume would be the reserve of Yahweh alone, although it is impossible to know whether the reader should infer that it is inappropriate for Moses to do so.

b. *Moses' Exclusion from Canaan*
*Moses' first account of his exclusion—Deuteronomy 1.37*. In 1.19–2.1 Moses gives his version of Israel's failure of nerve at Kadesh-Barnea during the spy episode and its aftermath. According to Moses the people's refusal on that occasion to obey Yahweh's command to go up against the land (v. 26) and to trust Yahweh to protect them (vv. 30, 31) resulted in Yahweh's decision not to allow any of that generation, except Caleb, to enter the promised land (1.35, 36). Yahweh's anger then spilled over onto Moses, who had pleaded with the people to have the courage to proceed (vv. 29-31). Moses says, 'Yahweh was angry with me on your account and said, "You shall not go in there"' (1.37). In other words, Moses claims that he was excluded from Canaan during

the time of the spy episode, which was prior to the 40 years of wandering, because Yahweh was angry at Israel for not trusting him to lead them into the promised land.

The narrator, of course, has a very different story. Some 38 years later[11] as the new generation is about to travel past Edom, Moses and Aaron are accused by Yahweh of 'not believing in me so as to treat me as holy in the eyes of the sons of Israel' (Num. 20.12). It is for this reason, according to Yahweh, that Moses is to be denied entrance into the promised land. Exactly what Moses' sin was[12] in this narrative is at this point irrelevant. For the narrator, Moses was excluded because of Yahweh's judgment on him for his disobedience at Kadesh. The narrator's character Moses claims that it was at the time of the spy mission a generation earlier when the people's disobedience brought judgment upon the innocent third party Moses as well as upon the people.[13]

*Moses' second account of his exclusion—Deuteronomy 3.26.* In 3.23-29 Moses speaks of a time after the conquest and distribution of Transjordan (cf. 3.18-20) when he pleaded[14] with Yahweh to reverse his decision to exclude him from Canaan. Moses claims that Yahweh's decision to reject Moses's last-minute plea was because he was still angry at Israel:

> But the LORD was angry with me on your account, and would not hearken to me; and the LORD said to me, 'Let it suffice you; speak no more to me of this matter' (3.26 RSV).

11. While the year is lacking in Num. 20.1 the narration of the death of Aaron follows directly upon the narration of the sin of Moses and Aaron. In Num. 33.38 we are informed that this took place in the fifth month of the fortieth year. The natural way to read the reference to 'the first month' is, therefore, the first month of the fortieth year.

12. The sheer number of views taken by interpreters, as discussed by for example Milgrom 1983, shows the difficulty of pinning down Moses' sin.

13. Mann (1979: 482) argues that vv. 37, 38 do not fit the context well. Notice the singular 'you' in v. 38 in contrast to the plural in v. 39. While too much must not be based on a change in number in the second person as this can be used as a rhetorical device, here I find Mann's argument convincing. If vv. 37, 38 are removed from the text, the remaining text reads just like the account in Num. 14.30, 31. Moses' comments about his own judgment are suspicious even without a knowledge of Num. 20.2-13.

14. So NJPSV. Craigie (1976: 127) notes that 'the verb used (Hithp. of *hānan*) is a strong one, implying a solemn request for the Lord to be compassionate'.

Moses is portrayed as fashioning his account of this episode in a way which draws the maximum amount of sympathy out of his hearers for his own, to him, tragic situation. First, Moses claims that he only made an attempt to convince Yahweh to reverse his decision after he had had to live with the burden which the decision brought upon him for 38 years. It was only after the death of the wilderness generation that the request was made. His claim of enduring this burden, apparently without complaint, for 38 years seems to be designed to attract his hearers' sympathy.

Secondly, Moses makes Yahweh's rejection of his request seem somewhat harsh by the use of a word-play. Again the ploy seems to be to gain sympathy—this time by claiming harsh treatment. He claims to have asked, 'Let me please go over (אעברה־נא) the Jordan'. Yahweh supposedly responded by really 'going over the top' (ויתעבר) in his anger (Mann 1979: 481).

Thirdly, the emphatic way in which Yahweh is alleged to have denied Moses' request, literally, 'That is enough. Do not continue to speak to me again on this matter' (Craigie 1976: 127), may also be designed to increase the hearer's sympathy for Moses.

Finally, Moses once again blames the people for his exclusion from the promised land: it was 'on your [Israel's] account' that Yahweh refused it. This statement and the similar ones in 1.37 and 4.21 are often used to exonerate Moses from any personal responsibility for being denied entrance to the promised land. Usually this is done on source-critical grounds.

Noth (1968: 146-47) argues that Num. 20.2-13, the narrative of Moses striking the rock, is an invention of P based on Exod. 17.1-7 in the interest of finding an excuse for Moses being denied entrance to the promised land. Similarly Deut. 32.48-52, referring back to that narrative, is a P insertion. In D's version, on the other hand, Moses is represented as bearing 'the guilt for the disobedience of the whole people' (Noth 1968: 146-47). But even if, for the sake of argument, we accept the traditional source analysis, this view is problematic. If Moses is judged along with the wilderness generation, although he is in fact completely innocent personally, why are Caleb and Joshua as well as the children exempted from exclusion from Canaan? Lohfink (1960: 403-407) suggests that the exilic readers who were taken into captivity through no fault of their own would identify with Moses who, though personally innocent, must bear the communal guilt. But why shouldn't Joshua and

Caleb also bear this communal guilt (Bertholet 1899: 6)? Mayes (1979: 147) seems to imply that Moses' role as leader makes the difference. But such a view fails to account for the fact that Joshua has in this respect, that is leading the people into Canaan, the same role as Moses and yet he is exempted.[15]

Some would go even further and assert that Moses died outside the promised land as a vicarious substitute for the people. Thus von Rad:

> The reason given, namely that Moses dies outside the promised land as a substitute for the people (v. 26 'on your account') is an important characteristic of the conception of Moses in Deuteronomy.[16]

With perhaps even greater theological development, Wright (1953: 339-40) speaking of 1.37 writes:

> The statement in vs 37 does not refer to this or any one single incident. It is rather an interpretation of the figure of Moses in a very different and more profound manner. He was unable to enter Canaan because he bore the divine 'wrath' on Israel's behalf, i.e. the denial of his dream was a vicarious burden laid upon him, not because of his own but on account of his people's sin (cf. 3.26; 4.21).

Similar views are expressed by Phillips (1973: 19), and Miller (1988: 251-53). While I would definitely not want to dismiss the tragic dimensions of Moses in Deuteronomy, surely this view is extreme. As Mann (1979: 486-87) has shown, the Hebrew vocabulary for substitution is lacking. While it is possible that Moses' exclusion from the land and his death prevented the *immediate destruction* of Israel the text gives no hint of such a notion. If the source-critical analysis is to be maintained, we are left only with questions. As Steuernagel long ago noted, 'The Old Testament has no solution for some riddles of history'(Steuernagel 1900: 14; my translation).

The narrator makes it clear (in Num. 20.2-12 and Deut. 32.48-52) to the reader, as opposed to Moses' hearers, that Moses is being portrayed as unfairly blaming the people and, by his silence over his own sin at Kadesh, denying his own responsibility in his tragic fate. The reader should also note that the narrator never gives an independent account of the conversation between Moses and Yahweh which Moses recalls in

---

15. The unfairness is only heightened if, with Mayes (1979: 126) we assume that Dtr had a spy narrative in which Joshua did not finally come to Caleb's support.

16. Von Rad 1966b: 45. In his *Old Testament Theology* (von Rad 1962: 294), he refers to Moses as 'suffering mediator'.

3.23-29. The narrator only gives Moses' own interpretation of that conversation and since the conversation centers on Moses' own personal role it is prone, at least potentially, to contain Moses' biases in a particularly obvious way. The reader has no way of confirming Moses' interpretation of the tone of the conversation, nor even that it ever actually took place within the narrative world.

*Moses blames the people a third time—Deuteronomy 4.21.* In 4.1-40, the final section of the first address, Moses turns from a rehearsal of the recent events in the nation's history to a plea that Israel would obey the teaching he is about to give them. Of particular concern to Moses is the tendency of the nation to lapse from the worship of Yahweh to the worship of the false gods of Canaan. Moses in 3.29 has just positioned Israel opposite the site of one such recent lapse, Baal-Peor. As Mayes notes, 'It is just at the point of Israel's first encounter with the forms of Canaanite worship that she receives her own life order' (Mayes 1979: 148). Moses draws on two past events, the sin of Baal-Peor (vv. 3, 4) and the revelation at Horeb (vv. 9-14) to warn Israel against now lapsing yet again into idolatry. He uses the first event to warn Israel of the severity of Yahweh's judgment on those who do so (vv. 3, 4a). He uses the Horeb experience to show the futility of trying to represent Yahweh, who has no form,[17] with the form of some created thing, and again reiterates the judgment on those who turn to idolatry (vv. 15-19, 23-28). The severity of Yahweh's punishment is further illustrated by Moses' own bitter personal experience (vv. 21, 22 with v. 24).

In this passage Moses, for the third time, blames the people for his being denied Canaan: 'Yahweh was angry with me on your account' (4.21). Verses 21 and 22 do not fit smoothly into the context.[18] They do illustrate that Yahweh is 'an eating fire, a jealous God', but it is almost as though Moses is a little too eager to remind his audience of his personal tragedy. Yahweh is not only a 'jealous God' (v. 24) but also a 'merciful God' (v. 31). He will even forgive the people of Israel after they have forsaken the first two commandments and have been exiled (vv. 25-31). But for Moses personally, he is 'an eating fire, a jealous God'.

Moses does not in this passage relate his denial to a specific event. Indeed Moses is not excluded from the promised land, as a future Israel

---

17. Technically Yahweh does, according to Num. 12.8, have a form (תמונת), but only Moses can see it.

18. Note how v. 23 follows naturally on from v. 20.

could be (vv. 25-27), for the heinous sin of idolatry. But Moses is excluded by this jealous God nevertheless. Moses does not further his case for the dangers of lapsing into idolatry by appealing to his own personal case. In fact it was not on account of Israel's idolatry that Moses was excluded even by Moses' own account (1.37), but because of Israel's lack of courage. Why then, does Moses here include his personal case yet again? It seems to me that its inclusion here serves only to magnify the jealousy and anger of Yahweh but not as those attributes show Yahweh's abhorrence of idolatry. The jealousy and anger of Yahweh are such, Moses would have his hearers believe, that they not only bring judgment down on those who disobey him but also on 'innocent bystanders' like Moses. It is as though Moses were saying, 'Yahweh is a jealous God all right. He even treats the loyal as though they were disloyal. I know this from personal experience. If he's so protective of his people's loyalty you must be extra careful not to do anything that could be construed as disloyal.'

*Yahweh holds Moses personally responsible for his exclusion from Canaan—Deuteronomy 32.48-52.* In 32.51 Yahweh makes it clear to Moses why he is being denied entrance into the promised land:

> [B]ecause you broke faith with me in the midst of the people of Israel at the waters of Meribath-Kadesh, in the wilderness of Zin; because you did not revere me as holy in the midst of the people of Israel (32.51 RSV).

It is ironic that immediately following Moses' recital of the song in which he castigates Israel for their unfaithfulness (ch. 32) the narrator quotes Yahweh reminding Moses of his own unfaithfulness. The passage merely confirms what even the first-time reader of the Primary History already knows; when Moses three times blames the people for his own exclusion from Canaan (1.37; 3.26; 4.21) he is in direct conflict with the narrator and with Yahweh who attribute his exclusion to Moses' own actions and words at Kadesh (Num. 20.2-13).

It could be argued that Yahweh's explanation for Moses' exclusion is rather feeble. After all, it is less than clear from Num. 20.2-13 what it is that Moses did or did not say or do which justifies Yahweh's punishment of him.[19] In this work, however, I operate with the assumption that

---

19. Milgrom (1983) discusses ten different suggestions by the medieval Jewish commentators alone. Certainly some of these are quite silly by the standards of present-day literary criticism but one is still left with more than one possibility and the nagging feeling that none of them is adequate. Could Yahweh have justifiably prevented

Yahweh is completely reliable and therefore always reflects the narrator's perspective. Whatever Moses' fault at Kadesh was, Yahweh and the narrator concur that Moses was indeed at fault and that this fault, and not Yahweh's anger at Israel over the spying episode 38 years earlier as Moses claimed, was the real reason for Moses being denied entry into Canaan. This is an obvious divergence in point of view between Yahweh and the narrator on the one hand, and Moses on the other.

## c. *Moses' Retelling of Israel's Recent Past*

One of the things that Moses is frequently portrayed as doing in Deuteronomy is recalling events in Israel's recent past and using the lessons drawn from his interpretation of those particular events as the basis for his exhortations to Israel to be faithful to Yahweh. A number of the events Moses retells have already been narrated in Exodus to Numbers. The reader is therefore enabled to compare Moses' version of events with the narrator's own version and possibly infer things about the way Moses is being portrayed as an interpreter of Israel's and his own past. While in general Moses' version of events corresponds fairly closely with the

---

Moses from seeing the fulfillment of his divine calling because he struck the rock instead of speaking to it when previously, in very similar circumstances, Yahweh had commanded Moses to do just that (Exod. 17.6)? Perhaps Moses' striking the rock twice indicates a stubbornness on his part to do things his way and not Yahweh's way? But this seems quite forced. The question which Moses asks in Num. 20.10 has even more possibilities: 'Hear now, you rebels; shall we bring forth water for you out of this rock?' Is it that Moses calls Israel 'rebels'? Hardly. The question itself could be read in two different ways that cast Moses in a negative light. Some (e.g. Budd 1984: 218) infer that the 'we' could be read as an attempt by Moses to claim credit for the miracle for himself and Aaron rather than giving credit to Yahweh. Personally I find this particular view difficult to square with v. 8b, 'You will bring water out of the rock for them!' If Yahweh said that they (and not he himself directly) would bring out water from the rock, how was it inappropriate for Moses to say the very thing that Yahweh had said? The question could imply doubt on the part of Moses as to whether the miracle was possible. But this seems hardly credible when the number of miracles that Moses had personally witnessed is considered. Nevertheless, whatever the exact nature of Moses' sin it is clear that the exact obedience of the earlier and parallel miracle (Exod. 17.6) is not duplicated here (Wenham 1981: 155). The point of this analysis is not to make one more attempt to solve a famous *crux interpretum* but to point out that the very ambiguity of the narrative toward the key question, 'How do Moses' speech, character, actions or lack of them correspond to Yahweh's judgment on him?', leaves the reader unconvinced that Moses has done anything seriously wrong.

narrator's version, there is some evidence that Moses is being portrayed as reshaping the past in such a way as to make Israel look marginally worse than they really were and to make himself look marginally better than he really was.

*Deuteronomy 1.9-18*. In 1.9-18 Moses retells the story of the delegating of some of his responsibilities onto others in Israel so that his burden could be eased. In the narrator's version of this episode in Num. 11.10-25 Israel had already left Sinai (Num. 10.13, 33) when Yahweh was angered by a second instance of the people's complaining. Moses complains to Yahweh:

> Why have you treated your servant so badly? And why haven't I found favor in your sight that you have placed the burden of the entire people upon me? Did I conceive all of these people? Did I cause them to be born so that you would be justified in saying to me, 'Carry them on your breast as a nursing mother carries a sucking child—all the way to the land which you swore to give to their fathers'? Where am I supposed to find meat to give to all these people when they cry to me saying, 'Give us meat to eat'? I cannot carry all these people by myself. Their burden is too heavy. If you're going to treat me like this then kill me now. Kill me if I find favor in your sight so that I will not see my own wretchedness (11.11-15).

Yahweh then decides to ease Moses' burden by imparting some of Moses' power to seventy leaders of the people (11.16, 17) and promises to give them so much meat, one cause of their complaint, that the Israelites will hate the thought of it (11.18-20). Moses expresses doubt at the possibility of such a task (11.21-22), then Yahweh reaffirms it (11.23).

In Deuteronomy we get an entirely different story. In addition to the chronological discrepancy which may be an indication that Moses is being portrayed as having suffered a minor memory lapse, Moses a) omits his complaint against Yahweh and his own expression of a lack of confidence in Yahweh's ability to do the miracle; b) instead claims his complaint was addressed to the people rather than to Yahweh;[20] c) treats the multiplication of Israel as a positive thing; d) implies that the practical solution to the problem, the delegating of authority, was his own idea,

---

20. Newing argues that this complaint should be seen as the duty of a vizier and not seen in a negative light. But, as he recognizes (1988: 417) there are no Near Eastern parallels for the role of vizier and furthermore Moses is still seen to be lacking in confidence in Yahweh's power even if we assume the hypothesis to be accurate.

not Yahweh's; and e) turns the 'burden' of the earlier narrative into 'weight, burden, and strife' (v. 12), thus making Israel seem to be worse than Moses had actually deemed them to be in the Numbers account.[21] When the reader compares Moses' version with the narrator's version, the reader recognizes that Moses is being portrayed as making Israel seem to be somewhat more burdensome than they 'really were' and himself somewhat more irreproachable than he 'really was'.

*Deuteronomy 1.19–2.1.* In this section Moses recounts the sending of the twelve spies (1.19-23); their positive report (1.24, 25); the people's refusal to trust Yahweh to lead them into Canaan (1.26-29; 32, 33) even though Moses attempted to reassure them of Yahweh's protection (1.29-31); Yahweh's judgment on that generation which included Moses himself (1.34-40); Israel's futile attempt to invade the land without Yahweh's approval or assistance (1.41-45); and their subsequent wandering for many days (1.46–2.1).

A comparison of Moses' retelling of the story with the narrator's version in Numbers 13 and 14 makes it clear that Moses is being portrayed as giving added emphasis to both Israel's failure of nerve and disobedience at an important juncture in the nation's history and his own positive role in trying to persuade them to proceed with the conquest immediately as Yahweh had commanded. In the Numbers narrative the spy mission is Yahweh's idea. In Moses' version it is the people's idea and Moses merely co-operates.[22] In Numbers the spies show the fruit (13.26) and give a brief positive account (13.27) which is immediately followed by a longer negative account (13.28, 29). This negative account is countered by Caleb (13.30) followed by a second negative account by the other spies (13.31). The narrator then reports a further and longer negative statement by the spies introducing it with, 'then they brought forth a false account of the land which they had spied out' (13.32-33). It is only after this third negative statement from the spies, tempered only by Caleb's lone encouraging statement, that the people lose their nerve and begin to cry out against Moses and Aaron and

21. Here I follow Craigie (1976: 98) in treating vv. 16-18 as an additional action separate from the delegating of authority. Thus Moses is not necessarily being portrayed as confusing Exod. 18 and Num. 11.

22. Polzin (1980: 85, 86) assumes that the very act of requesting spies shows a lack of courage on Israel's part, but this view is only sustainable if one ignores the Numbers account.

Yahweh (14.1-4). Moses and Aaron are very distressed by this (14.5) but it is Joshua[23] (who now surfaces for the first time) and Caleb, not Moses and Aaron, who make one more unsuccessful attempt to persuade the people to proceed with the conquest (14.6-9) before Yahweh steps in with judgment (14.12). Moses' appeal for pardon (14.13-19) is granted (14.20) but this is only a reprieve from immediate judgment as Yahweh decides that none of that generation will enter the promised land (14.21-35) and it is only an immediate pardon for the people, not their spies (14.36-38).

Moses has a subtly different way of telling the story. In Moses' version the spies return and give a positive report (1.25). Immediately, without any discouraging or negative report the people rebel (1.26) and murmur *in their tents* (1.27, 28). Moses then claims that it is *he* who gave an encouraging word (1.29-31)—not Joshua and Caleb as in Num. 14.6-9. Despite Moses' encouragement the people would not believe in Yahweh their God who, Moses reminds them, had given them plenty of proof of his care, protection and guidance by the fire and the cloud (1.32, 33; cf. Exod. 13.21-22). In Moses' version we hear of the spies' negative report only after the rebellion as the people murmur about it in their tents. In Moses' version there is a heightened sense of the people's responsibility and Moses is, if possible, even more innocent than in the narrator's version. Joshua and Caleb play no part at all according to Moses. He takes their positive role for himself.[24] What is of more significance is that after painting himself as completely innocent in the spy narrative,[25] Moses makes that very incident the basis for Yahweh's denying him entrance into the promised land. Moses' innocence is also highlighted by his emphasis on the contrasting guilt of the people.[26] Certainly the lack

23. As the Numbers narrative stands, it seems that Joshua at first went along with the majority but later switched to side with Caleb.

24. For a similar reading, though without noting the effect this has on the portrayal of Moses, see von Rad 1966b: 40-41.

25. The reader of Num. 13, 14 may even be wondering why Moses did not speak out on that occasion. Perhaps at this point in Deuteronomy the reader may assume that Moses is filling in details that were not recorded in the earlier narratives. Thompson (1974: 88) suggests that Moses' failure to speak out was the reason that Moses was judged along with the people at the spy incident. This, however, is an argument from silence and the reader already knows of another occasion (Num. 20.1-13) when Moses' 'sin' brought judgment down on him.

26. This highlighting of the people's guilt comes from: a) the order in which Moses tells the events—placing the rebellion before the negative report; b) the abbre-

of courage on the part of the people is as obvious to the reader of the narrator's version of events in Numbers as it is in Moses' version and his version certainly does not contradict the earlier account.

It should also be noted that one laudable action on the part of Moses which the narrator records in Num. 14.13-19, that is his intercession for Israel, is not repeated by Moses in Deuteronomy 1. If Moses was being portrayed as idealizing his past actions in a blatantly obvious and one-sided way one would have expected Moses to have retold that event in a self-congratulatory way. In fact he does not do so.

I conclude that while Moses is portrayed as making himself look slightly better and Israel slightly worse than in the narrator's account, Moses is not portrayed as being blatantly dishonest about himself or flagrantly jaundiced in his view of Israel.

*Deuteronomy 9.8–10.11*. Moses begins ch. 9 by assuring Israel of victory in the conquest (vv. 1-3) and by warning them not to assume once they have taken the land that they were able to do so because Yahweh was rewarding their moral rectitude (vv. 4-6a). He reminds them what a stubborn people they have proven to be (vv. 6b, 7) and then uses the golden calf incident (9.6-21, 25-29; 10.1-11) as well as other incidents (9.20-24) to prove the point. In Moses' retelling of the golden calf incident he seems to give more prominence to his role as intercessor than does the narrator in Exodus.

Moses' retelling of this incident is notable for the way in which the phrase, 'forty days and forty nights', is used as a structural signal. As Lohfink has shown, the resulting narrative ignores chronological sequence in order to emphasize the sequence 'covenant formation, covenant breaking, covenant renewal' (Lohfink 1963: 211-15). There are evidently three occasions on which Moses is on the mountain: the first to receive the stone tables (9.9-15), the second to intercede for Israel and Aaron (9.18-20, 25-29; 10.10, 11) and the third to receive the second set of stone tables (10.1-5). While the Exodus narrative refers to at least one other trip besides these three (Exod. 24.9-11), there seems to be no real conflict with Moses' account. Moses' account stands out in that he speaks of three periods of forty days and forty nights, during at

viation of the negative report in Numbers from 71 Hebrew words in three separate passages (13.28, 29, 31-33) to 13 Hebrew words in one passage (1.28); and c) changing from direct quotation of the spies' negative report in Numbers to a hearsay quotation of their report after the people had returned to their tents.

least two of which he went without food or drink while the Exodus account refers to only two periods of forty days and nights (Exod. 24.18; 34.28), during only one of which Moses fasted (34.28). Moses also informs his hearers of his successful intercession for Aaron (9.20) which is not recorded in the narrator's account in Exodus.

What, if anything, should be made of these variations? Perhaps, first of all, it should be recalled that for both the narrator and Moses, Moses is a great intercessor. He put his own life on the line for Israel (Exod. 32.32). Moses' version does, however, expand his role slightly. When Moses intercedes in Deuteronomy we twice hear that 'he fell before the Lord for forty days and forty nights' (9.18, 25), very long periods of intercession. Exodus does not report the duration of the intercession. In Deuteronomy Moses does not go on just one superhuman fast but at least two (9.9, 18) and he saves not only the people as a whole from destruction but Aaron in particular as well. Again, I would not want to place too much weight on this; after all, Moses does not mention that during the third trip he also fasted (Exod. 34.28) or the fact that he asked Yahweh to blot him out of his book rather than destroy Israel (Exod. 32.32). But the tendency to overemphasize his own role slightly, which we have already seen, may be showing itself again.

*Deuteronomy 5.22-23*. In this passage Moses tells of the events immediately following the giving of the ten words at Horeb. The passage divides into two units: a) 5.22-27, the people's request for Moses to serve as mediator for Yahweh's word in the future, that is after the people's fear of death when Yahweh spoke the ten words to them directly; and b) 5.28-33, Moses' recalling of Yahweh's private confirmation to him of the correctness of the people's request for Moses to be mediator. Moses then uses this as the basis (therefore, v. 32) for a call to obedience to the commandment (sg.), statutes and ordinances which, Moses claims, Yahweh has given him privately, and which he is about to pass on to Israel.

In this passage Moses is portrayed as giving his justification for his mediatorial role between Yahweh and Israel. Both units of the passage are paralleled in other parts of the Primary History. The first, Deut. 5.22-27, is paralleled by the narrator's account in Exod. 20.18-21 and by Moses' second account of it in Deut. 18.16. The second, Deut. 5.28-33, is paralleled by another Mosaic version of it in Deut. 18.17-20.[27]

27. I am not suggesting that the two Mosaic accounts of the conversation are contradictory, only that they are two records of at least parts of the same conversation.

In Exod. 20.18,19 we read:

> And all the people saw (perceived?) the thunder and the lightning and the
> sound of the trumpet and the smoking mountain and the people were
> afraid. And they trembled and they stood far away, and they said to Moses,
> 'You speak with us and we will listen but do not let God speak with us,
> lest we die'.

In Hebrew the people's speech is twelve words. In Deut. 5.24 the
people's speech is expanded into seventy-five Hebrew words. In Deut.
18.16 the speech is cast in the singular and re-worded but is still only
sixteen words. Why the disparity? Or, perhaps more importantly, what is
the nature of the disparity? In all three texts the people desire a
mediator, are afraid of having Yahweh speak directly with them, and
fear that death will be the consequence. The re-wording of the Exodus
version of the speech in Deut. 18.16 is quite within the bounds of what
one would expect in indirect discourse. The only fundamental change is
that the aspect of Moses' mediatorial office which Moses is emphasizing
is the prophetic aspect.[28]

In Deut. 5.24-27, however, Moses takes on, for the lack of a better
term, a superhuman status. The people, according to Moses, had believed
that a single direct conversation between God and humans would cause
their death. The Horeb experience, they admitted, had proved them
wrong (v. 24), but to continue to hear God's voice directly would result
in death (v. 25). They then ask:

> For who is there of all flesh who has heard the voice of the living God
> speaking from the midst of the fire as we have and has still lived? (v. 26)

The people are portrayed as saying, if I may paraphrase, 'What we are
experiencing (i.e. hearing God speak directly and not dying) is unique.
We had better not press our luck. Perhaps next time we will die. We had
better let someone who is truly unique, that is Moses, mediate for us.'
Thus Moses is portrayed as quoting Israel to the effect that Moses is
unique. He, contrary to 'all flesh' and all past experience, is able to speak

---

28. Here I concur with Childs (1985: 109):

> The most important point to make is that Moses was assigned a unique role within
> Israel, but one which at the same time encompassed such a rich diversity as to include
> practically every other office in Israel: deliverer, lawgiver, prophet, priest, psalmist and
> sage. However, the central focus of Moses' unique place rested on his role as mediator
> of the covenant. For this reason, the diversity of his roles turned on different aspects of
> his exercising of this covenantal authority.

with Yahweh repeatedly in a most direct way and yet suffer no ill effects. The people then pledge their obedience to Yahweh's law as given by Moses (v. 27). For the people, Moses would have us believe, Moses is in a different category from even the unique children of Israel who themselves are different from 'all flesh'.

Compared with the Exodus version, the account in Deut. 5.22-27 is longer and more elaborate and perhaps stresses the uniqueness of Moses in a more emphatic way. In addition, in Moses' version the profession of Israel's willingness to obey his word (as it in turn is Yahweh's word given to him) occurs before Moses actually begins to receive that word, while in Exodus the people only commit themselves to obedience after Moses has received and delivered 'the words of Yahweh and the ordinances' (Exod. 20.18, 22; 24.3). If we are to infer anything from this besides the fact that Moses may be being portrayed as having a slightly telescopic memory, it would be that Moses portrays the people as slightly more eager to have Moses as mediator and to obey the law which he receives as mediator than the narrator does in Exodus.

If that were the only difference between the two accounts I would be tempted to ignore it and perhaps explain it as part of the 'hortatory style' of Deuteronomy. But Moses goes on to record a conversation that he claims to have had privately with Yahweh immediately following the people's request in which Yahweh directed Moses to serve as mediator for him. The narrator does not include this conversation in Exodus. In Deut. 5.28-31 we read:

> And Yahweh heard the voice of your words when you spoke to me. And Yahweh said to me, 'I have heard the voice of the words of this people which they have spoken to you. Isn't what they have spoken good? Oh, that they always had an attitude such as this, to fear me and to keep all my commandments, so that things would go well with them and with their children forever. Now you tell them to return to their tents but you stand here beside me and I will speak to you all the command, statutes, and ordinances which you will then teach them and they will do (them) in the land which I am giving to them for a possession.'

Thus according to Moses his mediatorial role is based not only on the people's request because they feared Yahweh's presence but also on the clear desire of Yahweh that Moses perform such a role. His mediatorial role had a unique divine sanction. Some would even go so far as to argue that the attitude of Israel which Yahweh compliments (v. 29) is not their commitment to obey his law (v. 27b) but their desire that

Moses be the mediator of that law (v. 27a).[29] Certainly the text as it stands is ambiguous at this point. The reverential fear which leads Israel to ask for a mediator is perhaps just as desirable from Yahweh's point of view as is the commitment to obey the law once given through the mediator. Perhaps it is the attitude which underlies both the request for a mediator and the pledge of obedience that bring Yahweh's favor. In any case, the legitimacy of Moses' mediatorial role is given a much more secure foundation in Moses' version of events than in the narrator's. Is this an indication of excessive pride on Moses' part? In view of the generally positive view taken of Moses' role by the narrator this seems unlikely. But Moses certainly is portrayed as retelling this event in a way that exalts his own role as mediator.

d. *Moses Reinterprets the Law*
In 4.2 and 13.1 Moses claims that his words are inviolable, that is not to be added to or taken from. The rationale for this inviolability is Moses' claim to have received the words which he gives from Yahweh (4.5, 40). But Moses is portrayed in Deuteronomy as doing to Yahweh's words what he forbids others doing to his own words, that is altering them by adding to them or taking from them. In 1.5 the narrator informs us that Moses does not dictate the law; he explains it. Here our question is, 'Does Moses' interpretive activity ever lead the reader to infer that Moses oversteps the bounds of his legitimate role of interpreter?'

*Moses' version of the ten words—Deuteronomy 5*. Moses twice makes a distinction within his words between those words which Yahweh spoke to Israel directly at Horeb (the ten words) and the 'commandment, statutes, and ordinances' (5.31) or just 'statutes and ordinances' (4.13, 14), which are only indirectly Yahweh's word, since Moses received them privately at Horeb and was directed to teach them to Israel. In the process of teaching them to Israel Moses obviously interprets them.

Just as the previous generation of Israel first heard the ten words from Yahweh's own voice (Exod. 20.1-17) and later heard Moses teach them the statutes and ordinances which he had received privately on the mountain (Exod. 24.3), so in Deuteronomy Moses first quotes the ten words to the new generation of Israel (Deut. 5.6-21) and then explains to them the commandment (sg.), statutes, and ordinances (6.1; 12.1).

With the distinction that Moses makes between the ten words and the

29. Craigie (1976: 166) seems to imply this as does von Rad (1966b: 60).

statutes and ordinances, one would expect that Moses would be very careful in quoting the ten words to be scrupulously accurate. The ten words were not meant to be interpreted by Moses according to the distinctions which he himself makes between the ten words and the other laws.

In 5.2-5 Moses calls the new generation to relive the original giving of the ten words:

> The LORD our God made a covenant with us at Horeb. Not with our fathers did the LORD make this covenant, but with us who are all of us here alive this day. The LORD spoke with you face to face at the mountain, out of the midst of the fire, while I stood between the LORD and you at that time to declare to you the word of the LORD, for you were afraid because of the fire, and you did not go up into the mountain (RSV).

Moses then quotes Yahweh giving the ten words at Horeb (5.6-21). However, when one compares the narrator's version of the ten words in Exod. 20.2-17 with Moses' version it is clear that Moses is portrayed as making a number of minor and major changes; both deleting from and adding to the narrator's version.

Perhaps it could be argued that the changes are all in substance minor. After all the prohibition against coveting surely applies to one's neighbor's field even though it is not specifically mentioned by Yahweh in Exodus. Further, changes in the word order[30] or substitution of synonyms for the 'sake of variation only' (Mayes 1979: 172), the presence or absence of the conjunction,[31] and the fuller form of words[32] are, by most standards, relatively minor variations. But what of the more substantive changes? Can they be explained as having no real consequence for the characterization of Moses?[33] Craigie[34] would view even the differences in the motivation for the sabbath commandment as minor and capable

30. In the prohibition of coveting, Exodus has house, wife, servants, maidservants, ass. In Deuteronomy the order is wife, house, field, manservant, maidservant, ox, ass.

31. In Deuteronomy the conjunction is added in vv. 10, 18, 19, 20, and twice in v. 21. Deuteronomy lacks the conjunction once in v. 21.

32. In v. 9 Deuteronomy has the full form אבות. In v. 16 the short form יאריכן. Both in contrast to Exodus.

33. By this I mean in changing the common view that the deuteronomic Moses is portrayed as a wholly reliable transmitter of Yahweh's word.

34. Craigie 1976: 156: 'The positive formulation of the commandment has some small differences which distinguish it from the form of the commandment in Exod. 20.8-11, and which are further evidence of the hortatory style in which the commandment is presented in Deuteronomy.'

of explanation in terms of the 'hortatory style' of Deuteronomy. Perhaps one could argue that the important issue in terms of the ten words is the commands themselves and not the motivation clauses,[35] which are (on this view) quite appropriately changed as Israel faces changing circumstances. But even the commands themselves are changed in 'small' ways.[36]

If Moses' interpretative activity includes altering even the ten words, which are not alterable (4.13, 14; 5.31), at least not in the same sense that the statutes and ordinances are, should the reader conclude that Moses is being portrayed as overstepping his legitimate interpretative role? In my view, the strong evidence for convergence in point of view between the narrator and Moses in general which we have already discussed argues against such a conclusion. Instead, I would argue that the reader who accepts the reliability of the narrator and of Yahweh, and is not therefore interested in deconstructing this text,[37] should infer that Moses is being portrayed as somehow unique as an interpreter of Yahweh's word. In the narrator's view, it is quite appropriate for Moses to alter Yahweh's word—even the ten words themselves—and then tell others not to alter his own words—words which he obtained by altering Yahweh's words. It is not appropriate, however, for others to do what Moses had done, unless it be the prophet or prophets like Moses of which he later speaks (18.15) but which had not arisen in Israel (34.10).

One could, of course, conclude that Moses, when he alters the ten words, is being portrayed as overstepping his legitimate role as interpreter of Yahweh's word. It seems to me that this conclusion, however, sets the reader at odds with the narrator who claims that Moses speaks in accordance with all that Yahweh had commanded him concerning Israel (1.3).

*Deuteronomy 18.9-22.* In 18.16-20 Moses gives his second account of his private conversation with Yahweh at Horeb when Israel asks that Moses serve as mediator (cf. 5.28-31). Our analysis will be clearer if we put the two accounts side by side.

---

35. This is a common procedure used to discover the 'original' form of the ten words. See, for example, Mayes 1979: 162-63.

36. 'Remember' (זכור) in Exod. 20.8 is 'keep' (שמור) in Deut. 5.12.

37. While this text seems an obvious place where a deconstructive analysis might prove illuminating, it is not within the scope of this work to pursue such an avenue of inquiry.

And you said, 'Behold Yahweh our God has made us see his glory and his greatness, and his voice we have heard from the midst of the fire. Today we have seen God speaking with man and lived. But now, why should we die? For this great fire will consume us; if we continue to hear the voice of Yahweh our God any longer we will die. For who is there of all flesh who has heard the voice of the living God speaking from the midst of this fire, as we have, and still lived? You go near and hear all that Yahweh our God will say and you will speak to us all that Yahweh our God speaks to you and we will hear and we will do (it) (Deut. 5.24-27).

[J]ust like all that you asked of Yahweh your God at Horeb, when the congregation gathered saying, 'Do not let me continue to hear the voice of Yahweh my God and let me no longer see this great fire. I cannot keep seeing it or else I will die' (Deut. 18.16).

While Moses has in 18.16 reworded the request and placed it in the first person singular (something the ancient versions didn't like[38]), it is clear that Moses is referring to the same occasion in both passages. Yahweh's response in each case is strikingly different.

And Yahweh heard the voice of your words as you spoke to me; and Yahweh said to me, 'I have heard the voice of the word of this people which they spoke to you. Isn't all they have said good? Oh that they always had such an attitude to fear me and to keep all my commands forever, in order that things should go well with them and their sons forever. You say to them, "Return to your own  tents". You stand right beside me and I will speak unto you all the commandment and statutes and ordinances which you will then teach them to do them in the land which I am giving them to possess' (Deut. 5.28-31).

And Yahweh said to me, 'What they have spoken is good. A prophet I will raise up for them from the midst of their brothers, like you. And I will put my words in his mouth and he will speak unto them all that I command him. And the man who does not give heed to my words which he will speak in my name, I will require it from him. But the prophet who presumes to speak words in my name, which I have not commanded him to speak or who speaks in the name of other gods, that "prophet" will die' (Deut. 18.17-20).

---

38. See *BHS*, p. 319.

Clearly one text (ch. 5) exalts the role of Moses as mediator while the other (ch. 18) refers to the continuity of his role for there is to be at least one other who will fill it. Perhaps conflict is not the right word to use of the relationship between these two texts. It is possible to imagine a scenario where Yahweh affirms Moses as mediator and then also informs him that this 'office' or role will be continued in Israel.

Perhaps the existence of two very different accounts can be explained by inferring that Moses is being portrayed as using a rhetorical strategy. Moses' strategy may be to affirm his (unique?) divine sanction to deliver and interpret the law before he does so in chs. 12–26. For Moses to include the fact that he is not alone in his task but that one or more others will, in the future, perform the same function would in his view have undermined the immediacy and relevant authority of the law. Moses wants his law to be taken with the utmost seriousness and so he affirms his unique right and responsibility to communicate that law before he delivers it.

After he has begun to deliver the law in 12.1 the knowledge that Yahweh will continue to speak through one or more prophetic inter-mediaries may in Moses' view be a necessary reassurance to an Israel which is about to face the future without him. It is to be noted that the same obedience that Moses expects to be given to his word is also, in the view of Yahweh (i.e. the Yahweh of Moses), to be granted to the future prophet or prophets. The future intermediary figure(s), in other words, has the same authority status as does Moses. The fact that he waits until ch. 18 to tell his listeners about other mediatorial figures can be explained by the rhetorical strategy of Moses.

However, the reader still has difficulty in accepting Moses' version of events. The reader wonders whether it really makes sense for Yahweh to speak of the continuation of prophetic mediators to Moses during the initial making of the covenant. Before Israel has shrunk back from the conquest (Num. 14) and especially before Moses has sinned (Num. 20) and been excluded from Canaan, the succession of Moses was not a relevant question. It has to be asked whether Moses has the sequence of events right, especially since the narrator reports no such conversation in Exodus.

But if the reader assumes that Moses is being portrayed as inventing the conversation in ch. 18, what motive could be attributed to Moses in linking what he claims are both parts of a conversation which he had with Yahweh at Horeb? Self-justification? Hardly. By delivering the account in ch. 18 in addition to the one in ch. 5 Moses undermines his unique status. According to ch. 18 he is unique in his own generation but not absolutely unique. Another will take up the same function.

There is a fairly obvious answer to the reader's question. In 18.18 Yahweh's words sound strangely familiar. They are not the people's words, since they asked for Moses to be a mediator; they did not ask that there be others to follow in Moses' line. In fact these words seem to be Moses' own words in 18.15. What this text appears to show is Moses being portrayed as putting his own words into the mouth of Yahweh. At Horeb the people had not asked for a future person or persons like Moses to mediate for them. They wanted Moses to mediate for them then and there. It was Moses' own promise that, 'Yahweh your God will raise up to you a prophet from your midst, from your brothers' (18.15). He justifies this promise by referring to the fear of the people at Horeb of continuing to hear Yahweh's voice directly without a mediator. They asked Moses to serve as mediator (18.16). Yahweh said that their request (for Moses to be mediator and for them to obey Moses' mediated instruction) was a good one. Somewhat irrelevantly Yahweh then supposedly promised to raise up a future prophet or prophets from the midst of their brothers like Moses (18.17). Yahweh didn't answer the people's request for Moses to mediate because Moses has apparently put his words (18.15) into Yahweh's mouth (18.18). The roles are reversed. Before, Yahweh would speak, Moses would listen and then convey Yahweh's word to Israel, perhaps with a few minor modifications. Here Moses speaks; Yahweh listens and repeats what Moses said.

Unless one assumes without any evidence that the narrator is leading the reader to infer that Moses has the right to put words into Yahweh's mouth this text makes it particularly difficult not to conclude that the reliability of Moses as a conveyor of Yahweh's word is suspect in this particular instance.

### e. *Moses Takes Over Yahweh's Roles*
*Moses' claim to give the land to Israel—Deuteronomy 3.12-22.* In Moses' account of the distribution of Transjordan to the two and one-half tribes the first-time reader encounters for the first time the interplay within Moses' speech between attributing an action or the arrival of a state of affairs to Yahweh and attributing the same action or arrival of a state of affairs to Moses. In 3.12-22 on six occasions Moses is reported as saying, 'I gave' (נתתי) in relation to the entire Transjordan (v. 13), some part of it (vv. 12, 13, 15, 16) or its cities (v. 19). By contrast,

Yahweh is once said to have given the Transjordan (v. 18) and once Moses says that Yahweh will be or is giving the Cisjordanian portion of the land to the other nine and one-half tribes (v. 20). In addition, we are informed that the region of the Argob was taken (לקח) by Jair, not given by Moses or Yahweh (v. 14).

Within the narrative world of Deuteronomy it is true to say that Yahweh gave the land to Israel and Moses gave it to the Transjordanian tribes. It is also true to say that while Yahweh gives the land it must still be taken in battle by a human agent. It is difficult to know what, if any-thing, the reader should make of this observation. Is Moses portrayed as taking credit that should belong to Yahweh? Is the reader to assume that it is right and appropriate that Moses take credit for his part in leading Israel to victory or are we to assume that some sort of interplay between divine sovereignty and human agency is being hinted at? Asking these questions is easier than answering them, but the phenomenon of Moses attributing words and deeds to himself that the reader might expect to be attributed to Yahweh is not limited to this pericope.

*Moses speaks as though he is Yahweh.* Driver notes a series of texts in Deuteronomy (7.4; 11.14, 15; 17.3; 28.20; 29.3) in which, 'the discourse of Moses pass[es] insensibly into that of God'.[39] It seems clear that these texts, or at least some of them, imply that in normal speech, without any warning or verbal or textual indicators, Moses can suddenly slip into and out of divine speech in the first person. This phenomenon could then be viewed by the reader in a positive or a negative light. Negatively, this phenomenon could be viewed as Moses being portrayed as misusing his function as conveyor of Yahweh's word and, at least potentially, attempting to claim a status for himself and his word in his hearer's eyes that they would not ordinarily give to them. If viewed positively the reader could infer that this is one way the narrator uses to confirm the divine origin of Moses' speech and seeks thereby to elevate Moses' status as mediator in the reader's eyes.

*Deuteronomy 7.4.* Moses warns Israel, having defeated the inhabitants of Canaan, to utterly destroy them without mercy (7.2) and to avoid all social contact with them, especially intermarriage (7.3). Moses then gives his reason for recommending this harsh treatment:

39. S.R. Driver 1902: 99. I see no reason to include 5.11 in this list as Driver does.

> For they would turn your sons from following *me*, to serve other gods;
> then the anger of the LORD would be kindled against you and he would
> destroy you quickly (7.4 RSV, my emphasis).

In the apparatus of *BHS*, Hempel suggests, but without textual support,
that MT's מאחרי, that is 'following me', should read יהוה מאחרי, that is
'following Yahweh', evidently assuming that יהוה has dropped out in the
process of transmission. Another possible explanation is that the *yod* in
MT could be understood as an ancient abbreviation for Yahweh which
was later misunderstood as a suffix (G.R. Driver 1961: 119-20). While
either of these views is a possible explanation of this text both are
uncertain.

*Deuteronomy 11.14, 15.* In this passage Moses states that if Israel obeys
his command to love and serve Yahweh then:

> I will give the rain for your land in its time, the early and the latter rains,
> and you will harvest your grain and your wine and your oil; and I will give
> grass in your fields for your beasts and you will eat and be satisfied
> (11.14, 15).

The referent of the 'I' in both vv. 14 and 15 is Moses and yet in v. 17
Moses refers to *Yahweh* shutting up the heavens so that there would be
no rain. If we take MT as it stands Moses is portrayed as slipping into
and out of divine speech without any warning. This passage has textual
difficulties. In v. 14 the Samaritan Pentateuch, the Vulgate, a Qumran
mezuzah text (DJD III: 161), and most of the Greek manuscripts assume
an original, 'he (Yahweh) will give'. In v. 15 the Vulgate and a Cairo
Geniza manuscript omit the phrase 'I will give' altogether while the
Samaritan Pentateuch and some Greek texts assume an original, 'he
(Yahweh) will give'.[40] In this case, however, the MT has a strong
argument in its favor in that it is the harder reading (Mayes 1979: 215).

*Deuteronomy 17.3.* Here Moses legislates the death penalty for anyone
who breaks the covenant by worshiping other gods. The issue of interest
in 17.3 to us is that Moses recommends the death penalty for worshiping
and serving gods, 'which I [Moses] have forbidden'. While this is a
possible case of Moses reverting to divine speech without warning, it is
by no means certain. It is true that Moses had personally forbidden the
worship of other gods (13.1-18) and it therefore seems that it could be

---

40. On the textual evidence in general see *BHS*, p. 306.

entirely appropriate for Moses to refer to his own, as distinct from
Yahweh's, prohibition of idol worship.

*Deuteronomy 28.20.* In this section Moses warns Israel that if they
disobey Yahweh's commandments which he had just finished delivering
in chs. 12–26 they would be cursed (28.15-20a). He then gives the reason
for Yahweh sending his curses upon them. It would be, 'on account of
the evil of your doings, because you have forsaken me [Moses]' (RSV).
It seems odd that Moses would assert that Yahweh would curse Israel
because they had forsaken Moses. More probably, this is an example of
Moses reverting to divine speech.[41]

*Deuteronomy 29.5 (Eng. 29.6).* Recalling Yahweh's miracles by which
he had delivered and sustained Israel during the Exodus and Wandering,
Moses turns in this passage to his own role:

> I have led you forty years in the wilderness; your clothes have not worn
> out on you; and your sandals have not worn off your feet; you have not
> eaten bread, and you have not drunk wine or strong drink; that you may
> know that I [Moses] am the LORD your God (29.5, 6 RSV).

This text contains an example of Moses reverting to divine speech in the
first person without any warning or textual clues.[42]

*Summary.* We have seen that in at least three places (11.14, 15; 28.20;
29.5) and possibly in two others (7.4; 17.3) Moses is portrayed as
slipping into and out of divine speech in the first person, that is speaking
as though he was Yahweh, without in any way alerting his hearers.
There is no way I know of to decide whether the narrator is intending
for the reader to evaluate Moses' activity in these passages in a positive
or a negative light.

f. *Summary and Conclusions on Divergence*
I have argued that Moses is in clear conflict with the narrator over the
reason for Moses' exclusion from Canaan. Moses blames the earlier
generation of Israel in a self-justifying way while the narrator puts the

41. There is some limited textual evidence for changing 'me' to 'the Lord' or
'him', i.e. Yahweh (*BHS*, p. 335), but the criterion of the harder reading is a strong
argument in favor of the MT.
42. *BHS*, p. 339, notes that Codex Vaticanus, in v. 5b reads: 'so that you may
know, that this (is) the Lord your God', but cites no other evidence of textual variation.

blame on Moses himself. We have also seen good evidence that Moses is portrayed as retelling the past in such a way as to make himself look better and conversely Israel look worse than they really were according to the narrator. I have noted that on one occasion (18.18) Moses may be being portrayed as overstepping his legitimate role as conveyor of Yahweh's word by putting his own words into Yahweh's mouth. Elsewhere, however, the narrator leads the reader to infer that Moses' interpretative activity is quite acceptable.

Finally, while it is clear that Moses is seemingly portrayed as taking over some of the roles the reader would ordinarily expect to be the reserve of Yahweh alone it is not clear that the narrator is leading the reader to assume that this is necessarily an inappropriate thing for Moses to do.

## 4. *Conclusions*

The strength of the evidence for the habitual convergence in point of view between the narrator and Moses must not be disregarded when the reader attempts to synthesize the evidence for convergence with the evidence for divergence. If the narrator is presumed to be reliable, as here, it is clear that Moses is an essentially reliable character who can usually be trusted to be a mouthpiece for the narrator's perspective. The exceptions to this general rule are, relatively speaking, minor. Moses cannot be trusted when he blames the people entirely for his own exclusion from Canaan or when he retells events in a way that is self-congratulatory. Further the reader infers that it is inappropriate in the narrator's view for Moses to put his own words into Yahweh's mouth as he may have done in 18.18.

But at both the beginning (1.3, 5) and the end (34.10-12) of Deuteronomy the narrator makes it clear that Moses is an essentially reliable character. While my specific interest in this chapter has been the examination of the evidence for the unreliability of Moses—and I have found some—the overall perspective of the narrator must not be forgotten. The narrator's final evaluation of Moses is very positive indeed.

> And there has not arisen a prophet since in Israel like Moses, whom the LORD knew face to face, none like him for all the signs and wonders which the LORD sent him to do in the land of Egypt, to Pharaoh and to all his servants and to all his land, and for all the mighty power and all the great and terrible deeds which Moses wrought in the sight of all Israel (Deut. 34.10-12 RSV).

Chapter 2

## THE RELIABILITY OF JOSHUA

### 1. *Introduction*

This chapter is an examination of the reliability of Joshua as a character within the book of Joshua.[1] The introductory section of the book (1.1-9), which serves to prepare the reader for what is to follow,[2] introduces four themes which are the key components of the narrative portrayal of Joshua as it unfolds.

First of all, in 1.2, 3 Yahweh assures Joshua that he is giving (v. 2), or has already given (v. 3), the land to Israel. A central dichotomy of the book is the fact that even though this is so, Israel, and consequently Joshua as its leader, must acquire the land through military force if Yahweh's promise is to be fulfilled. The relationship between Yahweh's giving and Israel's taking the land is central to the plot of the book and to the portrayal of Joshua.

Secondly, in 1.5b Yahweh promises to be with Joshua just as he was with Moses. The development the reader sees in Joshua from being the subordinate of Moses to a leader in his own right, with a stature of his own, is a key to the analysis of the narrative portrayal of Joshua.

Thirdly, Joshua is given divine encouragement three times in the opening section (vv. 6, 7, 9). Joshua's development as a character is shown by the fact that he begins as a character who seems to need the encouragement of others, but ends up being a character who gives encouragement to others.

Finally, Yahweh directs Joshua to be very careful to obey the law of Moses (vv. 7, 8). Joshua's obedience or otherwise to Moses' written

1. The Primary History serves as the wider literary context for my analysis. It is not part of my purpose to examine the pentateuchal narratives which concern Joshua except as they impinge directly upon the book of Joshua. For this see Schäfer-Lichtenberger 1989.

2. Polzin (1980: 74) terms this passage a 'thematic reprise'.

Torah and to the oral Torah of Yahweh is important for the reader's evaluation of the reliability of Joshua.

It is the thesis of this chapter that within the book Joshua *develops* into a fully reliable character who has a status that is independent of Moses, who is as successful as he can be at his central tasks, and who is a trustworthy servant of Yahweh and an entirely reliable guide to the narrator's point of view.

### 2. *The Land: Yahweh's Gift or Israel's Achievement*

a. *Introduction*

In 1.11 Joshua instructs the people to cross the Jordan 'to go in to *take* possession of the land which Yahweh, your God is *giving* to you to possess it'. The seeming dichotomy between the land as Yahweh's gift and the land as Israel's acquisition is made plain in this single clause. On the one hand, Yahweh gives the land. On the other, Israel must fight to win it. Yahweh will guide the course of the battle but Israel must take up the sword. As Israel's leader Joshua's own understanding of how these seeming opposites work together, and his actual behavior in alternatively relying on Yahweh to act on Israel's behalf and acting himself, is important in evaluating him as a character. The reader asks, 'How much does Joshua rely on Yahweh to do and how much does he take to be his own responsibility?', and then, 'How is the reader to evaluate Joshua in light of the way in which he understands and acts upon this central dichotomy?'

b. *Joshua the Military Strategist*

*Introduction.* One of Joshua's primary roles is that of general of Israel's forces. Joshua says and does a number of things on his own initiative without Yahweh's prior authorization which the reader would expect any ordinary military leader to say and do. Joshua's actions and words demonstrate that he is not a passive bystander in the conquest but plays a full and integral part in it. Joshua takes the human part of the divine/human equation very seriously.

*Prepare your provisions—Joshua 1.10, 11.* In 1.2 Yahweh instructs Joshua to cross the Jordan without specifying the exact timing of the crossing. Joshua prepares the people by instructing them to prepare their food for the journey across the Jordan which, Joshua says, will happen in three days' time.[3] It is possible that the reader should infer that Joshua intends the people to attain food from sources other than the daily provision of manna that was still falling (Josh. 5.12) since manna could not be stored overnight (Exod. 16.19, 20; cf. Woudstra 1981: 64-65). The use of the word צידה supports this since it is usually used of food stored for a journey of some length.[4] If Joshua is to be so understood this shows that he relies on the ordinary human means of feeding an army as opposed to relying solely on the divinely given manna. But even if this is not the case Joshua shows a common-sense concern for the administrative details of moving a large group of people into a hostile environment.

*Reassurances from the Transjordanian tribes—Joshua 1.12-18.* Here Joshua uses his own military common sense by ensuring that his forces are as strong as possible. He seeks reassurances from the Transjordanian tribes that they will make good their pledge to Moses (Num. 32.20-22) to send their fighting men across the Jordan with the other tribes to assist them in the conquest.

*The spies sent to Jericho—Joshua 2.1.* In sending the spies[5] Joshua acts on his own initiative and once again his actions indicate military common sense.

*The taking of Jericho—Joshua 6.* In this narrative Yahweh first gives instructions to Joshua about how the city is to be taken (vv. 3-5). Then Joshua directs the priests and the people about how to carry out the battle strategy (vv. 6, 7). Finally, the narrator records how Joshua's instructions were carried out (vv. 8-16), explaining that the people acted 'as Joshua had commanded [them]' (v. 8).

There are three principal differences between what Yahweh directs Joshua to tell the people to do and what they actually do. First, Joshua

3. For the chronological difficulty see Woudstra 1981: 65, 79.
4. BDB, p. 845; Gen. 42.25; 45.21; Exod. 12.39; Josh. 9.11; Judg. 20.10; 1 Sam. 22.10.
5. Polzin (1980: 85, 86), because he treats the Deuteronomic History as his wider literary unit, accepts Moses' implied rebuke of the people for initiating the original spy mission (Deut. 1.22). Joshua's action in sending the spies is therefore viewed by Polzin in a negative light. Num. 13.1, 2, however, attributes the idea to Yahweh. Since the Primary History is our wider textual unit Joshua's sending of spies is no grounds for the reader assuming that Joshua lacks courage or is somehow otherwise deficient in sending them.

divides the troops which are to accompany the ark into 'the armed men' (חלוץ) who are to walk in front of the ark (v. 7) and the rest or 'rear guard' (RSV) who are to follow it (v. 9). Secondly, Yahweh directed that trumpets were to be blown on the seventh day (v. 4). In the event the trumpets are also blown on each of the first six days (v. 13). Finally, Joshua changes the signal for the battle cry from a trumpet blast[6] to his own verbal signal (v. 16).

The reader should not make too much of these changes since they are relatively minor. They do, however, demonstrate that Joshua displays a certain freedom in the way he carries out even fairly specific battle strategies which Yahweh gives him. Like any general he assumes he has the freedom to make minor adjustments in tactics on his own authority.

The reader could infer that Joshua's alterations are designed to enhance the surprise element in the battle strategy. If the inhabitants of Jericho only heard the trumpets blowing on the seventh day they would in all probability realize that this was a signal for the battle to begin and prepare themselves accordingly. By having the trumpets blown every day Joshua could be trying to prevent them from being tipped off as to the day of the attack. The changing of the signal for the battle cry from a trumpet blast to Joshua's own verbal signal could also serve this purpose. If the reader makes such an inference Joshua is seen to be a competent military strategist even as he carries out Yahweh's orders. This inference is, however, uncertain.

*The first battle at Ai—Joshua 7.2-5.* After the defeat of Jericho Joshua decides on the next target and sends spies to reconnoiter Ai (v. 2). The spies return and recommend that only two or three thousand men be sent to take the city since they consider it to be a relatively soft target (v. 3). Joshua, perhaps erring on the side of caution, sends three thousand men (v. 4).

If it were not for v. 1, the first-time reader could attribute the defeat at Ai to bad military planning by Joshua. After all, at the second battle Joshua decided that even with Yahweh's help 35,000 troops in all would be needed just for the ambush party (8.3, 12). The reader might also infer that the narrator is making an implicit rebuke of Joshua for not waiting for Yahweh's directive before plunging recklessly ahead in the first battle with Ai. But the narrator rules out such speculation in v. 1.

---

6.    This 'blast' (משך v. 5) is to be distinguished from the blowing (תקע) which was to occur during the seven circuits around the city.

Israel's defeat is the result of Achan's sin and Yahweh's concomitant anger against the nation (7.1), not Joshua's weak strategy.

The passage does reveal, however, Joshua's understanding of the relationship between Yahweh's giving the land and Israel's responsibility to take it. Joshua here seems to operate under the assumption that it is his responsibility to carry out battle plans as he sees fit and Yahweh's to ensure that the nation is victorious. Thus he does not see the need to consult Yahweh over the battle with Ai[7] and he prosecutes the battle with his best judgment.

Joshua's complaint against Yahweh over the defeat at Ai shows this. Joshua, in all sincerity, blames Yahweh for the defeat. It does not seem even to occur to Joshua that Israel's defeat might be due to something other than Yahweh's failure to protect Israel. He blames Yahweh because he has no knowledge of Achan's sin and he can see nothing wrong in the approach he took to the planning and the execution of the battle.

*The second battle at Ai—Joshua 8.* After the punishment of Achan and his family for violating the ban Yahweh directs Joshua to attack Ai once again (8.1). Yahweh's words to Joshua on this occasion point in a quite striking manner to the creative dialectic between the land as Yahweh's gift and the land as Israel's military conquest. On the one hand Yahweh encourages Joshua not to fear or be dismayed (v. 1) and promises Israel victory (vv. 1b, 2a). On the other hand, Yahweh instructs him to take *all* the fighting men with him (v. 1a) and to lay an ambush behind the city (v. 2b). In other words, Yahweh, having seen his nation defeated with a force of 3,000 men, tells Joshua to take no chances this time by taking all the military men and by using an ambush. Yahweh promises to give them victory, but for Yahweh, as well as for Joshua, the land being a divine gift does not preclude using the best military planning available.

Joshua shows that he understands this dialectic in a similar way to Yahweh. Having been directed to lay an ambush, Joshua sets one of 30,000 men so that the ambush party alone outnumbers the inhabitants of Ai by a significant margin (30,000 to 12,000). Further, after spending the first night among the people, Joshua reinforces the original ambush party by adding another 5,000 troops for a total of 35,000 (8.12) and spends an extra night before proceeding with the battle. This may indicate a certain cautiousness on Joshua's part in military matters. The size

7.    The choice of Ai as a target makes military sense as an attempt to divide the potential enemy into two parts by gaining control of the middle of the land first.

of the ambush party in relation to the enemy, the specific details of the
ambush, the reinforcement of the ambush party, and the additional
night's delay all show caution and military common sense. Joshua relies
on Yahweh's promises, but he also ensures that he has a better army.

*The defeat of the southern coalition—Joshua 10.1-15.* In this narrative
Israel faces a coalition of several kings who are threatening Israel's new
treaty partners, the Gibeonites. Joshua and his military force leave the
camp at Gilgal for Gibeon (v. 7). On the way Joshua receives Yahweh's
promise of victory (v. 8). Joshua then carries out a surprise attack by
marching all night and coming upon them 'suddenly' (פתאם; v. 9). Next,
Yahweh throws the opposition into a panic (v. 10a) and as a result Israel
defeats them at Gibeon and chases them to Azekah and Makkedah
(v. 10b). As they are fleeing Yahweh again lends assistance by throwing
hailstones down upon them (v. 11). Joshua then commands Yahweh to
stop the sun from going down so that Israel will have light to fight in
(vv. 12, 13), and Yahweh obeys (שמע ב; v. 14) him.

The narrative alternates between describing Joshua's and Israel's part
in prosecuting the battle, and Yahweh's part in seeing that Israel is
victorious. Joshua and Israel act in vv. 7, 9, 10b, 12, 13, 15. Yahweh acts
or responds in vv. 8, 10a, 11, 14.

Interestingly, the two sides of the divine/human equation are com-
bined in a remarkable way in vv. 12-14. Joshua, in a sort of role reversal,
commands Yahweh to act and Yahweh obeys (v. 14). What Joshua
seeks, that is more daylight so that his forces can complete the rout, is
what any general would seek in the circumstances. But Joshua is no
ordinary general. He gets those things for which ordinary generals only
hope. Joshua orders Yahweh, as though he were a subordinate, to use
his power to stop the sun. The divine and human sides of the conquest
are merged. A human agent Joshua temporarily takes upon himself the
role of Yahweh and Yahweh temporarily takes on the role of Joshua's
subordinate by obeying his instructions.

*Mopping up in the south—Joshua 10.16-43.* This passage records the
actions of Joshua and Israel from the time of the stopping of the sun
until Israel's return to the camp at Gilgal (v. 43).[8] The portrayal of

8. Since the return to the camp at Gilgal is already reported in v. 15, vv. 16-43
are out of chronological sequence and serve to fill in some details that are lacking in
the earlier narrative in vv. 7-15. Boling and Wright (1982: 277) remove the difficulty
by excising v. 15, which is missing in the LXX, and treating vv. 12-14 as a digression.

Joshua in 11.16-43 is strikingly different from the portrayal of him given in 11.8-15. In vv. 16-43 Joshua prosecutes the battle without recourse to direct divine intervention or even explicit divine guidance.

During the battle against the southern coalition Joshua is informed that the five kings who lead the coalition have hidden themselves in the cave at Makkedah (vv. 16, 17). Joshua tells his soldiers to prevent the kings from escaping by setting a guard and rolling great stones against the mouth of the cave (v. 18). The rest of the forces are to keep chasing the fleeing enemy (v. 19). After the pursuit has finished, Joshua gathers his victorious forces at Makkedah, where he uses the public execution of the five kings to encourage his forces to believe in their ultimate victory against their enemies (vv. 21-27). There follows a series of battle reports in which one city after another falls to Joshua in rapid fashion.

In vv. 16-43 Joshua chooses which cities to attack and in what order and uses ordinary military means to achieve success. The rapidity of Joshua's success is due to the fact that 'Yahweh, the God of Israel fought for Israel' (v. 42), but there is no indication that Joshua is given the sort of direct divine intervention or explicit divine guidance in the mopping up operation which he received in the initial battle.

*The northern coalition—Joshua 11.1-15.* Here Joshua again uses the surprise attack (v. 7). He also uses 'all his people of war' (RSV), apparently judging that the incredible size of the opposition (v. 4) requires as large a military force as possible, once again indicating military common sense.

*Summary and conclusions.* We have seen that Joshua consistently acts in ways which suggest that he takes his responsibility in leading Israel to take the land by force quite seriously. He uses ordinary military strategy and common sense in his leading of Israel's armed forces. He makes sure his army has sufficient provisions (1.10, 11) and that it is as large as possible by having the Transjordanians join them (1.12-18). He sends spies to obtain key information about the enemy (2.1; 7.2). It is possible that he modifies Yahweh's battle plans for Jericho in order to maximize the surprise element. He uses the surprise attack on two occasions (10.9; 11.7) and an ambush on another (8.3-22). He matches the size of his army to the relative strength of the opponent (7.3; 11.7). He displays caution by sending the largest number of troops that might be needed, rather than the least with which Israel might achieve success (7.4; 8.3, 12). He uses a military execution to give encouragement to his troops (10.25). He sometimes chooses where to attack (7.2; 10.29, 31, 34, 36, 38), while on other occasions his battle plans are determined by Yahweh (6.2-5; 8.1) or circumstances (10.1-6, 33; 11.1-5).

From this the reader infers that Joshua operates with the assumption that Yahweh's guarantees of victory do not absolve him of the responsibility of using his best military judgment.[9] Yahweh also displays an appreciation of the importance of strategy (8.2). The reader infers, therefore, that since Yahweh is a very reliable guide to the narrator's point of view in general, and since Joshua displays the same attitude to the divine/human dialectic as Yahweh, Joshua is also a reliable guide to the narrator's point of view on this central issue.

c. *Joshua the Trusting Servant*
*Introduction.* Joshua shows a reliance on Yahweh to do things for Israel militarily which ordinary generals do not depend on their gods to do for them. Joshua shows that he recognizes that while it is his responsibility to use sound military judgment Israel still will not succeed in taking the land unless Yahweh fights for Israel.

*Taking Jericho—Joshua 6.* Even if the reader assumes that Joshua's modifications of Yahweh's instructions concerning Jericho have a military purpose as suggested above, the most obvious point about those instructions should not be missed. As a human battle strategy Yahweh's plans make little sense. The main weapon is the people's shout which Yahweh promises will bring down the walls of Jericho. It is a miracle which is the decisive factor in the defeat of Jericho. Joshua may make modest alterations to Yahweh's plans, but he retains the most important part of the strategy, that is relying on Yahweh to perform a miracle.

*Joshua's complaint—Joshua 7.6-9.* As noted above, Joshua's complaint to Yahweh over the defeat at Ai shows that he operated under the assumption that Yahweh was to be trusted to ensure victory.

*The second battle with Ai—Joshua 8.* With Israel defeated at the first attempt to take Ai, Yahweh directs Joshua to attack them again. The strategy for taking Ai, an ambush, seems a very human one, but it comes

---

9.  Cf. Butler 1983: 115: 'Divine assurance does not exclude human wit and action.'

from Yahweh, not from Joshua. As noted above, Joshua does show caution by sending a very large ambush party and then reinforcing it, but Joshua relies on Yahweh for: a) the encouragement needed to face an enemy who has already beaten Israel (v. 1); b) the general strategy (v. 2); and c) the use of the javelin as the signal for the ambush to be sprung (v. 18). It may be a very human-sounding battle plan, but Joshua relies on Yahweh for it; he does not think it up himself.

*The sun stands still—Joshua 10.8-15.* Here Yahweh does not just give an overall battle strategy and perform a single miracle as at Jericho. He kills the enemy soldiers directly with hailstones (v. 11) and even stops the sun so that the battle may continue. The dramatic and direct way in which Yahweh intervenes in this battle is remarkable (v. 14). Even though Joshua takes the initiative in a more direct way in this passage he also displays a greater reliance on Yahweh's intervention than elsewhere.

*Yahweh helps the mopping up—Joshua 10.16-43.* The recounting of the mopping up of the southern coalition seems to progress naturally. Joshua moves from one city to the next in a fairly logical fashion and defeats the enemy in battle. There are no reports of miracles or any other sort of direct divine intervention. But, from another point of view, Yahweh seems very much directly involved in the battles. Punctuating the narrative at various points are statements which indicate that Yahweh is guiding the course of the battles (vv. 30, 32, 42) and that Joshua recognizes that Israel is winning, not because of its superior military prowess, but because Yahweh is helping them (vv. 19, 25).

*The northern campaign—Joshua 11.1-20.* Faced with an enemy army, 'in number like the sand of the seashore' (v. 4), Joshua receives reassurance of victory from Yahweh. The narrator also informs the reader that 'Yahweh gave them into the hand of Israel' (v. 8). Joshua thus shows reliance on Yahweh for encouragement and for victory in battle.

d. *Conclusions*

The dichotomy between the land as Yahweh's gift and Joshua's and Israel's responsibility to take the land by force is only an apparent dichotomy, not a real one. The narrator makes it clear that both aspects of the apparent dichotomy are simultaneously true. Joshua demonstrates that he understands the complementary nature of these seeming opposites, and because he does understand, the reader infers that, in regard to this crucial issue, Joshua is a purveyor of the narrator's point of view.

Joshua acts as though it is his responsibility to execute the military aspects of the conquest as he sees fit. Yahweh's responsibility is to give encouragement (8.1) and specific advice about the battle when it is needed. It is also Yahweh's responsibility in Joshua's view to ensure that Israel is victorious in battle by intervening in a direct or an indirect fashion as called for by the specific circumstances. There is nothing in the narrative to indicate that Joshua gets the balance wrong between using his own initiative on the one hand, and relying on Yahweh to act on the other hand. Joshua uses military common sense, but he does not rely on this exclusively. He expects Yahweh to intervene, but he does not sit back and expect Yahweh to do it all. He leads Israel to go in and take possession of the land, but he recognizes that ultimately it is Yahweh who gives the land. In this he concurs with the narrator's point of view.

## 3. *As I Was With Moses, So I Will Be With You*

### a. *Introduction*

In 1.1 Moses is described as 'the servant of Yahweh' and Joshua is described as 'Moses' minister'. The last time Joshua is given an epithet in the book he is called, 'the servant of Yahweh' (24.29). The development of Joshua from being Moses' subordinate into a person who has a status that is no longer dependent for its definition on his former relationship to Moses is a key part of the portrayal of Joshua. By the end of the book Joshua has stepped out from under the shadow of Moses and has a relationship with Yahweh that is parallel in many ways to Moses' own relationship to Yahweh.

### b. *Joshua Assumes the Place of Moses*

*Introduction.* As Childs has noted, '[T]he figure of Joshua, especially in the first eleven chapters, is often consciously set in a typological relation to Moses' (1979: 245). The reader notes that some of Joshua's actions, roles, and experiences are reminiscent of those of Moses. While Joshua is not, and never becomes, a second Moses except in a very weak sense,[10] he does take Moses' place as Israel's leader and comes to have a status

---

10. Butler (1983: 282-83) notes that Joshua attains the title reserved for Moses only after his death. He continues, 'The point being made is that the title, "servant of Yahweh" belongs supremely to Moses. No man can claim the title for himself and use it to rule others. Others must confer it in respectful memory.'

in the eyes of Israel, Yahweh, and the reader which is similar to that of Moses.

*The authority of Joshua's word—Joshua 1.15-18.* In 1.5 Yahweh promises to be with Joshua as he was with Moses. The Transjordanians draw the reader's attention back to that promise by expressing the wish that it be fulfilled (v. 17b). They also promise to give to Joshua the same obedience that they claim to have given to Moses (v. 17a) and express the view that disobedience to Joshua's word, like disobedience to that of Moses, should be a capital offence (v. 18). Yahweh's promise to Joshua in v. 5 has started to be fulfilled. One of the results of Yahweh being with Moses had been that Israel had come to have great respect for him and for his word. The Transjordanians express that same sort of respect for Joshua and his word.

*Crossing the Jordan—Joshua 3.7; 4.14.* Josh. 3.7 and 4.14 form an inclusio around the crossing narrative. In 3.7 Yahweh promises to exalt Joshua in the eyes of Israel that very day, that is the day of the crossing. Yahweh's stated purpose in exalting Joshua is that the nation will come to recognize that Yahweh is with Joshua in the same way that he has been with Moses. In 4.14 the narrator informs the reader that the promised exaltation has in fact taken place. The result is that Israel stands in awe of (ירא) Joshua just as they have stood in awe of (ירא) Moses. As Woudstra (1981: 94) remarks:

> The parallel with Moses' position after the Red Sea crossing is striking (cf. Exod. 14.31b). Joshua, like Moses, is accepted as God's accredited spokesman. The fear and the respect the people had felt for Moses is transferred to Joshua.

Joshua makes the parallel between Moses leading Israel through the Red Sea and his own leading of Israel across the Jordan explicit in his speech to the people after the crossing (v. 23). By means of the miraculous crossing Yahweh gives to Joshua a similar role for the conquest generation that he gave to Moses for the Exodus generation.[11]

*Holy ground—Joshua 5.13-15.* Just as Moses was instructed during the burning bush episode to take his shoes off because he was standing on

---

11. Hamlin 1983: xiii: 'The sea crossing out of a land of slavery is balanced by the river crossing into a land of freedom.'

holy ground (Exod. 3.5), so here Joshua is instructed to do the same and for the same reason (Josh. 5.15). In both instances the human figure was about to lead Israel to victory over a formidable adversary, has an experience of the numinous, and receives assurances that Yahweh would grant him victory in the struggle. Joshua thus receives a divine affirmation of his commission to lead Israel to victory which is strikingly similar to the experience of Moses at his call. Joshua takes another of the roles of Moses. He, like Moses, is the recipient of a divine commissioning.

*Joshua the intercessor—Joshua 7.6-9.* After the initial defeat at Ai Joshua questions Yahweh over the defeat and reminds him that Yahweh's own reputation with the Canaanites could suffer if Israel is allowed to be defeated in battle. The scene recalls at least two occasions in the career of Moses when he used the argument about Yahweh's potential loss of reputation as part of the basis of his intercession on behalf of Israel (Exod. 32.11-13; Num. 14.13-19; Woudstra 1981: 125) Joshua thus functions as the intercessor for his generation much as Moses was the great intercessor for Israel in an earlier generation.

*The rod of Joshua—Joshua 8.18-23.* In this narrative Joshua stretches out a javelin as a signal for the ambush at Ai to begin (v. 18)—which results in Israel's victory over its enemies. This is reminiscent of the story of Israel's battle with Amalek (Exod. 18) where the elevating of Moses' rod causes Israel to prevail in battle (Gray 1986: 93). In both instances a stick is held out or raised, leading to victory. Joshua's javelin, unlike Moses' rod, has no magical properties. Its function is merely that of a battle signal. But Joshua's action does parallel Moses' in a striking way and leads the reader to infer that Joshua is portrayed as functioning in a way that is similar to the way Moses once functioned.

*Implacable foes—Joshua 11.20.* The stubborn refusal of the kings of Canaan to make peace with Joshua is attributed to the fact that Yahweh hardened their hearts (Josh. 11.20) much as he had hardened Pharaoh's heart (Exod. 9.12). Thus both Moses and Joshua face adversaries whose stubborn refusal to capitulate was caused by Yahweh's direct intervention and resulted in a greater defeat for the enemy.

c. *Joshua Completes the Work of Moses*
Moses was commissioned by Yahweh to bring Israel out of Egypt so that he could then lead them into the promised land (Exod. 3.8). The

taking and allotting of the land was the natural conclusion to Moses' life's work. He was not, however, permitted to fulfill the second part of his basic task as Israel's leader. It was Joshua who first conquered and then divided the land of Canaan for Israel (11.23). In this sense Joshua completed the unfinished work of Moses. Just as Yahweh was with Moses during the Exodus, so Yahweh was with Joshua during the conquest and distribution of the land.

But Moses' work can also be viewed from another angle. In a limited sense, Moses did lead Israel in a conquest and distribution of land, that is the conquest and distribution of Transjordan. Admittedly, the Transjordan's legitimacy as a authentic part of the promised land is questioned in the books of Numbers and Joshua (Jobling 1986: 88-134). This may give the reader reason to question whether Moses really was distributing the promised land to the two and one-half tribes or not. Nevertheless, Moses' actions in conquering and then distributing Transjordan is a sort of model for Joshua's task of conquering and then distributing Cisjordan (Josh. 13.8-33).

In particular, Moses conquers (Num. 21.21-35), sets the boundaries for the two and one-half tribes (Num. 32.1-42), and then appoints three cities of refuge in Transjordan (Deut. 4.41-43). Joshua does the same for Cisjordan (Josh. 11.23; 20.1-9).

### d. *Joshua Fulfills Moses' Promises about Specific Inheritance Rights*
In Numbers, Yahweh, through Moses, makes promises concerning future rights to inheritances within the promised land to Caleb (14.24), the daughters of Zelophehad (27.1-11), and to the Levites (35.1-8). Joshua fulfills these promises when he oversees the distribution of the land.

In 14.6-12 Caleb asks Joshua for the right to conquer and claim as his inheritance 'this hill country' (v. 12). The basis for Caleb's claim is Moses' alleged assurance to him following the spy episode.[12] Joshua grants Caleb the inheritance he desires and in doing so fulfills the promise that Yahweh gave through Moses in Num. 14.24 and Deut. 1.36.

In Josh. 17.3, 4 the daughters of Zelophehad come to Eleazar and Joshua and remind them of Yahweh's promise through Moses to them that they would receive an inheritance alongside their fellow kinsmen

---

12. In fact the narrator only records Yahweh's rather vague promise in Num. 14.24, which Moses quotes in Deut. 1.36, that Caleb would have *an* inheritance without giving a specific location for it. The reader might infer from this that Caleb is rather conveniently reinterpreting the assurances which Yahweh gave through Moses.

(Num. 27.1-11). Joshua fulfills Moses' promise to them by granting them an inheritance among the brothers of their father (17.4).

In Josh. 21.1, 2 the Levites remind Eleazar and Joshua of Yahweh's command through Moses that they be given cities and pasture lands within the territories of the other tribes (Num. 35.1-8). Joshua fulfills this promise by granting the Levites 48 cities within the other tribes' borders (21.3, 41, 42).

### e. *Conclusions*

We have seen that Joshua takes over many of the specific roles of Moses, performs actions which are strikingly parallel to his, and even experiences a divine revelation that is quite like the revelation which Moses experienced at his call. We have also seen that Joshua is portrayed as completing the unfinished work of Moses by conquering and distributing Cisjordan and that he fulfills Moses' specific promises concerning individual inheritance rights for special cases within the promised land. Joshua functions in ways that the reader would expect Moses to function given the circumstances. In one sense Joshua surpasses Moses in that he, unlike Moses, actually finished Moses' life's work, that is the conquest and distribution of Cisjordan. When in 24.29 the reader notes that Joshua now receives the epithet from the narrator which was previously reserved for Moses alone,[13] that is the servant of Yahweh, the reader concludes that Joshua attains at the end of his life a status in Yahweh's and the narrator's eyes (and therefore in the reader's since the narrator and Yahweh are assumed to be reliable in this work) which is similar to the status of Moses. Yahweh's promise in 1.5 to Joshua has come true. Joshua eventually steps out from under the shadow of Moses. He is 'the servant of Yahweh' for his generation just as Moses had been for the previous one. He is no longer Moses' subordinate, but has a status which is defined on the basis of his own relationship to Yahweh and not in terms of his past relationship to Moses.

### 4. *The Encouraged Becomes the Encourager*

#### a. *Introduction*

Three times in the opening divine speech Yahweh uses an encouragement formula in speaking to Joshua (vv. 6, 7, 9). An analysis of the

---

13. Butler (1983: 283) notes that Joshua only uses this phrase of himself 'as a formula of self-humiliation before the deity in prayer (5.14)'.

vocabulary of encouragement formulae in the Primary History indicates that Joshua is the recipient of an extraordinary amount of encouragement from both Yahweh and others. Joshua also receives and gives encouragement without the specific vocabulary being used. While the reader is not given enough information to enable specific inferences to be made about the internal psychology of Joshua, it does seem clear that a process of development occurs in Joshua so that in the latter stages of his life he gives more encouragement than he receives.

b. *Encouragement Vocabulary*
Within the Primary History, in potentially dangerous or daunting circumstances, individuals or groups of individuals are encouraged to have the fortitude necessary to face the task ahead or their present difficult circumstances. In these situations the vocabulary used is fairly typical. This encouragement can be stated in positive or negative terms. In positive terms either 'be strong', חזק, and/or 'be courageous', אמץ, is used. In negative terms the person or group is told *not* to 'fear', ירא, and/or 'be in dread', ערץ, and/or 'be dismayed', חתת, and/or 'tremble', חפז. Often these words occur in clusters as in the phrases 'be strong and of good courage' (Deut. 31.6, 7, 23; Josh. 1.6, 7, 9, 18; 10.25) and 'do not fear or be dismayed' (Deut. 1.21; 31.8; Josh. 8.1; 10.25).

The striking thing about the use of these words in formulae of encouragement is how often Joshua is, or is supposed to be, the recipient of the encouragement, or is himself the giver of the encouragement. Of 51 instances in the Primary History in which one or more of the six Hebrew words just mentioned is used in formulae of encouragement, Joshua is, or is supposed to be, the recipient in thirteen instances and his generation is the recipient in a further seven instances. By contrast no other person or group receives encouragement more than once except Joseph's brothers (twice; Gen. 43.23; 50.19), Moses (twice; Num. 21.34; Deut. 3.2), and Moses' generation (four times; Exod. 14.13; 20.20; Num. 14.9; Deut. 1.29). Of the seventeen times Yahweh or his angel uses this vocabulary in speaking to humans, the words are addressed to or concern Joshua ten times (Deut. 1.38; 3.28; 31.23; Josh. 1.6, 7, 9, 18; 8.1; 10.8; 11.6). Besides Joshua, Yahweh only uses the vocabulary more than once in addressing Moses (twice; Num. 21.34; Deut. 3.2).

The extraordinary amount of encouragement which Joshua receives leads the reader to make one or both of the following inferences. First, the reader might infer that Joshua is an excessively timid person and

therefore needs more encouragement than others. Secondly, the reader
might infer that Joshua receives so much encouragement because the
tasks which he faces are far more dangerous than those faced by others.
The conquest of Canaan, so the reasoning goes, with its oversized people
(Josh. 14.12), superior weaponry (Josh. 11.4; 17.16), and enormous
armies (11.4) was a challenge unparalleled in all of the Primary History,
thus the need for encouragement.

Of course, it is possible and perhaps even likely that the reader should
make both inferences. Joshua's challenges were quite threatening and
would seem all the worse to a person who was naturally somewhat timid
in comparison with Moses.

### c. *Joshua Develops into an Encourager*

*Introduction.* We are not given enough information as readers about
Joshua's internal psychology to enable us to come to a definite conclusion about why Joshua receives encouragement from others so often.
There is, however, a pattern of sorts which emerges from an analysis of
the vocabulary. Joshua develops from being a person whom others see
as in need of encouragement into one who, towards the end of his life,
no longer receives encouragement, but gives it. Whether the reader
should infer from this pattern that Joshua is represented as outgrowing
his early timidity, or infer that Joshua's success in the conquest made the
need for encouragement disappear, or both, is uncertain.

*The emerging pattern.* In the programmatic opening chapter of the
book, Joshua is encouraged to 'be strong and of good courage' four
times (vv. 6, 7, 9, 18). He is also told once not to be 'frightened or
dismayed' (v. 9). The high density of the occurrence of the vocabulary
of encouragement is striking and shows the reader that both Yahweh
and the Transjordanians assume that Joshua needs verbal encouragement as he contemplates crossing the Jordan and beginning the conquest.

Joshua is next addressed with this vocabulary when Yahweh calls
upon him to attack Ai, who have just previously given Israel their first
defeat in battle (8.1). Joshua's need for encouragement at this juncture is
quite understandable since Yahweh was asking him to confront a foe
that had already demonstrated that it could defeat Israel in armed
conflict.

In 10.8, the next occurrence of the vocabulary, Yahweh addresses
Joshua as he is about to face a coalition, in contrast to the king of a

single city, for the first time. Once again the need for encouragement is understandable. This time the foe was a much more formidable one and the battle was in fact indirectly caused by Israel's failure to consult Yahweh before making a pact with the Gibeonites (9.14). Joshua has to risk his forces to defend the Gibeonites, who had used deceit to trick Israel into making a treaty with them. The reader might infer that Joshua could be wondering whether Yahweh would allow Israel's defeat in this battle in order to teach Israel a lesson about not making pacts with the inhabitants of Canaan just as he had previously taught them a lesson about the sanctity of the ban by allowing their defeat at Ai.

In this instance Joshua needs no encouragement to set out as he did at Ai since he has already left Gilgal before Yahweh speaks to him (vv. 7, 8). Yahweh's message gives him the reassurance he thinks Joshua needs to continue to prosecute the battle.

During the battle which ensues Joshua displays a sort of self-confidence or daring which he never displays in previous narratives. He has the self-confidence to command the sun and the moon to stop so that his army would have sufficient daylight to complete the slaughter.

In commanding the sun to stop in 10.25 Joshua displays an incredible degree of self-confidence. It is not surprising after such a demonstration that the next time the vocabulary appears it is found in the mouth of Joshua who uses it to encourage Israel in their future battles (10.25). Joshua, who up until this point in the narrative had been the recipient of encouragement from others, is now the giver of encouragement to others. A transformation or development has occurred in Joshua. The encouraged has become the encourager.

Joshua acts out his new found self-confidence by personally executing the five kings (10.26) and then leading Israel in a massive and rapid assault on the key cities of the south (vv. 28-43). Joshua's leading role is highlighted in each battle by the use of third-person masculine singular verbs as though Joshua did all of the actual fighting and by giving Israel a subordinate role by using the phrase, 'and all Israel with him' or its equivalent (vv. 29, 31, 34, 36, 38, 43) almost as a parenthetical comment. The rapid pace of the narrative (six battles in twelve verses) leads the reader to infer a quick decisive victory.

Joshua receives encouragement only once more (11.6) and that when he is about to face the northern coalition which has an army 'in number like the sand that is upon the seashore' (11.4 RSV). While this is against the trend of development in Joshua we have noted, it can perhaps be understood as being necessitated by the fact that the army which Joshua faced was far larger than any he had ever faced previously.

The last time the vocabulary of encouragement appears (23.5, 6) it is again found on the lips of Joshua who gives a sort of final charge to Israel before his death. He says:

> Yahweh your God will push them back before you, and drive them out of your sight, and you shall possess their land, as Yahweh your God promised you. Therefore be very strong in order to keep and do all that is written in the book of the law of Moses (Josh. 23.5, 6).

c. *The pattern without the vocabulary.* It is not only an analysis of the passages where the vocabulary of encouragement is used which leads the reader to infer a transformation in Joshua. It is also inferred from an analysis of those passages where Joshua gives or receives encouragement without the use of the specific vocabulary.

In 2.9-11 Rahab addresses the two spies:

> I know that the LORD has given you the land, and that the fear of you has fallen upon us, and that all the inhabitants of the land melt away before you. For we have heard how the LORD dried up the water of the Red Sea before you when you came out of Egypt, and what you did to the two kings of the Amorites that were beyond the Jordan, to Sihon and Og, whom you utterly destroyed. As soon as we heard it, our hearts melted, and there was no courage left in any man, because of you; for the LORD your God is he who is God in heaven above and on earth beneath (RSV).

Rahab's words could be placed in the mouth of an Israelite reciting their faith in creedal form. Rahab has as much confidence in Yahweh as Israel or Joshua, if not more. When Joshua hears of this message (v. 23b) he concludes:

> Surely the LORD has given all the land into our hands; and moreover all the inhabitants of the land melt before us.

Joshua, the reader notes, not only receives encouragement from Yahweh (1.6, 7, 9) and the Transjordanians (1.18), but also from a prostitute living in the land!

Later in Joshua's life, after the defeat of the northern and southern coalitions, things have changed. It is now Joshua who encourages others to go to battle to win those parts of the land not yet conquered. In 17.14 the tribe of Joseph complains that their allotment of land is too small. Joshua suggests that their inheritance could be expanded by clearing the forested part of it (v. 15). The tribe of Joseph respond by noting that the

Canaanites with their iron chariots would prevent them from doing so (v. 16). Joshua then encourages them to believe that they could clear the forest even though the Canaanites are a problem because they would beat them in battle despite their weaponry (vv. 17, 18). Yahweh once encouraged Joshua when he faced iron chariots (11.6). Here Joshua encourages those who face that same threat.

In 18.1 the reader is told that the land lay subdued before Israel, but the reader also knows that only the tribes of Judah and Joseph have actually taken possession of their tribal allotments. In 18.3 Joshua berates the remaining seven tribes:

> How long will you be slack to go in and take possession of the land, which the LORD, the God of your fathers, has given you? (RSV).

### d. *Conclusions*
We have seen that a pattern emerges in the portrayal of Joshua. Joshua begins by being the recipient of encouragement from others (1.6, 7, 9, 18; 2.9-11, 24; 8.1; 10.8; 11.6) and develops into a character who gives encouragement to others (10.25; 17.14-18; 18.3; 23.6). The pattern is not a simplistic one of continual upward progress, for Joshua receives encouragement from Yahweh on one occasion even after he had stopped the sun. But the pattern is, nevertheless, clear.

## 5. *Joshua Applies the Torah*

### a. *Introduction*
In 1.7 Yahweh charges Joshua to have the strength and courage necessary to keep and act upon the Torah of Moses without deviating from it. Since the Torah is something which Yahweh gave to Moses (Deut. 1.3), to obey Moses' Torah, whether oral or written, is to obey Yahweh's Torah (Josh. 11.15; 20.2). Thus Joshua has three sources of Torah which he is to obey: a) the written form of Moses' Torah (1.8); b) the oral instructions of Moses to Joshua; and c) the oral instructions of Yahweh to Joshua directly. The reader asks not whether Joshua applies the Torah faithfully (he does), but how he applies it and whether or not the narrator gives implicit and/or explicit approval to the ways he does so.

### b. *Joshua Obeys Yahweh's Instructions*
We have already discussed the way in which Joshua carries out Yahweh's oral instructions in military contexts. Joshua sometimes modifies Yahweh's instructions slightly, perhaps for military ends, but in

general he obeys Yahweh's instructions while using his own judgment on the specifics of applying them. For example, Joshua obeys Yahweh's instructions to place an ambush against Ai, but he chooses its size and to reinforce it later. Joshua displays a similar sort of obedience, but with freedom on specific matters, in responding to Yahweh's oral instructions which concern other matters.

In 3.8 Yahweh directs Joshua concerning the priests' role in the crossing of the Jordan:

> And you shall command the priests who bear the ark of the covenant,
> 'When you come to the brink of the waters of the Jordan you shall stand
> still in the Jordan' (RSV).

When Joshua relays this message to Israel he does so quite freely. He addresses his message to the people, not the priests (v. 9a). He introduces his message as though it were a prophetic oracle rather than a simple instruction (v. 9b). He spells out in detail the stopping of the waters of the Jordan, which is at most presumed in Yahweh's directive (3.13) and he uses the anticipated stopping of the waters as the basis for guaranteeing the success of the conquest (v. 10). Further he adds a command that twelve tribal representatives be chosen for some unstated purpose. It turns out that Joshua here obeys Yahweh's command concerning the tribal representatives before Yahweh even gives it. Just as Joshua anticipates the actual day of the crossing (3.5), he also anticipates that Yahweh will later need twelve tribal representatives (4.2, 3). The reader wonders how it is that Joshua knows what Yahweh is going to do before Yahweh even tells him. Perhaps the reader might infer that Joshua is following some pre-planned liturgy of which the reader is given no explicit indication (Soggin 1972: 86-88; Polzin 1980: 92). In any case Joshua uses a great deal of freedom in obeying this directive of Yahweh's.

In 4.2, 3 Yahweh directs Joshua to choose twelve tribal representatives, who are to carry twelve stones from the middle of the Jordan where the priests had stood to Gilgal. Joshua calls the twelve tribal representatives he had already chosen and relays Yahweh's command, giving his own interpretation of the significance of the stones (vv. 5-7). The twelve comply (v. 8) and then Joshua innovates by also setting up a second set of twelve stones in the midst of the Jordan where the ark stood (v. 9; Woudstra 1981: 92). Joshua invents an interpretation of the pile of stones at Gilgal for the twelve representatives (vv. 6, 7) and also for the people (vv. 21-24) and adds another pile which sits in the Jordan to parallel the one at Gilgal.

There is no indication in the narrative that the freedom with which Joshua carries out Yahweh's instruction in the crossing narrative is excessive from the narrator's point of view. Indeed, he is portrayed as obeying Yahweh's instructions at every point (1.2 with 3.1; 3.8 with 3.13; 4.2, 3 with 3.12; and 4.4, 8; 4.15, 16 with 4.17; 5.2 with 5.3; 6.4 with 6.15b).

### c. *Joshua Applies the Written Torah*
### i. *Introduction*
In 1.8 Yahweh commands Joshua to be careful to do according to all that is written in the book of the Torah. The first-time reader's initial question is, 'What exactly is the book of the Torah which Joshua is to obey?' The most obvious candidate is the book which Moses wrote down and was kept alongside the ark of the covenant (Deut. 31.9, 24) and which comprises some major portion of the present form of Deuteronomy, for example 12.1–28.69 or 4.41–31.24.

Joshua applies the Torah in Deuteronomy concerning: a) the ceremony at Ebal and Gerizim (Deut. 27.2-8; Josh. 8.30-35); b) the designation of the Cisjordanian cities of refuge (Deut. 19.1-13; Josh. 20.1-9); and c) the ban on conquered peoples and booty (Deut. 7.1-5; 20.1-20). While Joshua obeys the deuteronomic laws in a fairly straightforward fashion in the first two instances, his application of the ban rules is far more complex. The way Joshua applies the ban changes with circumstances, but since Yahweh is also portrayed as fitting the rules of the ban to the circumstances, Joshua does not receive the reader's opprobrium for his own free interpretation of the ban. In addition, Joshua adds to the written form of Yahweh's Torah (24.25, 26) and while this may technically contravene Moses' prohibition of adding to the Torah (Deut. 4.2; 13.1) once again Joshua receives no censure from the narrator or, consequently, the reader for doing so.

### ii. *Joshua Obeys Moses' Torah Strictly—Joshua 8.30-35; 20.1-9*
In 8.30-35 Joshua carries out Moses' instructions recorded in Deut. 27.2-7 to build an altar on Mt Ebal and hold a sort of covenant renewal ceremony there. Joshua carries out the instructions fairly strictly.[14]

In Josh. 20.2 Yahweh commands Joshua to 'appoint the cities of refuge, of which I spoke to you *through Moses*'. While Num. 35.6-34

---

14. Polzin (1980: 115-16) notes the addition of women, aliens, and dependants as participants in the ceremony.

records Yahweh originally giving the instructions concerning the cities of refuge to Moses personally, Moses relays them to Israel only in Deut. 19.1-13. Thus Joshua in 20.1-9 is obeying Moses' written Torah, of which Yahweh has just reminded him orally. Joshua obeys Moses' written instructions concerning the designation of Cisjordanian cities of refuge in a fairly straightforward manner (20.7-9).

### iii. *Joshua Applies the Ban Rules*
*Introduction.* In Deut. 7.1-5 Moses directs Israel to destroy utterly (חרם) the inhabitants of Canaan and their religious paraphernalia. In Deut. 20.10-18 Moses distinguishes between the treatment of Israel's defeated enemies, who are outside the land (vv. 10-15), and those inside it (vv. 16-18). Distant groups are to be offered peace for forced labor (v. 11). If the terms of peace are rejected, only the males are to be killed (v. 13) and the booty is to be enjoyed by Israel (v. 14). Groups inside the land, however, are to be utterly destroyed (v. 17) and everything that breathes killed (v. 16). Joshua's application of what seems to the first-time reader to be straightforward Mosaic legislation turns out to be far from simple, as the following discussion will show.

*The ban applied to Jericho—Joshua 6, 7.* The first case of a defeated people in the book are the inhabitants of Jericho. Joshua explains how the rules of the ban are to be applied to Jericho just before the people shout and bring down the walls:

> And the city and all who are in it will be put to the ban for Yahweh. Only Rahab the prostitute will live, she and all who are with her in the house, because she hid the messengers which we sent. However, you keep yourselves away from the banned things lest you ban them [for yourself] and take them from the banned things and put the camp of Israel under the ban and trouble it. But all the silver and gold and all the bronze and the iron is holy. It will go into Yahweh's treasury (6.17-19).

In applying the ban rules to Jericho, Joshua makes an exception of Rahab in clear violation of a strict reading of Deuteronomy 20. The oath which the spies gave to Rahab (2.17-20) was honored even though it was obtained in coercive circumstances (2.8-16). Rahab presents a problem for the strict application of the ban rules because she is a prostitute[15]

---

15. If Rahab is understood to be a fertility cult prostitute as argued by, for example, Mowinckel (1964: 13-15), the problem is intensified because she would be directly involved in a Canaanite cult which became such a temptation for Israel and was the rationale for the ban.

and lives in Canaan and yet trusts and fears Yahweh and helps Israel's cause by hiding the spies. Joshua never receives censure from the narrator either directly or indirectly for making an exception of Rahab and her household (6.25).

Joshua also interprets the ban by making another exception of the precious metals of Jericho which he directed were to go into the treasury. Once again this passes without any hint of the narrator's censure. Joshua's interpretation of the ban on precious metals is given Yahweh's implicit approval since he punishes Achan for keeping silver for himself in disobedience to Joshua's application of the ban rules. With these two exceptions Joshua applies the ban rules strictly at Jericho.

*The ban applied at Ai—Joshua 8.* After the punishment of Achan and his family for violating the ban on booty at Jericho, Yahweh directs Joshua to loosen the rules at Ai:

> And you shall do to Ai and its king as you did to Jericho and its king; only
> its spoil and its cattle you shall take as booty for yourselves (8.2a RSV).

Joshua faithfully carries out Yahweh's new rules concerning the booty (8.26, 27). Just as Joshua modified the ban rules in the case of Rahab, so Yahweh modifies them in the case of the booty of Ai. Yahweh's action shows that the Mosaic ban rules are not inviolable and must be applied as circumstances dictate. The reader may well infer that Yahweh modifies the rules about the booty at Ai because he has learned from the Achan episode that Israel could not be trusted to stay away from the booty and therefore the legislation was impractical in such circumstances (Gutbrod 1951: 73-75).

Yahweh's action also leads the reader to the inference that Joshua is not necessarily doing something wrong in the narrator's view when he modifies the ban rules in the case of Rahab. Yahweh's action leads the reader to infer that Joshua's action in modifying the ban at Jericho was probably acceptable to Yahweh.

*The ban applied to Gibeon—Joshua 9.* To the unwary Israelites the Gibeonites must have seemed to fit the Mosaic rules for the treatment of distant enemies quite precisely (Deut. 20.10-15). The only way they differed from Moses' scenario is that the Gibeonites came to Israel seeking peace while Moses legislated for circumstances when Israel was on the verge of attacking a distant enemy, but first offered it peace for forced labor (Deut. 20.10, 11). When Joshua is confronted with an enemy who claim to hail from a distant place and have evidence to prove it, and who offer servitude for peace (Josh. 9.11) he quite understandably, if naively accepts (v. 15). While Joshua should have asked for direction from Yahweh before proceeding to make the covenant (v. 14), it was out of ignorance and not out of rebellion that he contravened the ban rules. Upon discovering the Gibeonite ruse (v. 16), Joshua was faced with circumstances for which the ban rules did not legislate. Joshua could either break the solemn oaths which sealed the treaty and risk Yahweh's wrath (v. 20), or he could allow the treaty to stand and confirm the violation of the ban rules. Joshua chose the latter course, but he did make the Gibeonites pay for their deceit by making them take the lowest of positions within the covenant community.

Polzin (1980: 117-121) has noted that Joshua displays the same sort of mercy to the undeserving Gibeonites that Yahweh gave to the undeserving Israelites as noted by Moses in Deuteronomy 29. The Gibeonites in many ways parallel the Israelites in Deuteronomy 29. Joshua's merciful treatment of them has the solid precedent of Yahweh's merciful treatment of Israel. Joshua treats Canaanites who believe in Yahweh differently from the other inhabitants of the land. There is every reason to believe that Joshua is doing something right in the narrator's view in modifying the strict application of the ban rules in the case of Canaanites who have come to trust and fear Yahweh.

*The ban applied in the southern campaign—Joshua 10.28-43.* In the report of Joshua's defeat of the southern cities he applies the ban quite strictly. The repetition of a variety of stock phrases shows the comprehensiveness and strictness with which the ban is enforced: 'utterly destroyed' (vv. 28, 35, 37, 39); 'every person' (vv. 28, 30, 32, 35, 37 [twice], 39); 'as he did to the king of [Jericho]' (vv. 28, 30, 32, 35, 37, 39). The booty is not explicitly mentioned but it seems likely that the reader should infer that the policy first instituted at Ai of allowing the fighting men to take booty is still in force.

*The ban applied in the northern campaign—Joshua 11.1-15.* As in the southern campaign, Joshua is here portrayed as applying the ban strictly. Once again the narrator uses stock phrases which indicate this (vv. 8, 10, 11, 12, 14). The booty is here explicitly said to have been given to Israel (v. 13).

iv. *Summary*

We have seen that Joshua generally applies the ban rules quite strictly, but when the circumstances call for it, makes exceptions. When the enemy is hostile they are utterly destroyed. When the enemy trusts and fears Yahweh they are spared. The strict application of the ban on booty is altered, however, possibly because of the perceived difficulty, after the Achan episode, of keeping Israel from cheating.

d. *Joshua Adds to the Written Torah*

In Josh. 24.25, 26 we read:

> So Joshua made a covenant with the people that day, and made a statute and an ordinance for them at Shechem. And Joshua wrote these words in the book of the law of God.

While the translation and the exact significance of this verse is uncertain,[16] it is clear that Joshua added something in writing to the book of the law of God. It is even possible, though uncertain, that Joshua is being portrayed as inventing a certain law or laws and adding it (them) to the book of the law of God.[17] It is hard for the reader not to identify this book with 'the book of the law of Moses' in 1.7, 8; thus Joshua is seen to be supplementing Moses' written Torah.[18] In Deut. 13.1 Moses says, 'Everything that I command you, you shall be careful to do; you shall not add to it or take from it' (RSV). The first-time reader is presented with a dilemma. Moses directs that nothing be added to his Torah and yet Joshua is portrayed as doing exactly that. The reader's question is, 'In the narrator's view, is Moses too narrow in forbidding anything to be added to the Torah or is Joshua acting improperly by adding to an inviolable Torah?' The fact that both Joshua and Yahweh alter the

---

16. Among the difficulties are the significance of the singular 'statute and ordinance' and the referent of לֹו, which could be the collective noun or as Boling and Wright (1983: 529) suggest, the covenant.

17. Gray (1986: 181) claims that, 'The Hebrew means simply that he made the covenant binding as a decree (*hôq*) and a decision (*mišpāt*)', but he seems to grant that in the final form the words mean, 'the apodictic obligations of the covenant, and casuistic laws (*mišpātîm*) declared by the mediator of the covenant'.

18. Butler (1983: 277) comments, 'It [v. 26a] uses the language of the Deuteronomist and may well reflect an update of the tradition, identifying the statute and judgment of Joshua with the book of the Torah of God (cf. 1.7-8; 8.31-34; 22.5; 23.6). If so, then it may reflect the practice of revising the Torah itself, since here Joshua apparently adds the agreement he has made to the Torah.'

Mosaic ban rules without the narrator's explicit disapproval and perhaps with the narrator's tacit approval is crucial for this issue. If it is permissible in the narrator's view to alter the ban rules in some circumstances there is no inherent reason why Joshua should not alter it in other respects if the circumstances warrant it. In the case of 24.25, 26 Joshua adds something to the Torah book which is to remind Israel of their covenant promises to serve Yahweh. Since reminding Israel of their covenant obligations is obviously a worthwhile thing to do for our narrator, there is every reason for the reader to infer that Joshua's action is being implicitly commended to the reader.

e. *Summary*

We have seen that Joshua is portrayed as being basically obedient to Yahweh's and Moses' oral Torah and to Moses' written Torah. His obedience is not, however, mindless or slavish. In particular, Joshua applies the ban rules to fit the situation. His modifications of a strict application of the rules in the cases of Rahab and Gibeon, who trust and fear Yahweh, are in the narrator's view certainly permissible, perhaps even commendable actions. Joshua at first enforces the rules concerning booty strictly and is supported in this by Yahweh as is made evident by the latter's punishment of Achan. But that incident results in Yahweh loosening the rules concerning booty for the next battle and the rest of the narrative. Yahweh thus also modifies the ban rules to fit the situation and this gives the reader even more reason to infer that Joshua's modifications of the ban are not to be viewed in a negative way. Joshua adding to the Torah in 24.25, 26 is also, for the narrator, probably a commendable act. The reader concludes that as regards his obedience to Yahweh's and Moses' Torah, Joshua acts in ways that the narrator would deem appropriate and there is therefore no reason to doubt his reliability as an interpreter of the Torah.

## 6. *Conclusions*

We have discussed four major aspects of the portrayal of Joshua and in each case have concluded that for the narrator Joshua is a thoroughly reliable character. Joshua, in the narrator's view, has a correct under-standing of the proper balance between relying on Yahweh to act directly for Israel to give it the land and Israel's responsibility to act themselves, to take the land by force. Joshua neither abdicates his responsibility to Yahweh nor does he presumptuously depend upon his own ability and resources to the exclusion of relying on Yahweh. Joshua takes over the roles of Moses and *develops* into a figure who eventually steps out from under the shadow of Moses and becomes 'the servant of Yahweh' for his own generation just as Moses had been for the previous one. Joshua also *develops* from being a person who needs the encouragement of others into one who gives encouragement to others. In both of these cases of development Joshua is implicitly commended by the narrator to the reader. Finally, in Joshua's handling of the Torah of Yahweh and Moses, he is seen to act at least in a permissible way if not in a commendable one. I conclude that Joshua is a reliable character and his words and his actions are one way in which the narrator conveys his or her point of view.

Chapter 3

THE RELIABILITY OF ELIJAH

## 1. *Introduction*

This chapter is an analysis of the second-time reader's evaluation of the reliability of Elijah in the Primary History. This analysis differs significantly from the evaluation of the first-time reader who stops reading at 2 Kgs 2.12 (the ascension of Elijah), and even more so from the response of the reader who treats all (Gros-Louis 1974) or part[1] of the Elijah narratives as a narrative block without consideration of the preceding narratives, that is Genesis 1 to 1 Kgs 16.28, and from the response of the reader who does not give consideration to the narratives enmeshed within the Elijah narratives, that is 1 Kings 20 and 22. Due to the scope of the present work I have been forced to be selective in the amount of detailed consideration given to the effect the wider context might exercise on the reader's response.[2] I have therefore chosen to pay particular attention to the way the narrator portrays prophets or men of God and prophecy outside of the narratives about Elijah and Elisha but within Kings.

It is the thesis of this chapter that the first-time reader assumes that Elijah is portrayed as a very reliable character in 1 Kings 17 and 18 only to see this assumption called into question in ch. 19. It seems probable[3]

---

1.  Gregory 1990; Walsh 1982; and Cohn 1982.
2.  Gregory (1990: 137-47) discusses the 'numerous allusions' which 'invite the audience' to compare Elijah (unfavorably as it turns out) with characters in other Hebrew Bible stories in more detail than I am able to here.
3.  I use such words as 'probable', 'probably', and 'likely' in this chapter advisedly. It is possible for the Elijah narratives to be read as presenting a more idealistic figure than I have argued that he is portrayed as being. I would not want to claim that I have arrived at a definitive analysis of the reader's evaluation of the reliability of *any* of my four characters. But, in the case of Elijah, my analysis is less conclusive and is presented only as one credible analysis of the evidence.

that the first-time reader then reassesses the inferences which were previously made about Elijah's reliability and is likely to conclude that Elijah never was as reliable a character as the reader had at first assumed him to be.[4] In response to the rest of the Elijah stories (1 Kgs 21; 2 Kgs 1, 2), however, the first-time reader is likely to surmise that later in his life (in 2 Kgs 1) Elijah develops into a very reliable character. But the second-time reader is likely to question whether Elijah is being portrayed as totally reliable even in 2 Kings 1. The second-time reader comes to infer from the other stories about prophets in Kings that prophets generally are not necessarily reliable figures and do not always represent the narrator's point of view. From this and other considerations the second-time reader is, therefore, likely to conclude that even the reliability which Elijah appears to develop late in his life is questionable.

## 2. *The Self-Assurance and Charisma of Elijah*

a. *Elijah's Self-Assurance and Charisma in 1 Kings 17 and 18*
Elijah is repeatedly portrayed as facing daunting circumstances in which his words and/or actions display a remarkable degree of self-assurance and charisma.[5] He faces social superiors who possess the power and the inclination to harm him physically, and yet he delivers hostile messages which he knows are likely to provoke their wrath without flinching. He also demonstrates the ability to influence others to do his bidding. Elijah's very first words in the narrative display his self-assurance. An 'outsider'[6] who has neither welcome at, nor invitation to, Ahab's court, he delivers a message of divine judgment on Ahab's nation:

> As the LORD the God of Israel lives, before whom I stand, there shall be neither dew nor rain these years, except by my word (17.1 RSV).

4.	It may be that by the construction of the story itself the narrator has led the reader to assume things about Elijah which later turn out to be false or in need of radical qualification. If so, the narrator has been misleading the reader and the issue of narratorial reliability arises. This question, though of great interest, is not taken up in this chapter as I assume narratorial reliability.

5.	I use this word here in a non-religious sense of a special personal quality or power of an individual to influence others.

6.	Here I follow, for example, Gray (1970: 377) in reading, 'Elijah the Tishbite, of the settlers of Gilead'. Elijah is thus portrayed as an immigrant, and not a native resident, who hails from a marginal part of Israel, Gilead.

After delivering these words, Yahweh tells Elijah to hide himself since his life is under threat (v. 3). Elijah's oath promising a drought could not have been welcome news to the king who served Baal, the god of rain (16.31; Coogan 1978). The first-time reader is later informed that throughout the drought Ahab was desperately trying to find Elijah and, presumably, punish him (18.10). The reader's appreciation of the reality of Ahab's threat is reinforced by Obadiah's fear that he would be killed merely for not producing Elijah at a promised meeting (18.10-12). The king, whose wife had brutally purged the prophets of Yahweh, would presumably have no hesitation in killing Elijah.

The first-time reader's impression that Elijah possesses exceptional self-assurance is strengthened and reinforced by the record of Elijah's meeting with Ahab in ch. 18. Upon seeing Elijah, Ahab calls him 'troubler (עכר) of Israel' (v. 17). In what the reader must assume is a potentially life-threatening situation Elijah responds:

> I have not troubled Israel; but you have, and your father's house, because
> you have forsaken the commandments of the LORD and followed the Baals
> (1 Kgs 18.18 RSV).

Elijah commands Ahab to gather Israel and the prophets of Baal and Asherah to him at Carmel and Ahab complies. Because Ahab does not respond, the first-time reader infers that Elijah here displays such charisma and self-presence that the angry king who had been searching for Elijah abruptly ceases his accusations and obeys Elijah's directives. The first-time reader has not yet seen that Ahab characteristically wilts before strong personalities,[7] whether the personality be Elijah, Jezebel or Naboth, and can only assume at this point that Elijah's personal presence (his charisma) is so powerful that Ahab is intimidated into doing Elijah's bidding.

Elijah's stacking of the odds against himself and in favor of the prophets of Baal during the contest on Mt Carmel[8] also shows Elijah's supreme confidence as well as his courage. Certainly if Elijah had failed in his contest with the prophets of Baal he would have been greatly

---

7.  For a helpful demonstration of this point see Savran 1987: 151-52, who notes, 'The counterpoint to Ahab's submissiveness to God and prophet is to be found in the king's willing capitulation to *whoever* confronts him, regardless of politics or moral standards.'

8.  Elijah stacks the odds in favor of the prophets of Baal by choosing to be greatly outnumbered; letting them go first, thus giving them more time; letting them choose their own bull (v. 25); and dousing his sacrifice with ample portions of water.

outnumbered both by the prophets of Baal and the people of Israel and would have been in a very awkward situation which would have undoubtedly threatened his personal safety.

Elijah displays his charisma once again when he commands Israel to seize the prophets of Baal (18.40a) so that he (Elijah) could personally kill[9] them (18.40b). Even granting the startling demonstration of Yahweh's power which Israel witnesses (v. 38), it takes great self-confidence to command Israel to participate in the slaughter of 450 prophets who had the sanction of Ahab and Jezebel and whose death would almost certainly arouse Jezebel's wrath.

Elijah's self-confidence is also demonstrated in this scene by the way he addresses Yahweh. Yahweh had instructed Elijah merely to show himself to Ahab and promised that he would then send rain upon the land (18.1). The contest, a daring initiative it must be granted, is, as far as the reader knows, Elijah's idea (Gregory 1990: 104). When it comes time to win the contest, the wording of Elijah's prayer is far from timid or apologetic.

> O LORD, God of Abraham, Isaac, and Israel, let it be known this day that you are God in Israel, that I am your servant, and that I have done all these things at your bidding. Answer me, O LORD, answer me, so that this people may know that you, O LORD, are God, and that you have turned their hearts back (1 Kgs 18.36b, 37 NRSV).

Elijah displayed a similar sort of temerity in relation to Yahweh with his first recorded words in 17.1 where he promised the drought. While the first-time reader is led to expect that Elijah's oath will come true,[10] the fact remains that the reader is given no indication that Yahweh commissioned Elijah to speak these words. Further, to make the ending of the drought dependent on Elijah's personal word seems to indicate great confidence on the part of Elijah that Yahweh would indeed fulfill Elijah's words in Elijah's way, that is by bringing about the end of the drought through Elijah's word and not in some other fashion.

The first-time reader might presume that in addition to great confidence, this may also imply a degree of presumption on Elijah's part. Perhaps it is something other than self-assurance that leads Elijah to

---

9. The Hebrew word used for Elijah's slaughter of the prophets of Baal, שׁחט, is often used in sacrificial contexts. The narrator thus lets the reader in on a sort of joke; that is, the real sacrifice that day was to be the prophets of Baal, not the bulls that were sacrificed.

10. See the discussion of this point below.

announce a drought in the form of an oath ('by the life of Yahweh'), but it certainly includes an unusual degree of confidence that Yahweh would support Elijah by fulfilling Elijah's words. There is as little timidity in Elijah's claim to speak for Yahweh in 17.1, as in his prayer in 18.36, 37.

b. *The Hollowness of Elijah's Self-Assurance*
Having seen Elijah consistently display charisma and self-assurance before both human beings and Yahweh in chs. 17 and 18, the first-time reader is quite unprepared for Elijah's response to Jezebel's threatening message. Elijah's boldness of speech and actions before Yahweh in 18.36, 37, before Ahab in 17.1, and 18.18, 19 and before Israel and the prophets of Baal during the contest with the latter in 18.21-40 leave the first-time reader surprised at his response.

As though allowing him a head start, Jezebel, informed by Ahab of the fate of the prophets of Baal, sends a threatening message to Elijah:

> So may the gods do to me, and more also, if I do not make your life as the life of one of them by this time tomorrow (19.2 RSV).

The form of Jezebel's threat, a sworn oath, neatly corresponds to the form in which Elijah delivers his prediction of the drought in 17.1. Jezebel answers Elijah's hostile oath with a hostile oath of her own. But her oath is in the name of 'the gods', while Elijah uses Yahweh's name, the god who had just proved his own power and falsified Baal's claim to power at Mt Carmel.

Jezebel's threat seems full of pretense. Elijah has just experienced in a most dramatic way both the protection of Yahweh (17.2-16) and his awesome power (18.38, 46). Elijah has himself just proved that Baal is powerless. Israel has apparently been won over to his side. The reader asks how Elijah could imagine that in such circumstances Jezebel could really harm him.

The fact that she sends a messenger to Elijah first is not without significance. If she is so confident that she could defeat Elijah and his god Yahweh, why does she first send a messenger, thus enabling Elijah to escape, instead of a regiment of troops, as Ahaziah later did (2 Kgs 1.9, 11, 13)? Her sending a messenger leads the reader to infer that she is trying to trick Elijah into running in fear (De Vries 1985: 235). Unable to see the bluff behind Jezebel's threat Elijah runs away in fear of his life.[11]

---

11. The attempt to excuse Elijah for this action because he was tired (Auld 1986: 122; Nelson 1987: 122, 'Elijah burns out'), or somehow manic depressive (Auld

Elijah's sudden fear for his life does not last long, however, since one verse later he asks Yahweh to take it away (19.4)! Some commentators attempt to explain Elijah's response in psychological terms or to comment on how the lack of psychological coherence indicates divergent sources.[12] Nelson (1987: 126), while warning against such psychologizing in general, ends up by affirming the inevitability of such a reading in this case.

> While guessing at the psychological motivations of characters in narratives is usually a serious exegetical mistake, in this case the reader has been provided with so many explicit symptoms that the 'psychologizing' process becomes *inevitable* (my emphasis).

The motivation seems to be an understandable desire on the part of modern readers to empathize with Elijah's feelings and/or to excuse his actions. For Elijah to be so brave at Mt Carmel and then, almost immediately after, run away in fear at Jezebel's threats needs to be explained. If his original 'bravery' is assumed to be real and not just bravado, so the reasoning goes, Elijah must be suffering from the symptoms of exhaustion, excessive stress, and then depression. While this may help modern readers, who have experienced these symptoms (personally or vicariously) to identify with Elijah, this reading is based on the assumption that the reader's initial assumption about Elijah's courage was correct.

When the facts of the story line are kept in mind, however, such psychologizing is unnecessary. When Elijah finally meets characters who are non-compliant he demonstrates no remarkable level of charisma; that is, he does not influence them to do his bidding, and shows little self-assurance. In ch. 19 Elijah is confronted with two situations in which he is faced with the prospect of meeting two non-compliant characters, Jezebel and Yahweh. In each case Elijah's actions show that he is afraid to meet either of them.

Elijah is evidently so afraid of Jezebel that he does not even realize the element of bluff in her threat. He should have realized the bluff behind sending a messenger with such a threat and not sending a military or

---

1986: 122, 'After the heights of triumph come the depths of despair'; Sockman 1954: 160) is unconvincing. It is anachronistic to impose a modern reader's idea of psychological coherence on our reader (cf. Todorov 1977: 53-65).

12. De Vries 1985: 235: 'Psychologizing interpretations of this narrative have been hard put to explain how the triumphant, high-flying Elijah of 18.46 could suddenly become so frightened (19.3) and despondent (vv. 4-9), but of course this question does not arise for those who recognize the original independence of these passages.'

police force or going herself to confront him. If Jezebel was really so confident of overcoming Elijah why warn him? The reader knows that Yahweh, who had miraculously (?) preserved Elijah's life during the drought, who had raised the woman of Zarephath's son, who had caused fire to fall from heaven to consume the sodden sacrifice, and who had placed his hand on Elijah so that he could outrun the king's chariot, could certainly be relied upon to protect Elijah from Jezebel's threats. But Elijah gives no consideration to these factors. Instead of waiting for Yahweh's word to come to him as he did in 17.2, he runs away in fear.

Elijah also seems to be afraid, or at least unusually hesitant, to meet Yahweh. As Gregory[13] notes, in 17.1 Elijah claims to 'stand before' Yahweh (עמד לפני). When, however, at Horeb Elijah is asked 'to stand' on the mountain 'before Yahweh' (עמד לפני, 19.11) he has to be coaxed out onto the mountain by the 'still small voice' and can only bring himself to 'stand' (עמד) at 'the opening of the cave' (פתח המערה, 19.13). While the opening of the cave is presumably on the mountain, and therefore in some sense 'before Yahweh', since Yahweh is portrayed as being on the mountain, Elijah's response just barely qualifies as obedience. His earlier claim (17.1) and his intrepid approach to Yahweh in prayer (17.20, 21; 18.36, 37) as well as his confident delivery of apparently unauthorized words from Yahweh, have not led the first-time reader to anticipate Elijah's hesitancy. Yes, he is ashamed at how he ran away from Jezebel's threat ('I am no better than my fathers', 19.4), but that only demonstrates that he has suddenly become aware of his own weakness. While Elijah, evidently unmoved by the experience of Yahweh passing by (19.11, 12), still has enough self-assurance to repeat his complaint against Yahweh of being the only one left (19.10, 14), when he is invited to actually stand before Yahweh (v. 11), as he had earlier claimed (17.1), his response can only be described as hesitant, even fearful.

While the experience of failing to stand up to Jezebel's threat has brought some self-awareness to Elijah about the partially illusory nature of his own self-confidence, the reader comes to view Elijah's claim to 'stand before' Yahweh as somewhat hollow. Suddenly, what the first-time reader had thought was the narrator's affirmation of Elijah's courage becomes only Elijah's somewhat empty assertion.[14]

13. Gregory 1990: 101-102. Some translations obscure this point by paraphrasing 'before whom I stand' in 17.1 and 18.15 to 'whom I serve' (NJPSV, GNB, JB, NIV) or to 'whose servant I am' (NEB, REB).

14. Gregory (1990: 102), argues that the 'tentative response of Elijah' to the

## c. *The Second-Time Reading of 1 Kings 17 and 18*

The second-time reader is led to infer that Elijah only displays the signs of self-assurance and charisma when the people he confronts are relatively easily influenced or when he is immediately protected by Yahweh. In 17.1 as soon as Elijah utters his threat to Ahab, who, as I will argue, turns out to be a rather weak character, Yahweh takes Elijah into hiding to protect him. When Jezebel utters her threat, no word of Yahweh is immediately forthcoming and Elijah runs away in fear.[15] While Elijah is undoubtedly being portrayed as demonstrating an exceptional degree of self-assurance in proclaiming such an unpopular message directly to Ahab in 17.1 in the first place, the reader comes to question the depth of this self-assurance. Elijah is fearless before Ahab, but Ahab turns out to be a fairly acquiescent character. Elijah's 'courage' or self-assurance must, therefore, be reassessed by the reader. Jezebel, on the other hand, is consistently displayed as a strong character. Before her Elijah appears rather timid.

Elijah displays courage in confronting Ahab to announce the end of the drought, especially since Obadiah has just informed him that Ahab has been looking for him (18.10). But Ahab turns out to have more bark than bite. His first words upon encountering Elijah are: 'Is it you, you troubler of Israel?' (18.17 RSV). Whileat first sight this sounds threatening, his apparently immediate and uncontested compliance with Elijah's order to gather Israel and the prophets of Baal and Asherah to him at Mt Carmel, with no demand of an explanation from Elijah of his (from Ahab's point of view sinister) purpose, shows that whatever the tenor of his words, Ahab's actions lead the reader to infer that he can be a rather submissive character.

The portrayal of Ahab in this passage as a person who has a marked tendency to yield to strong personalities is striking. Elijah commands Ahab, without giving any reason, to gather the prophets of Baal and Asherah and the people to Mt Carmel (18.19). Ahab complies (v. 20). Ahab makes no attempt to establish the ground rules for the contest. He silently witnesses it. In fact, Ahab is so passive during the contest that

---

command to actually stand before Yahweh is the very moment when the 'alert audience' discovers the hollowness of Elijah's bravery and begins to reconstruct the story to view Elijah as, 'a prophet plagued by his own ego and exaggerated importance'.

15. If we repoint, 'and he saw' (וַיַּרְא), to, 'and he was afraid' (וַיִּרָא), as suggested by *BHS*, the point is reinforced that Elijah's fear was so immediate that he never gave Yahweh a chance to offer protection as he did in 17.2.

when he reappears in v. 41 the first-time reader may well be surprised to find him still there. He also passively witnesses Elijah's slaughter of the prophets of Baal without challenging Elijah in any way (v. 40). Elijah next commands Ahab to, 'Go up, eat and drink' (v. 41). Ahab's reaction is, '[He] went up to eat and drink' (v. 41).

The reason Elijah gives Ahab for eating and drinking is that he (Elijah) hears the sound of a rainstorm coming. For Ahab to obey such a command on the sole basis of Elijah's promise of rain implies that either Ahab, like Israel, has been won over to Elijah's side on the issue of Baalism versus Yahwism, or that Ahab is too afraid of the charismatic Elijah to stand up to him and refuse to do his bidding, or both. If the reader assumes that Ahab has been won over to Yahwism, for him to eat and drink is actually a demonstration of faith on Ahab's part, since as yet there is no tangible evidence of rain coming.[16]

Elijah's next command directs Ahab to descend the mountain in his chariot in order to avoid being stopped by the rains (v. 44b). Ahab obeys (v. 45b). At this point there is still no evidence of the torrential downpour which Elijah promises except a little cloud like a man's hand. Ahab, in following Elijah's order to descend the mountain is portrayed as being either too afraid to disobey Elijah which again indicates submissiveness, or as genuinely believing Elijah's prediction because he has come to recognize him as the representative of the god who controls the rains, Yahweh.

Ahab yields to Elijah at every point in this narrative. The reader infers that this is either because Ahab is a person who habitually yields to strong personalities or because he has converted, albeit temporarily, to Yahwism or a mixture of both reasons. But even if the reader assumes that Ahab underwent some sort of reformation, the fact that it soon disappears when he meets the next strong personality in his life, Jezebel, leads the reader once again to the conclusion that Ahab is somewhat spineless or at least easily influenced. For Elijah to face and overcome him is not necessarily to be regarded as a particularly notable feat of daring.

Elijah at first seems courageous in proposing the contest with the 450 prophets of Baal. But the prophets of Baal and the people of Israel who witness the contest turn out to be just as compliant as Ahab. Elijah sets up the terms of the contest. The prophets of Baal do not protest or

---

16. Nelson (1987: 119-20) argues that the eating and drinking is actually a feast of celebration in anticipation of the ending of the drought.

attempt to negotiate modifications. They obey Elijah. In 18.25 he commands the prophets of Baal in these words:

> Choose for yourself one bull and prepare it first, for you are many; and call on the name of your god, but put no fire to it (RSV).

In 18.26 we read of their compliance:

> And they took the bull which was given them and they prepared it, and called on the name of Baal from morning until noon (RSV).

It is notable that Elijah's terms for the contest are accepted without question. Wasn't there one prophet of Baal who thought 'this is too good to be true'? No. Elijah displays self-assurance and daring, but only to a relatively compliant group of rival prophets.

The people of Israel are no different. When Elijah proposes the terms of the contest they respond: 'The thing is good' (v. 24b). After the futile efforts of the prophets of Baal (vv. 26, 28, 29) and Elijah's sarcastic mocking of those efforts (v. 27),[17] Elijah commands the people to *come near* to him (v. 30). The response is, 'and all the people *came near* to him'(v. 30). Elijah then, having prepared the altar, the sacrifice, and somewhat mysteriously dug a trench around it (vv. 30-33a), gives orders that twelve jars of water in all be poured over the sacrifice and the wood (v. 33b). The drought had undoubtedly made water especially precious (Gros-Louis 1974: 187). Didn't any of the Israelites question the wisdom of wasting precious water on what may have appeared to be a prophet's whim? No. In the context it must be individuals from the assembled people of Israel who comply with Elijah's directives. Just as Israel came near when Elijah ordered them to, so they unquestioningly obeyed his order to pour precious water over the sacrifice.

The people's acquiescence to Elijah is further indicated by their response to Yahweh's devouring of the sacrifice and its excess water. When Elijah earlier suggested the terms of the contest he said, 'the God who answers by fire, he is God' (v. 24). After Yahweh answers by fire in a most convincing manner (v. 38) the people's response is:

> And when all the people saw it, they fell on their faces; and they said, The LORD, he is God; The LORD, he is God (18.39 RSV).

---

17. Rendsburg (1988) argues that the common view that in v. 27 Elijah mockingly wonders whether Baal's lack of response was due to his being busy defecating can be sustained without emending the text.

The people's words are in exact conformity with the original terms of the contest. Elijah's, 'he is God' (v. 24) corresponds precisely to the people's, 'Yahweh, he is God' (v. 39). Israel not only accept Elijah's terms for the contest without demurring, they respond with Elijah's very words when Yahweh wins the contest.

The final piece of evidence that Israel is portrayed as being easily swayed is their obedience to Elijah's command to seize the prophets of Baal so that they could be killed (v. 40). Killing the losers of the contest was not one of the originally agreed terms, so the people's obedience to Elijah is shown to go beyond even the previously agreed terms. It is one thing for the people to agree to the terms of Elijah's contest, to partici- pate in the necessary preparatory steps, and to acknowledge the winner of the contest. But to assist Elijah in killing the prophets of the god who had royal approval shows that the people have become putty in Elijah's hands. The fact that Israel's 'conversion' to Yahweh at Mt Carmel ends up being short-lived is significant at this point because it reinforces the second-time reader's impression of their submissiveness to Elijah. The people of Israel are no more easily swayed by Elijah at Mt Carmel than they were earlier swayed by Ahab's and Jezebel's Baalism and would later be swayed by that same Baalism after the events of that day had faded from their memories. The people of Israel are no threat to Elijah at all and the reader therefore surmises that, contrary to the reader's earlier assumption, Elijah's seeming daring and self-assurance in dealing with Israel is no necessary indication that he has extraordinary charisma.

### d. *Summary*

At first reading Elijah appears in chs. 17 and 18 to display formidable charisma and self-assurance. These qualities, however, seem to disappear when Elijah is confronted with the more formidable Jezebel and when he is asked to actually stand before Yahweh. The reader re-evaluates the nature of the seeming threat of Ahab, the prophets of Baal and the people of Israel. When this is done the reader discovers that Elijah only appears to display charisma and daring when dealing with people who are extraordinarily compliant and submissive toward him. When he faces more formidable adversaries his ability to influence them is apparently non-existent and his self-assurance seems somewhat hollow. It is only when the reader realizes that Elijah cannot summon up the courage to face Jezebel, and in a different way Yahweh, that Elijah's self-assurance is seen to be one part bravery and several parts bravado.

e. *Loose Threads*
When the reader comes to the conclusion that Elijah is portrayed as being truly afraid of Jezebel several loose threads in the story which are otherwise a mystery are more easily explained.

*1 Kings 18.19—the missing prophets of Asherah.* In 18.19 Elijah directs Ahab to gather to Mt Carmel the 450 prophets of Baal *and the 400 prophets of Asherah*, who eat at Jezebel's table. In v. 20 we read, 'so Ahab sent to all the people of Israel, and gathered the prophets together at Mount Carmel'. In its context 'the prophets' presumably number 850 in total, 450 of the god Baal and 400 of the goddess Asherah. But the prophets of the goddess Asherah never figure in the story again. When Elijah sets up the contest it is between two male gods, Baal and Yahweh, and the prophets who represent them: 450 anonymous prophets representing Baal, and Elijah representing Yahweh. The prophets of the female goddess and the goddess herself are not involved. Another female person is also not present even though she sponsored the prophets of Baal and Asherah by feeding them (18.19).

The person that Elijah does not invite to the contest is Jezebel and by his later response to a threat of Jezebel's that seems to be more full of bluff than substance, the second-time reader can provide a plausible reason. Elijah may be being portrayed as already being afraid of Jezebel and it could well be that this is the reason Elijah does not invite her even though she was a logical choice to be invited to such a contest. After all she was responsible for introducing into Israel the vitriolic form of Baalism which Elijah spent his life combating.

A specifically feminist reader might surmise that Elijah is afraid of Jezebel not just because of her strong personality but also because she is *female*, and he just cannot cope with a strong *female* adversary.[18] The fact that 400 prophets of a female deity Asherah must be assumed to witness the contest between two male deities, without either being drawn into the contest, or suffering the same fate as the prophets of Baal, is also of significance for the second-time reader, feminist or not. If a specifically feminist line were taken, the second-time reader might ask whether the exclusion of the prophets of Asherah from further action in the plot is evidence of male insecurity (Yahweh's representatives can only overpower the representatives of other male deities) or of a male chauvinistic ignoring of the importance of things feminine, or both.

18. A recent treatment, although not exclusively feminist, is Trible 1995.

In this work, in which our reader is not specifically feminist, the mention of the 400 prophets of Asherah and their absence from the further plot may be a clue on the basis of which the reader infers that something, or as it turns out someone, feminine is missing. Just as the prophets of Asherah are not involved in the contest, neither is another female authority figure, Jezebel. Elijah's failure to confront the prophets of Asherah may lead the reader to infer that Elijah's contest does not include all the relevant participants. By ignoring Jezebel, and not confronting her in the contest, the reader might infer that Elijah's daring is being portrayed as superficial. Elijah only demonstrates daring when he is able to control his adversaries fairly easily. What appears at first as a loose narrative thread actually is one of the very threads that, when given a good pull, could well unravel the bravery of Elijah to reveal his fear of his nemesis Jezebel.

*Why Elijah blames Israel for killing the prophets.* A second seemingly loose narrative thread which the reader is able to understand better by assuming that Elijah's avoidance of Jezebel is due to his fear of her is Elijah's statement to Yahweh that *the people of Israel* (not Jezebel) had slain Yahweh's prophets with the sword (19.10, 14). The narrator makes it clear that it is Jezebel, not Israel, who is ultimately responsible for the purge of Yahweh's prophets (18.4, 13). Ironically, the only prophets which Israel as a whole have in fact helped to slay, as far as the reader knows, are the prophets of Baal, not the prophets of Yahweh (18.40). While Elijah's claim that Israel had slain the prophets could be understood as the irrational exaggeration of an understandably depressed prophet (Nelson 1987: 126), the reader's assumption that Elijah fears Jezebel could lead the reader to another explanation which may be preferable. Perhaps Elijah blames Israel because he does not want to admit his own fear of Jezebel to Yahweh or take responsibility for his response to it. Significantly, he never mentions Jezebel in his complaint to Yahweh. Instead he blames Israel for what the narrator and Obadiah (18.4, 13) lay at the feet of Jezebel. Since the reader knows that Obadiah has informed Elijah of Jezebel's purge (18.13), the reader cannot infer that Elijah is ignorant of Jezebel's responsibility for the death of the prophets of Yahweh. By blaming Israel for the actions of Jezebel, Elijah may be being portrayed as avoiding admitting to Yahweh his real problem. The reader could well infer that Elijah is afraid of Jezebel and that is the real reason that Elijah is at Mt Horeb.[19]

The reader knows that at Mt Carmel Israel had shown themselves to be quite amenable to the recognition of the supremacy of Yahweh over Baal, even if this did not result in sustained loyalty to him. In fact Yahweh reminds Elijah in 19.18 of 7,000 in Israel who had remained loyal to him and would be preserved when Hazael, Jehu and Elisha carried out Yahweh's judgment on the nation. Even though Elijah blames the nation, Israel is not Elijah's major problem. Jezebel is. Elijah's failure to admit this, either before or after the theophanic phenomena, could lead the reader to infer that Elijah is either unable or unwilling to confront his own problem. On this supposition even Yahweh's 'still small voice'[20] could not shake Elijah into admitting or recognizing his fear of Jezebel. That one of the tasks Yahweh gives to Elijah is to anoint Elisha to replace him as prophet (v. 16) is not surprising if this view is taken. Until and unless Elijah either admits his fear of Jezebel and asks for Yahweh's help and/or overcomes that fear by directly challenging her, Elijah's work will be severely hampered and his development as a character stymied.

*Elijah's failure to confront Jezebel.* A third loose narrative thread is the fact that even after the experience of Horeb and Jezebel's involvement in the Naboth incident Elijah never directly confronts Jezebel. When Jezebel conspires to defraud Naboth of his patrimony and have him executed on trumped-up charges, Elijah is sent to confront Ahab, not Jezebel. While Ahab is as deserving of judgment in the Naboth affair as Jezebel, it is only Ahab whom Elijah directly warns of judgment.[21] Elijah is taken up into heaven without having ever met the woman who caused him such anguish.[22]

19. Auld (1986: 124), comments, 'To excuse his presence at the mountain, Elijah blames not Jezebel but the whole sorry national situation...'

20. For the difficulties in translating this particular expression note the variety in the standard translations: AV, RSV, 'still small voice; NJPSV, 'a soft murmuring sound'; NEB, 'a faint murmuring sound'; NRSV, 'a sound of sheer silence'.

21. On 1 Kgs 21.23 see below.

22. That Jezebel was not quite as formidable an opponent as Elijah thought her to be may be indicated by the rather routine way in which Jehu later deals with her (2 Kgs 9.30-37). The reader might, however, explain the different reactions of Elijah and Jehu to Jezebel by the fact that Jezebel softened with age or that she lost power after Ahab's death. It is, however, possible that the contrast between the ways Elijah and Jehu deal with her is meant to highlight Elijah's fear.

*Elijah's post-Horeb self-assurance.* Given that Elijah's fear of Jezebel and his hesitancy to stand before Yahweh could lead the reader to qualify his or her original attribution of self-assurance and charisma to Elijah in chs. 17 and 18, is there any evidence that suggests to the reader that Elijah changes after the experiences of ch. 19?

*1 Kings 19.19-21.* The record of Elijah throwing his mantle to Elisha (19.19) could lead the first-time reader to infer that even if Elijah has not completely recovered his self-confidence at least he is once again willing to follow Yahweh's directives. He is no longer sitting under a single broom tree contemplating death. He is once again doing Yahweh's work. But as we shall see, the second-time reader may be led to qualify this inference.

*1 Kings 21.* In ch. 21, the Naboth incident, Elijah again delivers a hostile message to Ahab, a sign of bravery and/or self-confidence in 17.1 and 18.18, 19. If anything, the reader is invited to assume that Elijah is even more confident and daring in confronting Ahab. This is seen by comparing the confrontation in 18.18, 19 with that in 21.20-24. In both passages Ahab addresses Elijah first, and on each occasion in an unfriendly manner. But the hostility of Elijah's reply is greater in the latter story than in the former. The first-time reader might well infer that Elijah's pre-Horeb charisma and self-assurance have returned and have even strengthened. Ahab is still some sort of threat to Elijah and yet Elijah makes the already hostile message which Yahweh commissions him to deliver (21.19), even more hostile (21.20-24). Whereas Yahweh had commissioned Elijah to deliver a message which only threatened Ahab personally, Elijah's message threatens his entire dynasty.[23] The first-time reader could easily infer that Elijah has regained his self-confidence, perhaps even without its previous superficiality.

But other factors lead the second-time reader to question this line of reasoning. First of all, while ch. 20 seems to show that Ahab does have some courage (v. 11—his response to Benhadad's threat, 'Tell him, "Let not him who girds on his sword boast like him who ungirds it"', shows that Ahab can display courage), it ends by portraying Ahab responding to a prophetic threat not by threatening the prophet, but by sulking (20.43). Again, in ch. 21, when Naboth refuses to sell his patri-

---

23. If v. 23 is considered part of Elijah's message and not as a parenthetical comment by the narrator, Elijah also threatened Ahab's wife Jezebel, albeit indirectly.

mony to Ahab, Ahab's response is not to threaten him or personally to concoct a plot against him as Jezebel does. Instead, unable to stand against the strong Naboth, he returns to his home and sulks in his bed—refusing to eat (21.4).[24] The reader here probably adopts Jezebel's point of view that Ahab is a bit of a weakling (21.7, 'Do you now govern Israel?', implying doubt). Elijah's increased hostility towards him in the Naboth incident is not, therefore, necessarily an indication of a return of, or an increase in, Elijah's self-assurance.

Secondly, a comparison of the confrontations between Ahab and Elijah in 18.18, 19 and 21.20 leads the reader to infer that Ahab is more easily intimidated by Elijah in the latter episode than he is in the former. In 18.17, upon finally seeing Elijah, Ahab says, 'Is it you, you troubler of Israel?' It must be remembered that up until this time Ahab has been seeking to find Elijah and punish him for causing the drought (18.10). By contrast in 21.20 he addresses Elijah with these words, 'Have *you* found *me*, O my enemy?' (my emphasis). The reader notices that whereas before Ahab had been seeking Elijah in order to harm him (18.10), here in 21.20 Ahab has been avoiding Elijah and does not want to be found by him. Ahab had evidently learned after the events at Mt Carmel to be afraid of Elijah. Also, the words which Ahab uses to describe Elijah in 21.20 are less threatening than those he used in 18.17. In 18.17 the word 'troubler' recalls how Achan had brought disaster upon Israel by violating the ban.[25] Ahab, by implication, accuses Elijah of similarly bringing disaster on Israel. In 21.20, however, Elijah is merely Ahab's personal foe, ('*my* enemy'). For Elijah to confront Ahab when the reader realizes that he is afraid of Elijah does not lead the reader to assume that Elijah has remarkable courage or self-confidence; it only shows Ahab's timidity.

Finally, the fact that Jezebel is either not addressed by Elijah directly, or perhaps not even indirectly in 21.20-24, could lead the reader to surmise that Elijah has not overcome his fear of Jezebel. Even if the reader assumes that v. 23 is part of Elijah's message and not the narrator's comment (as are vv. 25, 26), Elijah only refers to Jezebel. He

---

24. The Hebrew collocation used to describe Ahab's reaction, סר וזעף, is found only in these two passages (20.43; 21.4) in the Hebrew Bible. This reinforces the connection between the two incidents and thus reinforces by repetition the reader's impression that Ahab's response is feeble.

25. The Hebrew word for troubler (עכר) recalls the valley named after the Achan incident, Josh. 7.25, 26.

does not confront her directly even though she is at least as responsible as Ahab, if not more so, for the treachery against Naboth.

The fact that Elijah does not address Jezebel directly, if at all, and the fact that Ahab has been portrayed as somewhat weak-willed and afraid of Elijah leads the reader to the inference that Elijah is not necessarily being portrayed as any more brave or self-confident in ch. 21 than he was in chs. 17 and 18. As noted above, the first-time reader in all probability comes to the conclusion that Elijah's earlier courage and self-confidence were probably somewhat shallow characteristics. Chapter 21 gives the reader little reason to assume that they have deepened significantly.

*2 Kings 1.2-17.* The same, however, cannot be said of the reader's evaluation of Elijah's self-assurance after having read 2 Kgs 1.2-17. Here Elijah is portrayed as displaying more courage than earlier. Elijah prayed fervently in ch. 18 for Yahweh to burn up a single sacrifice, albeit a wet one. By contrast, in 2 Kgs 1, Elijah seems rather effortlessly to call down Yahweh's fire to burn up two entire military units and their commanders (vv. 10, 12). He shows no fear of their military might, nor of the king who stands behind them. It is only when the third commander takes a servile approach, begging that he and his men's lives be spared (vv. 13, 14), that Elijah goes down and addresses Ahaziah as requested (vv. 15, 16). Elijah evidently speaks to the dying Ahaziah in Samaria (v. 2), the capital of Israel, which is a potentially dangerous place for a prophet hostile to the regime then in power. The message which he delivers to Ahaziah face to face (v. 16) is just as hostile as his earlier indirect ones. Without flinching Elijah tells Ahaziah that he is about to die because he sent to ask a foreign god, Baal-zebub, for guidance. True, Elijah is reassured by the angel's words before he goes to address Ahaziah (v. 15). But this is only to be expected. As idealized an Elijah as we seem to have here would want to go down at Yahweh's bidding and not at the king's. There is, therefore, some evidence that Elijah's courage and self-confidence are deeper at the end of his life than those qualities had been earlier.

But even if 2 Kings 1.2-18 shows that some of Elijah's seeming bravery has returned the reader still cannot disregard the fact that Elijah never confronts Jezebel. This fact casts a shadow over Elijah even to the end. He might stand up to military units and their commanders. He might scold Ahab and his dying son Ahaziah. He might even take the risky step of going to the royal court in Samaria to deliver his message. But he never confronts Jezebel. While there could be other reasons which the reader might legitimately infer for why Elijah never confronts Jezebel (e.g. she may have lost her real power after Ahab died) it seems to me that the reader will probably be plagued by some doubts about the reality of Elijah's seeming transformation at the end of his life.

### 3. *Elijah's Reliability as Yahweh's Representative*

a. *Introduction*
One of the obvious roles which Elijah is portrayed as filling is his work as Yahweh's representative, which involves delivering Yahweh's word and performing certain authorized actions.[26] He both speaks and acts to or before a variety of different people. In some instances the reader is informed that Yahweh authorizes Elijah to deliver a message from him (1 Kgs 17.16; 21.17-19; 2 Kgs 1.3) or do something for him (1 Kgs 18.1; 2 Kgs 1.15). On other occasions Elijah merely claims to do so without explicit narratorial confirmation (17.1; 18.36). Occasionally both the message or action which Yahweh instructs Elijah to deliver or perform, and the message which he actually delivers or the action which he actually performs are recorded (1 Kgs 21.18, 19 with 21.21-24; 2 Kgs 1.3, 4 with 1.6, 16). In such instances the reader can compare the two versions in order to assess Elijah's performance. At other times the reader can only infer whether or not Elijah is being portrayed as a reliable representative of Yahweh.

As is the case with Elijah's charisma and self-assurance, Elijah is at first portrayed as being a very reliable representative of Yahweh. To the first-time reader he appears to deliver Yahweh's words reliably. But after reading to 1 Kgs 19.14, the reader comes to realize that Elijah's reliability as Yahweh's representative is not being portrayed as being absolute. The reader comes to surmise that Elijah in all probability does and says things on his own initiative while claiming Yahweh's authorization. The reader also comes to reassess whether Elijah's words and deeds, which the reader had previously assumed were quite reliable representations of what Yahweh had authorized Elijah to say or do, were in fact as reliable as the reader had at first assumed them to be.

---

26. Here I distinguish between actions which Elijah did in his personal life, treated in the next section of this chapter, and those public actions which Yahweh commissioned him to do as his representative which are treated here.

This all changes, however, in 2 Kings 1, where Elijah appears to the reader to be very reliable indeed. But even this seemingly idealistic portrayal of Elijah must be carefully qualified. In 2 Kings 2 Elijah is taken up into heaven by a whirlwind. He leaves the human scene without having confronted Jezebel and without having accomplished at least two of the three tasks Yahweh gives him to do in 1 Kgs 19.15-17. In addition, the narratives enmeshed within the Elijah stories help to create, and the subsequent narratives in 2 Kings reinforce, the reader's suspicion of the reliability of prophets and prophecy in general. This suspicion is quite naturally transferred to Elijah. The second-time reader comes to suspect that any claim by a prophet or prophetess to speak or act for Yahweh which is not given explicit narratorial confirmation could be being portrayed as the prophet's own invention. While Elijah may appear to the first-time reader to have developed into a truly reliable representative of Yahweh in 2 Kings 1, the second-time reader may well have genuine doubts about this. Moreover, even the first-time reader is influenced by the portrayal of prophets and prophecy in 1 Kings 13, 20 and 22, and may also, therefore, harbor some doubts about Elijah's reliability.

b. *Elijah's Reliability as Yahweh's Representative in 1 Kings 17 and 18*
*1 Kings 17.1-7.* Elijah first appears in the narrative in 17.1, where he uses an oath formula to announce the coming of a drought upon Israel, presumably because of Yahweh's displeasure at Ahab's introduction and promotion of Baal worship in Israel (16.30-33). Elijah's appearance in the narrative is somewhat sudden. The reader is given no prophetic call narrative nor any notice that Yahweh has sent Elijah to speak the specific message which he does against Ahab. He is not identified as a prophet or as 'a man of God' by the narrator and yet the first-time reader is not surprised that the drought which Elijah predicts does in fact occur (17.7). The first-time reader naturally expects that Yahweh's displeasure at Ahab's marriage to a Phoenician princess and his promotion of the worship of Baal will result in some sort of divine judgment on Ahab's household, just as it had in the cases of Jeroboam and his son Nadab (1 Kgs 12.26–13.6; 13.32–14.20; 15.29-30), Rehoboam (1 Kgs 14.21-28), and Baasha and his son Elah (1 Kgs 15.32–16.13).

The reader's expectation that Elijah's 'prediction' (technically it is a promise or oath) of divine judgment by means of a drought will probably come true is partially created by the record in 1 Kgs 16.34 of Joshua's seemingly unauthorized curse being fulfilled. Without any divine directive, Joshua had sworn an oath (וישבע) which laid a divine curse upon anyone rebuilding Jericho (Josh. 6.26). The oath threatened the death of the builder's firstborn and youngest sons, at the start and finish of the project, respectively. To the first-time reader it is a bad omen for Ahab that it is during his reign that this curse is fulfilled, thus creating the expectation that other curses might follow. Significantly, what was originally an unauthorized statement, apparently on Joshua's own initiative, is reported in 1 Kgs 16.34 as, 'the word of Yahweh which he spoke by the hand of Joshua, the son of Nun'. When the reader reads in the next verse that Elijah promises with an oath formula ('By the life of Yahweh') that a drought will come upon Israel, without any explicit indication from the narrator that Elijah's message is from Yahweh, the first-time reader naturally assumes that this too could be the word of Yahweh (in this case) by the hand of Elijah, even though the narrator does not explicitly say so. The first-time reader is not yet aware of the complex relationship between a human spokesman's words and Yahweh's words as depicted later in Kings.

The fulfillment of an apparently unauthorized prediction is not a guarantee that the reader is to infer that Yahweh had in fact originally given the word, even though not explicitly indicated in the narrative. There may well be other reasons for Yahweh to fulfill the prediction. For instance, Yahweh might fulfill a word because to not do so would discredit a valuable human emissary. Or he might fulfill one because the prediction, while not originally his idea, is in general accordance with his intentions in the particular circumstances and therefore he wants to fulfill it. In any case, the narrator invites the reader to assume that Elijah's message will be fulfilled. When the fulfillment actually occurs, the first-time reader quite properly infers, if only tentatively, that Elijah is being portrayed as a reliable messenger of Yahweh.

*1 Kings 17.8-16.* The reader's initial impression of Elijah's reliability as a messenger of Yahweh is given confirmation on the very next occasion when Elijah claims to utter a word from Yahweh, that is 17.14. In response to the widow of Zarephath's understandable reluctance to accede to Elijah's request for food, Elijah replies:

> Do not be afraid. Go! Do as you have said. But first make me a small cake of it and afterwards make one for yourself and your son. For thus says Yahweh, the God of Israel, 'the jar of meal will not be spent and the cruse of oil will not fail until the day Yahweh sends rain upon the earth' (17.13, 14).

The narrator immediately confirms that Elijah's message is, like Joshua's, 'the word of Yahweh which he spoke by the hand of [Elijah]' (v. 16). This confirmation comes not only by the direct statement just quoted, but also by the exact correspondence the narrator records between Elijah's prophecy and its fulfillment. Even though we have no record of Elijah receiving this message from Yahweh prior to its delivery, it appears to the reader that it is in fact Yahweh's message, and not a message which Elijah makes up and merely claims to be Yahweh's.

*1 Kings 17.17-24*. The story of the healing (or raising) of the woman's son (17.17-24) seems, at first, to establish for the reader Elijah's reliability as a spokesman for Yahweh yet again. The woman's words, upon having her son returned to her in good health, express what the first-time reader must assume is the narrator's point of view on Elijah.

> Now I know that you are a man of God and that the word of Yahweh is truly in your mouth (1 Kgs 17.24).

But upon further reflection the second-time reader realizes that something might be amiss in this idyllic picture which has been constructed of a pious woman of incredible faith and the totally reliable prophet whom Yahweh sends to her. To begin with, it seems very strange to the second-time reader, who has, as we will see, heightened suspicions about the reliability of prophets, that it is only after Elijah has restored her son to health that the woman recognizes that Elijah is a 'man of God' and that Yahweh's words are truly in his mouth. Had she not seen miraculous confirmation of Elijah's status every day as she scooped out the meal and poured out the oil and saw the jar and cruse refilled, as Elijah had predicted? Was this not ample evidence to a woman who supposedly has the faith to give her last morsel of bread to Elijah? When this and other factors are taken into consideration A. Graeme Auld's (1986: 110) suggestion that the reader could well assume that the woman might have been 'prevaricating a little over the extent of her supplies—to protect her family of course!' takes on added credibility.

If, for the sake of argument, we assume that the reader infers that the woman is lying, what textual evidence can be marshaled to support this assumption? In support are several factors. The first is the woman's situation. Even if she had more food than she admitted to Elijah, she was living in a famine and it would be very unwise, from her point of view, to give it away to someone else. Thus the reader does not have to assume that the woman was a habitual liar or an especially devious person in order to infer that she is at least exaggerating on this occasion.

Secondly, the narrator's description of the woman as 'the mistress of the house' (בעלת הבית, v. 17) could well be taken to imply that she was a woman of some substance.[27] The phrase 'mistress of the house' is found only here in the Old Testament, but the analogy of the use of the masculine equivalent yields the sense 'owner of the house' and does not necessarily imply great wealth.[28] Her house did, however, have an upper chamber large enough for Elijah's bed (v. 19) and the phrase 'her household' in v. 15 might imply that she had servants. This does not, however, prove that she had more food than she admitted to Elijah, but it is consistent with that interpretation.

Thirdly, as Auld (1986: 111) notes, the widow's sin which she alleges Elijah had brought to Yahweh's attention (v. 18) could be her sin of lying to Elijah about the extent of her reserves. Again, this is a possible inference for the reader to make, not a necessary one.

Fourthly, several pieces of evidence could be taken by the reader to imply underlying hostility on the part of the woman towards Elijah. This would give the reader further reason to suppose that she might be being portrayed as lying to Elijah in v. 12. A person hostile to another is unlikely to admit to that person during a famine the amount of food they actually have left. The fact that the woman lived in Zarephath, which belonged to Sidon, the Baalist Jezebel's home country (16.31), might give the reader reason to suppose that she would be unlikely to be sympathetic to a Yahwistic prophet from Israel. She even refers to Yahweh as, 'your [Elijah's] god', which implies that even though Yahweh had commanded her to feed Elijah (17.9), she did not at this point, at least, recognize Yahweh's authority over her. Even the word 'mistress' (בעלת) might be a clue to the reader that she was a worshiper of Baal (בעל). Again, this is not conclusive and these factors must be balanced by the fact that she did eventually give food to Elijah (v.15) and even provided lodging for him.

Finally, if the reader assumes that the woman is lying, the woman's words in v. 24 are seen to be literally true and not the emotional outburst of an overwrought mother who had just lost her son (Auld 1986:

27. In terms of the tradition history of the text it may well be that the mistress of the house in 17.17-24 is not to be identified with the widow of vv. 8-16 (De Vries 1985: 222). However, Elijah's description of her as 'the widow' (האלמנה, v. 20; cf. vv. 9, 10) makes it clear that the same woman is in view in the final form.

28. Cf. BDB, p. 127; Exod 22.7.

111). If she is lying about the extent of her provisions, she only really receives confirmation that Elijah is indeed a man of God when he becomes the channel through whom Yahweh miraculously heals her son. Up until then, if she was lying, she had seen no miraculous demonstration of Elijah's status. Again, this is not conclusive and the reader cannot be certain at this point.

While the story does not lead even the second-time reader to a clear decision about the veracity of the woman's statement in v. 12, the very fact that the narrative could be read in either way leads the reader to be cautious in assuming that the story is as simple as it might sometimes seem. If the reader infers that the woman is lying, the reader comes to view Elijah's statement in a different way. If the woman is truly impoverished Elijah's prediction is a genuine prophecy designed to reassure the woman who is being asked to take a step of faith. But if the woman is lying Elijah's prediction could lead the reader to infer that Elijah is somewhat naive. He promises enough food to last, implying that Yahweh will supply it miraculously, when in fact there is no need for a miracle at all, only generosity from the woman. He thinks he is the channel of a miracle when in fact he is the object of the woman's ruse. If the reader understands the story in this way the reader surmises that Elijah's reliability is not necessarily being affirmed in this story.[29]

*1 Kings 18.20-40.* In this passage Elijah proposes a contest between the prophets of Baal (and initially also the prophets of Asherah) and himself. There is no explicit indication by the narrator that the contest is Yahweh's idea.[30] This is only Elijah's claim (v. 36). In all probability the first-time reader is inclined to accept Elijah's claim that Yahweh directed him to set up the contest on Mt Carmel. The second-time reader, however, does not necessarily accept this claim. In two previous instances (17.1, 14), the first-time reader recalls that Elijah gave messages for which he claimed divine authorization. The narrator does not in those cases give *explicit* confirmation of Elijah's claim to have had divine authorization *prior* to the delivery of the messages. Nevertheless the messages are fulfilled as though they had Yahweh's prior authorization (17.7, 16). This

29. The reader could, of course, assume that Elijah knows that the woman is lying and so is not deceived by the woman at all. Elijah's prediction of a miraculous supply of food then has an ironic twist to it.

30. Gregory (1990: 104) and Wiener (1978: 11-12) suggest that Elijah is here acting on his own initiative.

leads the first-time reader to conclude that Elijah does not need the explicit prior confirmation of the narrator to be believed when he claims to speak or act for Yahweh. After all, didn't the drought come as Elijah predicted? Didn't the woman of Zarephath's food supply last as Elijah had said? Didn't the fire consume the sacrifice and thus authenticate Elijah's claim? The first-time reader also knows that the narrator sometimes only gives confirmation that a message which Elijah claims to be from Yahweh is in fact Yahweh's word after Elijah has delivered it (17.14, 16). Elijah's claim in 18.36 is, however, never given explicit narratorial confirmation.

c. *Is Elijah's Concern for his Own Status Excessive?*
But there is another important consideration which might lead the second-time reader to doubt the first-time reader's assumption that the contest with the prophets of Baal was Yahweh's idea all along, as Elijah claims. It is possible that the reader is being led to infer that Elijah is being portrayed as confusing his concern for his own status with his responsibility to be a reliable representative of Yahweh.

*1 Kings 17.1.* The concern which Elijah displays for his own status may be present in his very first prophetic message. Elijah swears on oath that there would be no dew or rain in Israel *'except by my word'* (17.1). Elijah is depicted here, not only as giving what could be an unauthorized message from Yahweh, but also as claiming to have been given the right to determine when the drought would end. According to Elijah, the drought will end only when he gives the word for it to end. Admittedly Elijah does later publicly recognize that Yahweh, not he, would send the rain (17.14). But it may be significant that in a message which the narrator never confirms as being authorized by Yahweh, Elijah should affirm the *essential* nature of his own role in bringing the drought to an end. According to Elijah, Yahweh could only send him, and not some other emissary to announce the ending of the drought.

*1 Kings 18.36, 37.* Elijah's concern in this prayer is not just with Yahweh's reputation. He wants Yahweh also to demonstrate that he is Yahweh's servant and that he is merely following Yahweh's directions in setting up the contest. But the reader knows that Elijah is not the only 'servant of Yahweh' and that in all probability he is not his only prophet, contrary to his claim (18.22).

Obadiah's very name means 'servant of Yahweh', and the narrator gives clear confirmation that he lived his name (18.3, 4). Obadiah was responsible for the protection and feeding of 100 prophets of Yahweh during Jezebel's purge. Just as Yahweh had protected (hid; סתר, 17.3) and fed (כלכל, 17.4) Elijah in ch. 17, so here Obadiah is portrayed as protecting (חבא, 18.4) and feeding (כלכל, 18.4) 100 prophets of Yahweh. The parallel between Yahweh and Obadiah (Yahweh's servant) is not lost on the reader. Obadiah was a truly pious servant of Yahweh. But Elijah seems to be portrayed as at least ignoring Obadiah's piety and his faithful service to Yahweh in difficult circumstances (see below) if not actually refusing to recognize them.

In his prayer in 18.36, Elijah in effect asks Yahweh to demonstrate to Israel that he is an 'Obadiah', that is Yahweh's servant. There is a pious 'servant of Yahweh' near to hand; however, it is not Elijah but Obadiah. The attempt of Elijah to establish himself as the servant of Yahweh and what could easily be understood as his dismissal of a true servant of Yahweh may indicate that, for Elijah the purpose of the contest on Mt Carmel is not just to establish Yahweh as Israel's God. The reader could quite easily infer that he also wants to establish himself as Yahweh's single truly loyal representative. As I will show he seems to ignore or refuse to recognize Obadiah's loyalty and, in effect, asks Yahweh to establish that he is truly Yahweh's servant.

*1 Kings 18.22; 19.10, 14.* Elijah's excessive concern for establishing his own status in the contest on Mt Carmel may also be being hinted at by his claim to be the only remaining prophet of Yahweh. He makes this claim, not only to Israel in 18.22, but also to Yahweh both before and after the theophanic phenomena (19.10, 14). Ironically, by killing the prophets of Yahweh (18.4), Jezebel had given a superficial sort of credibility in Israel's eyes to Elijah's claim to be the only prophet of Yahweh left. Even the first-time reader knows, however, that this claim is, in all probability, false (18.4). There were at least 100 prophets of Yahweh still alive but in hiding[31] and Elijah has at least heard of the existence of these prophets (18.13). The first-time reader may at first be inclined to view Elijah's claim to be the only prophet left as a noble effort to hide

---

31. There is no reason to suppose that the reader should infer that the 100 prophets were either now dead or no longer in hiding, although this is possible. Obadiah's fear of Ahab's wrath (18.12) and Jezebel's threat to Elijah (19.2) make it probable that the persecution of Yahwists was still going on.

the existence of the prophets which Obadiah had been hiding, whose secrecy would have been compromised if Elijah had publicly acknowledged their existence. When Elijah twice repeats this claim to Yahweh (19.10, 14), from whom Elijah has no reason to keep the existence of the prophets a secret, however, the first-time reader alters the earlier judgment, if in fact the judgment was made in the first place, and infers that Elijah is either unwilling or unable to face the obvious and well-known (18.13, 'Has it not been told my lord?') fact that many other legitimate prophets were still alive. Alternatively the reader might surmise that Elijah has such a narrow definition of just who is a loyal follower of Yahweh that it excludes Obadiah and the prophets he had been hiding.

*1 Kings 18.2-16.* In this passage Elijah, particularly by the way he treats and refers to Obadiah, seems to dismiss or ignore Obadiah's loyalty to Yahweh rather curtly. Obadiah recognizes that he has an obligation to Ahab as well as to Elijah and Yahweh. He admits that in some sense Ahab is his 'lord' (v. 10). But he also claims to have a genuine and over-riding loyalty to both Elijah and Yahweh. He also uses the word 'lord' of Elijah. In his speech in 18.9-14, Obadiah refers to Elijah as 'my lord' or to himself as 'your [Elijah's] servant' four times (vv. 7, 9, 12, 13). He also informs Elijah that he had 'revered Yahweh from his youth' (v. 12) and that he had more recently shown that reverence by risking his own personal safety by hiding and feeding 100 of Yahweh's prophets (v. 13). The narrator gives explicit *advance* confirmation of Obadiah's account of his own piety and his action in protecting the 100 prophets (18.3, 4). This prevents the first-time reader from ever assuming, even for an instant, that Obadiah is being portrayed as conveniently inventing the record of his faithfulness under pressure from Elijah. Elijah, however, gives no recognition to Obadiah and speaks to him as though he either does not believe Obadiah's account of hiding the prophets, or as though he assumes that they were not prophets who were truly loyal to Yahweh.

Obadiah shows his loyalty to Elijah with his very first words, 'Is it you, *my lord* Elijah?' Elijah's response may imply that he rejects Obadiah's professed loyalty to him and may be subtly accusing him of having compromised his faith with Ahab: 'It is I. Go tell *your lord*...' The reader knows that the narrator takes Obadiah's side on the issue of Obadiah's own piety. Elijah should have known about Obadiah's risky faithfulness in protecting 100 prophets of Yahweh and should have believed Obadiah's profession of loyalty to him when he addressed him as 'my lord'. By clearly taking Obadiah's side on this issue over against Elijah, the narrator shows that Elijah is somewhat jaundiced in his view of the faithfulness of others. He is either so blinded to reality that he denies the very existence of other prophets, or he is so rigidly judgmental of the orthodoxy and orthopraxy of other followers of Yahweh that he assumes that only he really counts in the arithmetic of the faithful.

*1 Kings 18.24, 39.* That one of Elijah's primary concerns in arranging the contest with the prophets of Baal is with his own status may also be subtly indicated by the word-play that Elijah sets up between the response of the people to the winner of the contest, and the meaning of his own name. 'Elijah' means either, 'Yahweh is my God' or simply 'Yahweh is God'. Elijah has told the people that the god who answers by fire, 'he is God' (18.24). When Yahweh wins the contest their response is naturally, 'Yahweh, he is God. Yahweh, he is God' (Noth 1966: 16ff., 70, 139ff.). The people's answer is very close in Hebrew to saying Elijah's name twice. Granted, in Elijah's name the 'Yahweh' and 'God' elements are in their shorter forms and in reverse order, but this is not a great obstacle to a fluent reader of Hebrew such as is our reader. It is not only Yahweh who wins the contest at Horeb. By a word-play, which Elijah sets up, the people also unwittingly declare Elijah the winner.

d. *The Unmasking of Elijah's Reliability in 1 Kings 19*
While the first-time reader probably would not assume merely from reading ch. 18 that Elijah has been concerned with his own status in setting up the contest, when the reader hears Elijah repeat his claim to be the only remaining prophet of Yahweh in 19.10 and sees him refuse to be shaken from his false concept of his own importance even after a remarkable revelation of Yahweh's presence (19.14), the reader is likely to begin to distrust Elijah's portrayal of himself. By his refusal to be shifted from his conviction that he is the only one left, even after a direct revelation of Yahweh, Elijah's egocentricity is 'unmasked' (Gregory 1990: 102). The reader then re-evaluates the inferences about Elijah which were previously made. As a part of this re-evaluation the reader comes to infer that the contest with the prophets of Baal is so inter-twined with Elijah's concern for his own position that it was possibly or probably not originally Yahweh's idea.

Granted, Yahweh does answer Elijah's prayer in 18.36, 37. But could Yahweh do otherwise? If Yahweh had not answered Elijah's prayer and won the contest, the people of Israel would have quite naturally assumed that Yahweh was just as impotent as Baal. If Yahweh had not answered Israel would never have come to understand the point of the drought. The drought was sent as a judgment on, and a warning to, Israel for their worship of Baal. If Yahweh had not backed up his prophet's contest, even though Elijah's motives in arranging it were not entirely selfless, Israel would have concluded that Yahweh had no more power than Baal to control the natural elements. If Yahweh could not answer with fire, there would be no reason for Israel to believe that he had control over the drought. Thus the point of the drought being a judgment would be lost on them. Elijah might be eccentric and perhaps even slightly egocentric (Gregory 1990: 102-104), but he is still on Yahweh's side. Elijah really gives Yahweh no alternative but to answer.

While it must be emphasized that the contest with the prophets of Baal is a daring initiative and one that helps to further Yahweh's purpose, it seems likely that the reader will ultimately infer that it was Elijah's idea. As such, his own desire to have his personal status publicly demonstrated and the egocentricity which this implies are mixed with his desire to see Yahweh vindicated in the very terms of the contest. While Elijah claims to have received a directive from Yahweh to set up the contest (18.36), subsequent events probably lead the reader to infer that this claim is unlikely to be true. Elijah does not simply represent Yahweh at Mt Carmel, he represents himself also.

### e. *Elijah's Reliability after Horeb*
*1 Kings 19.15-18*. Commentators often assume that 19.15-18 relates a recommissioning of Elijah[32] or a reconstituting of his position. In my view, this is a complete misreading of the chapter. Within the chapter there is no evidence to suggest that Elijah has been changed by his experience at Horeb. As Nelson (1987: 125) writes:

> The key to understanding these verses is the recognition that they fail to make any difference in Elijah's situation. Elijah is in exactly the same place after the theophany as before, complaining in exactly the same words (vv. 10, 14).

Yahweh does not recommission him at all. Instead he merely directs him to anoint his successors (19.15, 16) and chastises him for believing that

---

32. See for example De Vries's (1985: 232) title for this section, 'Yahweh Renews Elijah's Authority'.

he is the only faithful follower left (19.18). Elisha is to take Elijah's place as prophet (19.16). Elijah's job is effectively over. His only remaining work is to appoint his replacements.

Yahweh gives Elijah three tasks to complete. He is to anoint Hazael, Jehu and Elisha. They are to be Yahweh's instruments of judgment on Israel for the nation's disloyalty in serving Baal. Since Elijah, up to this point, has been Yahweh's instrument of judgment on Israel for its disloyalty, it is clear that these three are to carry on Elijah's unfinished work. Yahweh seems to be being portrayed as reasoning that if his own self-revelation could not alter Elijah's defeatist attitude, then he would simply use others to accomplish his purposes. The first-time reader could expect the story of Elijah to end very quickly. But perhaps, the reader might speculate, if Elijah at least faithfully performs his last instructions from Yahweh something of his reputation as Yahweh's representative can be restored. His personal role in Yahweh's purpose is, however, to be taken up by others.

*1 Kings 19.19-21.* In 19.19-21 Elijah seems to start well. His first action after Yahweh's instructions in 19.15-18 is to find Elisha and throw his mantle to him (19.19). While this is not 'anointing' as Yahweh had directed (v. 15, 16) it does seem close enough in its effect to constitute some sort of obedience to Yahweh's directive. Perhaps, the first-time reader speculates, Elijah has changed. But once again Elijah does things his way. As when Elijah predicted a drought and made its ending dependent on his word (17.1) and as in the contest on Mt Carmel (18.1-40), Elijah is not portrayed as acting in strict conformity to his divine instructions. But it does appear to the reader as though Elijah is performing a sort of ceremony which identifies Elisha as his successor.

The first-time reader's tentative assumption that Elijah might have accomplished the first part of his three-part commission is, however, undermined to a degree by subsequent events. Elisha asks Elijah for permission to return to 'kiss' his parents, promising to follow him thereafter. Elisha's intention turns out to be an honorable one. He is not rejecting Elijah's call. While the 'kiss' turns into a rather involved send-off party, the fact that Elisha expends his former means of livelihood in order to provide the food for the party is proof that he is sincere in his promise to follow Elijah. But notice how the ground has shifted. Elijah was directed to anoint Elisha to be prophet in his place (v. 16). Instead of transferring his prophetic authority to Elisha, Elijah ends up merely calling Elisha to follow him. In fact, the mantle which Elijah initially throws to Elisha must have been returned to Elijah, either literally or metaphorically, since Elisha only receives it permanently at Elijah's translation in 2 Kings 2. While Elijah is sent to anoint Elisha to be prophet in his place, Elisha ends up merely ministering to him, much as Joshua did for Moses.[33] This of course indicates to the first-time reader that, contrary to what Yahweh had said (v. 16), Elijah intended to continue to act as a prophet for some time. Why else would Elijah need someone to minister to him? True, Elijah did designate Elisha as his prophetic successor, but this is not the same thing as anointing him to be prophet in Elijah's place.

In the parallel cases of Hazael and Jehu, as soon as they are informed that they are to be king, they more or less immediately take action to begin serving as king. Hazael assassinates his master the next day and becomes king (2 Kgs 8.15). Jehu is immediately proclaimed king by the servants of Joram, the king he was to replace, and sets about to plan a coup. While the first-time reader may be unsure of precisely what Elijah has done to or for Elisha, the second-time reader recognizes the disparity with the cases of Jehu and Hazael and infers that Elijah does not really 'anoint' Elisha at this point in the narrative. If Elijah had truly anointed Elisha to be prophet in his place the second-time reader would have expected Elisha to begin doing his prophetic work more or less immediately. Elijah makes Elisha wait until the end of his life, which is some time away, before fulfilling (inasmuch as he ever fulfilled it) Yahweh's directive to anoint Elisha to be prophet in his place.

The first-time reader is in some doubt over just exactly what Elijah does do to Elisha in 19.19-21. The ambiguous rhetorical question which Elijah asks as part of his answer to Elisha's request to be given time to say 'goodbye' to his family is also the first-time reader's question. Just exactly what has Elijah done to Elisha? Has he anointed Elisha to be prophet in his place? Has Elijah rebelled against Yahweh's directive and decided to continue as prophet despite Yahweh's decision to replace him? Or, has he in some sense, done both? Or something else?

*1 Kings 20.35, 36.* In 20.35-43 a prophet speaking by the direction of Yahweh, and not on his own initiative (v. 35), asks a fellow prophet to

---

33. The Hebrew word used in 19.21 suggests this parallel. In Exod. 24.13; 33.11; Num. 11.28; Josh. 1.1, Joshua is Moses' 'minister' (משרת). In 1 Kgs 19.21 Elisha 'ministered' to (וישרתהו) Elijah.

strike him. This unusual request turns out to be part of the first prophet's prop for delivering a message of judgment against Ahab because he had allowed Benhadad to go free. The prophet who is asked to strike his fellow prophet, however, refuses to do so (v. 35b). Surprisingly the first prophet then delivers a prophetic word of judgment against the prophet who refused to strike him.

> Because you have not obeyed the voice of the LORD, behold, as soon as you have gone from me a lion shall kill you (v. 36a RSV).

Like clockwork the prediction is fulfilled: 'And as soon as he departed from him a lion met him and killed him' (v. 36b RSV). The reader is left with a dilemma. How was the prophet who disobeyed to know that Yahweh had indeed given the first prophet such an unusual message? Further, how could he have known that the punishment for not obeying such a bizarre request would be so incredibly harsh?

But this is not the first time the reader has read of a lion killing a prophet for unwittingly disobeying a command of Yahweh. The story, in 1 Kings 13 of the man of God from Judah has left the reader in a similar dilemma. The man of God from Judah is originally ordered by Yahweh not to eat or drink in Israel, or use the same road to return home (vv. 9, 17). The man of God is very careful to obey this command until he is tricked by another prophet into believing that Yahweh has rescinded his order. The reader is informed that the old prophet has lied (v. 18), but the man of God from Judah is in a hopeless situation. If he refuses the old prophet's offer of hospitality he might be guilty of disobeying a command of Yahweh. If he accepts it, he runs the risk of disobeying another word of Yahweh. The man of God unfortunately decides to believe the old prophet's word. Ironically, while the man of God is in the very process of eating and thus disobeying Yahweh's original command to him, the old prophet, who has just given him a false prophetic message, suddenly gives him a true one. As with the prophet in 20.35, 36 so also this 'disobedient' man of God is sentenced to death outside of his homeland Judah. The sentence is carried out immediately and by a lion (1 Kgs 13.24).

The reader of 20.35, 36 cannot help but put these two stories together and ask just what they imply about the narrator's point of view on prophets and prophecy. The conclusions which the reader comes to includes a recognition that, for the narrator, prophets and prophecy itself are not to be naively trusted. If a prophet can lie and fool an apparently innocent and obedient fellow prophet into disobeying Yahweh, with literally fatal consequences, how can the reader know without a reliable narrator's help when a prophet is lying or when he is telling the truth? In short, the reader can't. If genuine prophets are killed by lions for mistakenly disobeying directives of Yahweh, what chance has the reader of sorting out which prophet's word to trust and when to trust it?

Elijah has claimed to have received messages from Yahweh which the narrator does not confirm (17.1; 18.36). The reader has inferred that Elijah sometimes does things on his own initiative and for mixed, if not clearly self-centered, motives. The reader already knows that Elijah is not always to be trusted. Chapter 20 adds to the reader's suspicion, first aroused in ch. 13, that even prophets of Yahweh can be deceptive and dangerous. While the first-time reader may have given Elijah the benefit of the doubt on non-confirmed prophetic messages in the past, after reading ch. 20 the reader is likely to be more hesitant to trust prophets who appear in the narrative in the future. When Elijah does appear again the first-time reader is more cautious in accepting any unverified claims which Elijah makes to speak or act for Yahweh.

The reader would probably also tend to solidify any suspicions which might have been entertained, even if momentarily, about Elijah's earlier unverified prophetic words or actions by reassessing the inferences made previously in reading those passages.

*1 Kings 21.1-29.* If Elijah's absence from the narrative in ch. 20 has led the first-time reader to wonder whether or when Elijah will return to the narrative, the reader's curiosity is ended when the narrator informs the reader that Yahweh sends Elijah, and not some other prophet[34] to Ahab with a message of judgment against him for his complicity in the murder of Naboth (21.18). While Yahweh had spoken earlier as though Elijah was to be replaced as prophet (19.16), he evidently must have had a change of heart about him. The first-time reader surmises that whatever Elijah did to Elisha in 19.19-21, as far as Yahweh was concerned it did not result in Elisha immediately taking over Elijah's work. After 19.21 Elisha disappears from the narrative until the events leading up to the translation of Elijah in 2 Kings 2. Up until that point Elijah functions as

---

34. In ch. 20 Yahweh does send other prophets. This increases the narrative tension and creates interest in the first-time reader, who wonders whether Elijah will ever reappear in the narrative. It also tends to confirm once again the reader's suspicion that Elijah's claim (18.22; 19.10, 14) to be the only prophet left is likely to be untrue.

at least one of Yahweh's principal prophetic spokesmen.[35] The reader also infers that, in Yahweh's view at least, Elijah has changed enough for him to again be useful as a prophetic intermediary.

'But if Elijah had changed enough to be a useful representative of Yahweh once again', the first-time reader asks, 'has he changed completely or will there still be at least some elements of weaknesses of the old Elijah reappearing?' That the latter is probably the case is seen by the way in which Elijah alters the message which Yahweh gives him when he delivers it to Ahab. Yahweh directs Elijah:

> And you will speak to him saying, 'Thus says Yahweh, "Have you murdered and also confiscated property?"' And you will speak to him saying, 'Thus says Yahweh, "In the place where the dogs licked the blood of Naboth the dogs will lick your blood, yes yours"' (21.9).

The message which Elijah actually delivers, however, is strikingly different.

> I have found you, because you have sold yourself to do what is evil in the sight of Yahweh. Behold, I will bring evil upon you; I will utterly sweep you away, and will cut off from Ahab every one who urinates against the wall, bond or free, in Israel; And I will make your house like the house of Jeroboam, son of Nebat and like the house of Baasha, son of Ahijah because of the anger to which you have provoked me and (because) you have made Israel sin. The one who dies from Ahab's house in the city, the dogs will eat and the one who dies in the field the birds of the air will eat (1 Kgs 21.20-22, 24).

At least four things concerning this message are of importance for the reader in the evaluation of Elijah. The first is the depth of the non-correspondence between the message which Yahweh commissions Elijah to deliver and the message he actually delivers. The reader's expectation is that a reliable messenger will deliver his master's message in as exact a form as possible. Yahweh's message is directed specifically at Ahab's sin of complicity in Jezebel's plot to have Naboth unjustly executed so that Ahab's desire to own Naboth's vineyard could be fulfilled. The punishment is to be his own death at the place of Naboth's execution with the prediction that he, like Naboth, would suffer the indignity of having 'dogs' lick up his blood. By contrast, Elijah's message is a dynastic doom oracle, modeled on those of Ahijah in 1 Kgs 14.10, 11 and Jehu in 16.3, 4, which threatens the end of Ahab's entire dynasty.

---

35. In 1 Kgs 20 and 22 other prophets besides Elijah take center stage, so Elijah is not Yahweh's only prophetic representative.

While this dynastic doom oracle is not contrary to Yahweh's purpose since he does fulfill it, albeit in the reigns of Ahab's sons Ahaziah and Joram, Elijah is again portrayed as claiming that his message is a word from Yahweh without narratorial confirmation of this claim.

Secondly, it is not only the contents of Elijah's oracle which diverged from the message Yahweh authorized him to deliver; it is also the form. The 'I' of Elijah's message is Elijah himself, not Yahweh.[36] The form in which Elijah delivers his unauthorized message is in the divine first person without any introductory formula such as, 'Thus says Yahweh'. Yahweh had instructed Elijah to use this formula twice in the message he authorized Elijah to deliver in 21.19. In all probability, the reader should not infer from this that Elijah is here represented as suffering from delusions. He is not portrayed as claiming that he personally would bring evil upon Ahab's house, killing every male, bond or free. But by omitting the introductory formula for divine speech the narrator portrays Elijah as appearing not just to speak for Yahweh, but as speaking *as* Yahweh, that is as taking over his speech rather than merely delivering or quoting it. The reader has seen this phenomenon previously in the case of Moses[37] but Elijah is no Moses[38] and what might be permissible for Moses is not necessarily permissible for other prophets. By delivering his message in the divine first person without an introductory formula for divine speech, Elijah seems to be being portrayed as confusing his role with Yahweh's and as claiming a status which he did not have.

The reader has recognized this concern for his own status previously in the portrayal of Elijah, and therefore is unlikely to attribute it here to a momentary lapse by the narrator or by Elijah. In addition, when the reader has given due weight to the suspicion of prophets and prophecy which 1 Kgs 13.11-32 and 20.35, 36 have helped engender along with Elijah's past record of a heightened concern for his own status, it is

36. If v. 23 is read as part of Elijah's words the initial impression that Elijah is speaking in the divine first person is quickly modified. But even if v. 23 is read in this way, the impression that Elijah initially gave Ahab and the reader, that he spoke as though he were Yahweh, still has its impact on the reader. That this causes difficulties for modern readers is shown by the fact that the Good News Bible solves the problem by supplying, 'So the LORD says to you', before the beginning of the first-person message in v. 21.

37. Cf. Chapter 1 above.

38. See Childs 1980 for the view that Elijah is portrayed as falling short of the pattern of Moses.

hard, though not impossible, to imagine the reader not inferring that Elijah is again being portrayed as speaking on his own initiative and in a manner that is somewhat self-aggrandizing.

Thirdly, this passage is important to the reader's evaluation of Elijah because of the suddenness with which it is portrayed as being delivered. The narrator creates this impression of suddenness by failing to provide a narrative of Elijah traveling to meet Ahab to deliver it. The authorized message finishes at the end of v. 19. With no record of Elijah's trip, the narrator transports the reader immediately to a conversation between Ahab and Elijah. The first words of v. 20 are, 'Ahab said to Elijah', with no notification as to how Elijah had come to speak to Ahab.

The impression of the suddenness of the message is also created by the way Elijah is portrayed as launching into his speech without giving Ahab an opportunity to respond.

> Ahab said to Elijah, 'Have you found me, O my enemy'. He answered, 'I have found you, because you have sold yourself to do what is evil in the sight of Yahweh. Behold I will bring evil upon you.'

As in 18.17-19, Elijah does not even give Ahab a chance to respond verbally. Elijah does not even stop to say, 'Thus says Yahweh'.

The suddenness with which Elijah delivers his message could lead the reader to infer that Elijah is portrayed as speaking in anger here. Certainly his message is far more harsh than the message Yahweh commissioned him to deliver. What Yahweh had given as a personal judgment on Ahab turns into a judgment against Ahab's entire dynasty when Elijah delivers it. It is almost as though Elijah rushes to 'tell off' Ahab.

When Ahab responds to Elijah's message with the outward signs of repentance, Yahweh informs Elijah (but not Ahab!) that he has decided not to bring down the evil of dynastic doom during Ahab's own lifetime because Ahab has 'humbled himself'. At least Ahab would not have to witness the destruction of his dynasty personally. Yahweh's original sentence (21.19), however, which Elijah never delivers to Ahab, is not delayed until a later generation but is fulfilled with some precision in 1 Kgs 22.37, 38. In other words, Yahweh freely modifies Elijah's message of dynastic doom, but his own word of judgment, which applies to Ahab personally, he does not modify. This may be a clue designed to lead the reader to infer that Elijah's words are a bit rash and certainly do not have the same immutability in this case as Yahweh's actual words.

Fourthly, this passage is important for the reader's evaluation of Elijah because Elijah's message is delivered to Ahab, and not also to Jezebel.

Even if v. 23 is read as part of Elijah's message, and not as a narratorial intrusion,[39] Elijah's message is still delivered to Ahab, not Jezebel. Since it was Elijah's fear of Jezebel and his inappropriate response to that fear that seems to have led to the partial undoing of his prophetic work, it may be significant for the reader's evaluation of Elijah that he does not deliver a message directly to Jezebel. He does not confront the person most directly responsible both for the death of Naboth and Elijah's personal crisis in 1 Kings 19. While Elijah may be rehabilitated to a degree in 1 Kings 21, it is by no means a total rehabilitation.

Granted, Yahweh sends Elijah to Ahab, not to Jezebel. The reader could therefore reason that it is not Elijah's fault that he does not go to Jezebel directly. Yahweh sends him to Ahab and he obeys. But the reader could just as easily infer that Yahweh sends Elijah to Ahab because he realizes that Elijah is incapable of confronting Jezebel directly. There is no way for the reader to be certain, but it is not lost on the reader that the person most directly responsible for the injustice of the Naboth incident is Jezebel, and she never receives a direct prophetic rebuke from Elijah.

*Summary.* While the fact that Yahweh once again chooses to send Elijah to deliver a message of divine judgment against Ahab, when in 19.16 it appeared to the first-time reader that Elijah's work might be over, shows that Elijah has been somewhat rehabilitated in Yahweh's eyes since the events of Horeb. When, however, the reader analyses the way in which Elijah is portrayed as altering Yahweh's word when delivering it, both in content and form, the reader could easily infer that Elijah has not changed all that much. He still seems to be overly concerned with his own status, even to the point of momentarily speaking as though he were Yahweh and not just an intermediary. He still lurches out on his own initiative and says things which Yahweh has not authorized him to say. He is still somewhat more zealous[40] than even Yahweh to call down

---

39. There is a strong, even if not totally conclusive, argument that v. 23 is a parenthetical narratorial aside to the reader. If v. 23 is removed from vv. 21 to 24, the parallel with the two previous oracles of dynastic doom, 1 Kgs 14.7-11 and 16.1-4, is clear. Verse 23 breaks the parallel and thus appears as a sort of intrusion. Verse 23 is probably better viewed as the second half of Yahweh's message against the royal family in v. 19 than as part of Elijah's message.

40. Gregory (1990: 102) notes that Elijah's claim to be 'very zealous for Yahweh, the God of hosts' (19.10) is actually a usurpation of a divine quality. Elijah's zealotry is part of the portrayal of Elijah's confusion of his own role with Yahweh's.

judgment on the king of Israel. He still has only faced Ahab. The reader may, therefore, conclude that while Elijah has been rehabilitated to serve once again as Yahweh's principal intermediary, he is still the Elijah who has some of the same faults as he had displayed earlier and which led to his humiliation before both Jezebel and Yahweh in ch. 19.

The reader's doubts which arise about Elijah's reliability as a prophetic representative of Yahweh in 1 Kings 21 are given confirmation by the fact that the story of Naboth in 1 Kings 21 immediately follows the second[41] story of a prophet who is killed by a lion for disobeying a command from Yahweh when the prophet has no sure way of knowing that the specific command is from Yahweh. The suspicion of prophets and prophecy that the reader has gleaned from reading 1 Kgs 20.35, 36 and its related text in 1 Kgs 13.11-32 reinforces the reader's suspicion about Elijah's prophetic work in 1 Kings 21. If prophecy is a logically mysterious phenomenon, in which it is difficult, without the reliable narrator's help (which we do not have in 1 Kings 21), to distinguish true from false messages, the reader quite naturally infers that Elijah's prophetic activity may also be questionable.

*1 Kings 22.1-40.* The reader's doubts about Elijah's reliability as a prophet acquired from reading chs. 13, 20 and 21 are further strengthened in this passage, where prophecy and prophets are shown to be, if possible, even more problematic than they were in 1 Kings 13, 20 and 21, and in the previous Elijah narratives.

One of the major themes of the chapter is trickery or deception. Micaiah, when pressured by Ahab's messenger to give an encouraging oracle concerning Israel's prospects in retaking Ramoth-Gilead militarily (22.13), solemnly promises, 'By the life of Yahweh I will only speak what Yahweh says to me' (21.14). When, however, he actually delivers his first message, it is such a transparently deceptive prophecy that Ahab knows that he is being disingenuous and reminds Micaiah of his supposed tendency not to speak the truth (or truly) when he speaks in the name of Yahweh (v. 16). He also reminds him that he had many times previously forced Micaiah to promise[42] not to lie when he spoke for Yahweh. The irony of Ahab warning Micaiah only to speak the truth, and thereby encouraging Micaiah to give a prophetic judgment which would predict

---

41. The other is 1 Kgs 13.11-32.

42. The Hebrew, משבעך, is Hiphil with a causative sense; cf. BDB, p. 989.

Ahab's own death, is remarkable. Micaiah's first message is not, formally speaking, a true one. In fact it is an almost verbatim quote of the false message which the 400 other prophets had been giving (22.6, 15).

Zedekiah and the 400 prophets are also deceptive. They prophesy in Yahweh's name[43] (vv. 11, 12) and not in the name of some foreign deity. Thus they are not portrayed as prophets of Baal or Asherah. The reader, however, must wonder just how it has come about that Ahab, who himself served Baal (16.31) and whose wife Jezebel was such a zealous promoter of Baal, has 400 prophets of Yahweh at his court. Had his seeming repentance in 1 Kgs 21.27-29 resulted in his expelling prophets of other gods and consulting only Yahwistic prophets? How could it be, if this were so, that Jezebel tolerated this? The reader's suspicion of these prophets is shared by Jehoshaphat, who asks that another prophet of Yahweh be consulted (v. 7). The 400 prophets purport to be Yahweh's prophets and yet the reader cannot trust them. Once again prophets are seen to be untrustworthy. In this case these particular prophets are untrustworthy in that they tell Ahab what he wants to hear.

In his third message (22.19-23) Micaiah claims that in his use of prophets even *Yahweh* is deceptive. Micaiah's explanation for the disparity between the messages of Zedekiah and the 400 prophets (22.6, 11, 12) and his own (22.17) is not, surprisingly, that he is a true messenger of Yahweh and they only pretended to be. On the contrary, according to Micaiah, Zedekiah and the 400 prophets of Yahweh had received genuine revelations from Yahweh. Unfortunately, from Ahab's point of view, the revelation which Yahweh sent to the 400 prophets is, according to Micaiah, the work of a lying spirit sent to entice Ahab into a battle in which he would be killed.

But the reader is unlikely to accept at face value Micaiah's claim that Yahweh is deceptive. If Yahweh had really wanted to deceive Ahab, would he have given Micaiah knowledge of his plan so that he could reveal it to Ahab and thus risk thwarting his own objective of deceiving Ahab? This seems unlikely to the reader. While Micaiah claims that Yahweh is deceptive, in fact the reader infers that it may well be once again Micaiah who is full of artifice.

It is impossible for the reader to know when Micaiah is telling the

---

43. In v. 6 *BHS* has אדני as the name for God but notes that a Cairo Geniza text and many other Hebrew manuscripts read יהוה. If we take the *BHS* reading as it is the 400 prophets only claim to be Yahweh's prophets *after* Jehoshaphat questions their authenticity.

truth. He speaks five times in the story. In the first speech (22.15) it is so transparent that he is lying that Ahab rebukes him and instructs him to tell the truth. In the second (22.17), he completely reverses his first message and seems to imply that Israel was about to become shepherd-less, that is kingless. In the third speech (22.19-23), he claims that Yahweh is deceptive, but this message cannot be trusted unless the reader is prepared to infer that Yahweh is not very clever when it comes to arranging a deception![44] His fourth speech (22.25), to Zedekiah, is never said to be fulfilled and the second-time reader is left to wonder whether it does or does not come true or whether it is in fact a genuine message from Yahweh at all. His final message (22.28), really a summary of the result of the second message, is in fact fulfilled (22.37). When the reader considers that Micaiah lies (22.15) and invents messages (22.19-23) and yet also seems to be able to predict the future accurately (22.17, 28, 37) and yet that he is also clearly a prophet of Yahweh who courageously speaks for Yahweh against Ahab on numerous occasions (22.8, 16), the reader is in a quandary about prophets. Can prophets be trusted? Sometimes. Can a true prophet be distinguished from a false one? Sometimes. Micaiah is a deceptive character and he represents prophets and prophecy generally in that it is very difficult for the reader to sort out when a prophet or prophetess is deliberately lying, when prophets are inventing their own messages and when they are delivering Yahweh's. Since this passage is enmeshed within the Elijah narratives, it tends to increase the reader's suspicions about his prophetic activity.

While Micaiah's notion of Yahweh sending a lying spirit to his own prophets is not necessarily to be trusted by the reader as an accurate representation of the narrator's point of view, Yahweh is portrayed by the narrator as using trickery to bring about Ahab's demise. Ahab, having received Micaiah's message and having imprisoned the recalci-trant prophet (22.26, 27), takes steps to avoid what he evidently thinks is his predicted but avoidable fate. By disguising himself, and having Jehoshaphat dress in a way designed to trick the Syrians into thinking that the latter is the king of Israel, Ahab thinks he can outwit the Syrians, Yahweh, and perhaps also his supposed ally Jehoshaphat. But

---

44. One could, of course, argue that Yahweh is very clever in arranging a deception since by having Micaiah reveal it Ahab is tricked into not really believing it. While this is possible, the fact that Ahab has Jehoshaphat dress up like him indicates that Ahab did believe the message to some extent and tried to thwart its fulfillment.

the ruse does not work and Ahab is struck down by a 'aimless'[45] shot which has remarkable accuracy (v. 34). Ahab's trickery is turned on him when his wounded body is propped up in his chariot to deceive his own troops and those of his enemies into believing that he is supervising the battle. An 'aimless' arrow is Yahweh's trick on Ahab, as is the fulfillment of Yahweh's own undelivered message of judgment on Ahab (1 Kgs 21.19; 22.37, 38). Ahab did not know that even though Yahweh had put off the fulfillment of Elijah's dynastic doom oracle until the time of Ahab's sons (21.27-29), Yahweh's own message, which predicted Ahab's personal doom and which Elijah never delivered (21.19), had not been delayed in its fulfillment.

The deceptiveness of prophets and prophecy is a central motif in this passage. The first-time reader is likely to become even more hesitant about trusting Elijah's unauthorized messages and actions after reading this chapter.

*2 Kings 1.2-18.* In contrast to what we have just noted the next story in which Elijah's prophetic work is displayed presents a dramatically different Elijah. As in 1 Kgs 21.17-24, the reader of 2 Kgs 1.2-18 is able to compare the message and actions which Yahweh instructs Elijah to deliver and perform with the message he actually delivers, and the actions he actually performs. When the reader has done so he or she infers that Elijah is being portrayed as a very reliable conveyor of Yahweh's word and it turns out that he is also seemingly a very reliable performer of authorized prophetic actions. Just as Elijah's self-assurance returns to something like its pre-Jezebel proportions in 2 Kings 1, so Elijah's prophetic reliability seems to return. In fact, he seems to be a more reliable messenger than he ever was in 1 Kings 17 and 18. Gone is the Elijah who changes and/or invents things to do and/or say and then claims Yahweh's authorization. Gone is the Elijah who shows excessive concern for his own role as Yahweh's prophetic representative.

In 2 Kgs 1.2-18 Ahab's son Ahaziah is bedridden through a household accident. He sends messengers to inquire of Ekron's god, Baalzebub,[46] as to his prospects for recovery. As the messengers are on the way,

---

45. The Hebrew, לתמו, literally means 'innocently' (BDB, p. 1070), i.e. with no intention of harming Ahab.

46. As often noted, Baalzebub, 'lord of flies' is probably the narrator's deliberate and sarcastic corruption of Baalzebul, 'lord of princes'. So Robinson 1976: 18.

Yahweh's messenger[47] directs Elijah to go and meet them and deliver a word from Yahweh. The narrator records Elijah's response simply as: 'and Elijah went' (v. 4). Since the actual delivery of the message is not recorded the reader can only infer its contents from the message which the messengers claim Elijah gave them. Their message is so close to the original message that the reader infers that Elijah has conveyed the message with what is for him remarkable precision.

| | |
|---|---|
| Is it because there is no God in Israel that you (pl.) go to inquire of Baalzebub, the god of Ekron? Now therefore thus says Yahweh, 'You shall not come down from the bed to which you have gone up, but you shall surely die' (2 Kgs 1.3b, 4). | Thus says Yahweh, 'Is it because there is no God in Israel that you (sg.) go to inquire of Baalzebub, the god of Ekron? Therefore, you shall not come down from the bed to which you have gone up, but you shall surely die' (2 Kgs 1.6). |

Elijah eventually also delivers this message, which was originally intended for Ahaziah's messengers, to Ahaziah himself.

> Thus says Yahweh, 'Because you sent messengers to inquire of Baalzebub, god of Ekron—It is because there is no God in Israel to inquire of his word? Therefore you shall not come down from the bed to which you have gone up, for you will surely die (2 Kgs 1.16).

It may be significant that Elijah is not commanded to deliver this particular message to Ahaziah. He is simply directed to go down from the hill to meet the king (1.15). In light of the way Elijah has seemed to create messages from Yahweh in the past, the first-time reader may be somewhat surprised that Elijah does not create one in this circumstance, especially since Elijah seems to have been given the freedom to do so by Yahweh's messenger. But Elijah is changed. Instead of inventing a word from Yahweh and then expecting him to confirm it as the reader suspects has happened previously, Elijah is very careful in this situation to speak only the words which he knows (and the reader knows) Yahweh wants spoken. He even prefaces his message with the formula, 'Thus says Yahweh', something he neglected to do in 1 Kgs 17.1 and 21.20-22, 24. This ensures that Elijah's words and Yahweh's are carefully distinguished, something the reader could reasonably expect of a reliable prophet.

Elijah has not only changed in terms of the accuracy of his delivery of Yahweh's messages, and the care which he exercises in distinguishing

---

47. Here I assume that Yahweh's messenger is a completely reliable representative of him.

divine words from his own words. He has also changed in his willingness to do exactly what Yahweh wants him to do, and only that. This contrasts sharply with the way he has been portrayed earlier. In 18.1 Yahweh directs Elijah to show himself to Ahab. Elijah does this but, through Obadiah, not directly, and then probably invents an elaborate contest with the prophets of Baal (1 Kgs 18.21-40). In 2 Kgs 1.2-18 Elijah is portrayed as being much more careful to do exactly as directed and only makes major decisions when given divine direction to do so. In 1.3 Elijah is directed, 'Arise, go up to meet the messengers of the king of Samaria and say to them...' In 1.4b we read of Elijah's response, 'And Elijah went'. In 1.15, in contrast to 1 Kgs 19.3, Elijah waits for the messenger's directive before going to meet the king of Israel. The messenger reassures him, 'Go down with him; do not be afraid of him'. In 1 Kgs 19.3, Elijah does not wait for Yahweh's directive and fear overcomes him. Here he waits for a directive and receives the reassurance he needs not to be afraid. Elijah's reaction to the messenger is, 'So he arose and went down with him to the king'. In both these cases, the scrupulous accuracy with which Elijah performs authorized actions is notable in light of his past performance.

Even in the case of Elijah's uncommissioned action of calling down fire on the first two captains, the first-time reader is struck by how different Elijah is in comparison with the Elijah who has to plead with Yahweh at Carmel to burn up one stationary sacrifice. Here Elijah seems effortlessly to call down fire from heaven on two mobile groups of fifty soldiers and their captains. Since Yahweh responds immediately this suggests that Elijah is acting in strict conformity with Yahweh's will and thus does not need to plead with him to do his bidding. Even though the reader is not informed that Elijah is explicitly authorized by Yahweh to call down fire, the ease with which it happens suggests that Elijah is not acting merely on his own initiative.

Elijah's concern for his own status, displayed in the earlier narratives, is also changed in 2 Kgs 1.2-18. While Elijah does ask Yahweh to verify his status as 'man of God', this title is not one which Elijah has sought for himself on his own initiative as was the title 'your servant' in 1 Kgs 18.36. Instead Elijah merely uses the title which the captains of fifty use to address him. The captains were implicitly claiming that the king had authority over a designated representative of Yahweh, that is a man of God. The king did not like the negative message which he had received from Elijah and therefore sent troops to threaten him. But in this case

Elijah's message is so precisely Yahweh's message that the threat is really one directly against Yahweh and his right to bring judgment down upon a king of Israel who served other gods. Elijah does nothing by himself to draw attention to his status as Yahweh's representative. This is in contrast to the way he is portrayed in the contest with the prophets of Baal on Mt Carmel.

The first-time reader must wonder how it has come about that Elijah has changed so radically. Nothing in the story seems to explain the change. The second-time reader probably suspects that ultimately the change turns out to be incomplete. Elijah never confronts Jezebel and he never fulfills two of the three tasks which Yahweh gives him to do at Horeb. But even for the second-time reader, the post-Horeb Elijah does seem to develop, even if not perfectly, into a reliable representative of Yahweh.

### f. *Prophetic Unreliability in 2 Kings 2–25*

The first-time reader has gained a certain suspicion of prophecy from 1 Kings 13, 20 and 22, not to mention the Elijah narratives themselves. This suspicion of prophets and prophecy is confirmed, if not heightened, for the second-time reader by reading the narratives which follow the Elijah narratives, that is 2 Kings 2–25. The reading of these chapters only reinforces the first-time reader's distrust of some of the words and deeds of prophets who, like Elijah, claim to speak or act for Yahweh without narratorial confirmation of their claims, that is 1 Kgs 17.1; 18.36, 37. The second-time reader, after finishing Kings, reassesses the reading of the Elijah narratives with a heightened or at least confirmed sense of the potential unreliability of prophets and this has its effect on the reader's evaluation of Elijah's reliability. While a detailed consideration of the portrayal of prophets and prophecy in 2 Kings 2–25 is outside of the scope of this work, two examples will be used to demonstrate that the unreliability of prophets is a consistent part of the portrayal of prophets and prophecy in these chapters.

*Elisha's unreliability.* For detailed consideration of Elisha's unreliability as a prophet the reader is referred to the following chapter. Here only the briefest of examples must suffice. In 2 Kgs 8.10 Elisha is portrayed as lying or at least being involved in deceit when giving a prophetic oracle. Benhadad, the Syrian king, is ill, and he sends Hazael to Elisha, who is conveniently in Damascus, to inquire of Yahweh as to whether he will recover. Elisha gives this message to Hazael:

> Go, say to him, 'You shall certainly recover'; but Yahweh has shown me
> that he shall certainly die.

Elisha plainly lies or at least instructs Hazael to lie when pretending to give a true answer. Ironically, Benhadad does not die from natural causes. He dies because Hazael goes from his meeting with Elisha and kills him. A prophet of Yahweh, to whom Elijah has promised a double portion of his spirit (2 Kgs 2.9, 10), uses his prophetic gift to encourage Hazael to accomplish Yahweh's stated purpose (1 Kgs 19.16) by giving a false message to his master and then killing him. This reinforces the reader's view that prophets are not necessarily to be trusted when they claim to give a word from Yahweh.

*Huldah the prophetess—2 Kings 22.14-20.* Huldah's prophecy is given in response to the request of a committee sent by the pious Josiah to inquire concerning the judgment of Judah for its disobedience to the strictures found in the recently rediscovered book of the law of Yahweh (2 Kgs 22.8-13). Huldah's words of unremitting doom (vv. 15-17) are fulfilled in Nebuchadnezzar's conquest (24.1, 2). But she also gives a more encouraging message for Josiah personally:

> But as to the king of Judah, who sent you to inquire of the LORD, thus you
> shall say to him, 'Thus says the LORD, the God of Israel: Regarding the
> words which you have heard, because your heart was penitent, and you
> humbled yourself before the LORD, when you heard how I spoke against
> this place, and against its inhabitants, that they should become a desolation
> and a curse, and you have rent your clothes and wept before me, I also
> have heard you, says the LORD. Therefore, behold, I will gather you to
> your fathers, and you shall be gathered to your grave in peace, and your
> eyes shall not see all the evil which I will bring upon this place' (2 Kgs
> 22.18-20 RSV).

The reader is reminded of Ahab's humbling of himself in 1 Kgs 21.27 and Yahweh's promise in response that 'the evil' of the total destruction of his dynasty would be put off until the next generation (1 Kgs 21.29). The reader recalls that Ahab still died a violent death, even though his dynasty was not destroyed during his own lifetime (1 Kgs 22.37, 38).

In Huldah's prophecy, the pious Josiah seems to be promised something better than Ahab was. Huldah promises in Yahweh's name (vv. 15, 18, 19) that Josiah would not, like Ahab, have to see 'the evil' come in his own lifetime. But unlike Ahab (cf. 1 Kgs 21.19; 20.42), the pious Josiah would be 'gathered to [his] grave in peace' (2 Kgs 22.20). This seems only just to the reader since Josiah is portrayed as an unambiguously good king (2 Kgs 22.2). The first-time reader's expectation is that Josiah will live a long life, die of old age, and be buried in his family grave in peace.

In fact, however, Josiah does not die in peace, but is killed in the prime of life (at age 39, 2 Kgs 22.1) by Pharaoh Neco (23.29, 30). It is not entirely clear whether his death is in battle or whether Neco killed him during what was intended by Josiah to be a peaceful meeting. In any case the first-time reader is shocked to find that even the most righteous of Judah's kings, who did not veer from the pattern of David (22.2), who 'turned to Yahweh with all his heart and with all his soul and with all his might, according to all the law of Moses' (23.25), died a violent death even though Huldah, the prophetess who was otherwise reliable, had clearly predicted that he would be gathered to his grave in peace.

Even though Huldah is correct in her prediction about the irreversible doom coming upon Judah, she is wrong about Josiah. The record of Josiah's violent death upsets any confidence the reader might still be harboring about the ability of prophets to know the mind of Yahweh unless he explicitly reveals it and does not later modify his intentions. Huldah's mistaken assurance to Josiah shows that the reader cannot trust unverified prophetic messages, even when the unwitting reader's sense of justice leads to the assumption that the message is from Yahweh. Yahweh (or perhaps it is just the course of events) is far too unpredictable for his actions to be accurately predicted, even by the ablest prophet, unless Yahweh commissions a message, and does not later modify it. The effect of this on the reader's evaluation of the reliability of Elijah will probably be for the second-time reader to be even more suspicious of Elijah's unauthorized messages unless explicit confirmation is given that Elijah speaks for Yahweh.

g. *Conclusions on Elijah's Reliability as Yahweh's Representative*
While to the first-time reader Elijah appears at the outset of his story to be a thoroughly reliable representative of Yahweh, as the story progresses the reader begins to question this initial impression. In ch. 18 Elijah seems to do things in his own way and to be preoccupied with his own status as Yahweh's representative. When in ch. 19 he is confronted with a direct revelation of Yahweh it becomes apparent to the first-time reader that Elijah has been too concerned with his own status all along. His inability to take responsibility for his own weaknesses and his refusal or inability to recognize that he is not the only human channel of

Yahweh's work available leads Yahweh to look to others to do his work. Elijah is to be replaced.

But for some unexplained reason Yahweh gives Elijah a second chance. However, in his delivery of Yahweh's message to Ahab in 1 Kings 21, Elijah still displays some of his earlier weaknesses, for example, the tendency to draw attention to his own status, to do things his own way, and to speak with his own words when speaking for Yahweh.

In 2 Kgs 1.2-18, however, Elijah seems to have inexplicably changed into a very reliable representative of Yahweh. But the fact that Elijah is taken up in a whirlwind without confronting his nemesis Jezebel and without completing two of the three tasks Yahweh had given him at Horeb serves as a counterweight against the reader giving an overly idealistic reading of Elijah, even in 2 Kings 1. Elijah does change at the end of his life, but not enough to convince the reader that his change is absolutely complete.

Just as importantly, the steady reinforcement of the unreliability of prophets and prophecy, which the narrator provides the reader in 1 Kings 13, 20 and 22, and in the portrayals of the prophetic work of Elisha and Huldah, may well lead the reader to have a presumption of distrust for any prophet, Elijah included. This acquired distrust for prophets means, in practical terms, two things. First, the reader no longer assumes, if she or he ever did, that Elijah's actions necessarily have the narrator's approval or represent the narrator's point of view just because Elijah is a prophet. Other considerations must enter into the reader's evaluation. Second, the reader no longer assumes that Elijah's prophetic words have been given to him by Yahweh just because he claims that this is so. This acquired distrust of prophets and prophecy affects the second-time reader's evaluation of Elijah even in 2 Kings 1 where he seems to have changed. While the first-time reader might assume that Elijah has changed out of all recognition in 2 Kings 1, the second-time reader infers that Elijah is not necessarily to be trusted without narratorial confirmation. Even Elijah's seeming transformation in 2 Kings 1 may be incomplete and does not necessarily completely convince the second-time reader.

## 4. *Elijah the Submissive Servant*

### a. *Introduction*
While some of Elijah's actions have already been discussed in relation to his work as Yahweh's representative, in this section we will address

Elijah's obedience to Yahweh more generally. Much of the discussion does, however, presuppose our earlier treatment of the relevant texts.

Elijah's very first words, 'By the life of Yahweh, *before whom I stand*', contain an implicit claim that he had an intimate relationship with Yahweh. The phrase, 'before whom I stand', is sometimes paraphrased as, 'whom I serve' (NJPSV, GNB, JB, NIV). While this translation obscures the connection between Elijah's claim in 17.1 and his reticence to actually do what he claimed to have always done in 19.11-13, the translation does capture the sense of the expression. Elijah claims to be Yahweh's loyal servant, ever standing in his presence, waiting to do his bidding. As De Vries notes, this phrase means that Elijah, 'served as one of [Yahweh's] intimate counselors and obedient ministers' (De Vries 1985: 218).

The pattern which emerges in the reader's evaluation of this claim is similar to the pattern we have seen in the reader's evaluation of Elijah's charisma and self-assurance, and of his role as Yahweh's representative. Elijah at first seems to be true to his claim in 17.1 to be an obedient servant. But the truth of this claim by Elijah is seen to be undermined by Elijah's subsequent actions, both by the way Elijah responds to Yahweh's instructions, and by what he does without Yahweh's authorization. Once again the events of ch. 19 serve as a sort of negative turning point in the reader's evaluation of Elijah's obedience to Yahweh, and once more Elijah seems to be reformed in 2 Kings 1. The second-time reader, however, in keeping with the pattern we have observed, ultimately qualifies the initial impression about the depth and permanence of Elijah's seeming reformation in 2 Kings 1. The reader ends up by assuming that Elijah is portrayed as being a changed person at the end of his life but it is likely that the reader still has doubts about just how much Elijah has really changed.

b. *Elijah's Submissiveness in 1 Kings 17 and 18*
Yahweh's first instruction to Elijah (1 Kgs 17.3, 4) directs him to travel to the brook Cherith, and hide there. The brook is to be Elijah's source of water during the drought and ravens (or perhaps Arabs; cf. Gray 1970: 378-79) are to provide his food. In this instance, as Gregory (1990: 104) notes,

> Elijah's obedience is thoughtless; what Yahweh commands he does. When
> Yahweh sends him to Cherith, he follows the command exactly.

Elijah also follows Yahweh's second command fairly closely. This time he is to, 'Arise, go to Zarephath and dwell there' (17.9). A widow is to provide sustenance for him on this occasion. She, however, seems more reluctant to provide food for Elijah than the ravens had been, and Elijah is forced to play a more direct role in the process of receiving his food. In the earlier incident his food was brought to him. Here he has to ask (v. 11), attempt to calm the woman's fears (v. 13a), challenge her to trust Yahweh (v. 13b), and then deliver a reassuring oracle from Yahweh (v. 14). While Yahweh does not explicitly authorize Elijah to do and say these things there is no reason for the reader to suspect that Elijah says or does anything which Yahweh does not want him to say or do. In fact the narrator is careful to confirm that in giving his oracle (v. 14) Elijah is in fact delivering Yahweh's word (v. 16). The woman's understandable hesitance forces Elijah to play an active part in obtaining his own food.

Yahweh's third directive to Elijah, 'Go show yourself to Ahab' (18.1), however, shows the gap between Yahweh's command and Elijah's execution begin to widen (Gregory 1990: 104). Elijah's initial response to this directive, 'So Elijah went to show himself to Ahab' (18.2a), suggests to the first-time reader that Elijah's compliant attitude to Yahweh's instructions is about to be reinforced by yet another example. But the story takes a surprising turn. Elijah's next appearance in the narrative is in the presence of Obadiah, not Ahab. Elijah uses Obadiah to arrange a meeting with Ahab. At that meeting, contrary to the first-time reader's expectation, Elijah does not announce Yahweh's decision to send rain upon the earth. Instead he contrives a contest in which, as we have seen, his own personal role as Yahweh's representative is highlighted. Elijah claims to have merely obeyed Yahweh in fashioning the contest (18.36), but the second-time reader comes to surmise that it is questionable whether Elijah was really acting under Yahweh's instructions when he announced the contest. The gap between Yahweh's explicit command and Elijah's execution of that command is widening further. During the Carmel incident Elijah acts on his own initiative and with an excessive concern for his own part in Yahweh's purpose.

c. *Elijah's Non-Compliance in 1 Kings 19*
*1 Kings 19.1-14.* Once again ch. 19 functions as a turning point in the Elijah narratives. The gap between what the reader presumes Yahweh and the narrator would want Elijah to do and say and what he actually does and says is first revealed by his failure to wait for Yahweh's word when he receives a threat from Jezebel. In 17.2 by contrast, Elijah does wait for such a word, obeys it, and thereby demonstrates his obedience to Yahweh. There Elijah is evidently at Ahab's court and yet he does

not leave until instructed to do so by a message from Yahweh. Here, Elijah has not yet even arrived at the court itself. He is merely at the entrance to Jezreel (18.46). Instead of waiting for a message from Yahweh, he flees in fear (19.3). This leads the first-time reader to infer that Elijah's actions are not always directed by Yahweh. Sometimes, as in this instance, he acts before giving Yahweh a chance to lend assistance.

   In the theophany pericope (1 Kgs 19.9-18) Yahweh instructs Elijah, 'Come out; stand on the mountain before Yahweh' (v. 11). The reader's expectation is that a truly submissive servant would have obeyed such a directive, especially one who claimed to 'stand before' Yahweh. Instead Elijah remains in the cave while Yahweh passes by (v. 11). After the theophanic phenomena Elijah does move, but only out to the entrance to the cave. Ironically he wraps his mantle, the symbol of his prophetic power, around his face, evidently to hide himself from Yahweh behind it.[48] It was similarly at the entrance to Jezreel where he failed to face Jezebel, another daunting personality. In contrast to Moses, who stood on Mt Sinai as Yahweh both stood with him there and also passed by before him (Exod. 34.5, 6), Elijah is very hesitant to face Yahweh. His words of complaint, spoken both before and after the theophany, show that he is unwilling to budge from his somewhat self-pitying assumption that he was the only one left. The theophany has no effect on his stance. Instead of admitting his weaknesses and asking for forgiveness, a sign of a willingness to be obedient, Elijah shows the opposite. He reasserts his dubious claim to be the only one left.

*1 Kings 19.15-21.* Elijah fails to obey Yahweh's directives in 19.15-17. While Yahweh instructs him to anoint Hazael, Jehu and Elisha in that order, he never anoints any of them, and he never goes to Damascus as Yahweh clearly instructs him. While the reader has no reason for supposing that the order of the anointings is highly significant (the reader would probably be satisfied that Elijah had obeyed Yahweh's directive if Elijah anointed all three of the men in any order), it is significant that Elijah does not go to Damascus to anoint Hazael as Yahweh commands him.

---

   48. Slotki (1950: 139) relates this to Moses hiding his face because he was afraid to look upon God (Exod. 3.6). But this was at the beginning of Moses' service. Elijah had been representing Yahweh for some time. Gray (1970: 411) compares this to the theophany to Moses in Exod. 33.21ff. But there Yahweh hides Moses for his own protection, not because Moses was afraid to look at him (v. 18).

Furthermore Elijah does not strictly obey Yahweh's instruction even in the case of Elisha. Yahweh's directive is that Elijah should 'anoint' Elisha. He never explicitly does so. The ambiguity of what exactly Elijah did to or for Elisha in 1 Kgs 19.17-21 has already received analysis. In addition, as the first-time reader will see, even at Elijah's translation he does not anoint Elisha. The fact that Elisha designates Hazael as king of Syria and has Jehu anointed is not a commendation of Elijah, but of Elisha.

d. *The Transformation of Elijah into a Compliant Servant in 2 Kings 1.2-18*
As noted earlier, Elijah's compliance to the directives of Yahweh's messenger in this passage is remarkable for its precision. In v. 3 he is directed to 'Arise, go up to meet the messengers of the king of Samaria', and deliver a message. Without demur Elijah goes (v. 4). The scrupulous accuracy with which Elijah delivers the message is seen by comparing vv. 3 and 4 with v. 6.

In v. 15 the messenger of Yahweh directs Elijah, 'Go down with him [the captain]; do not be afraid of him'. Elijah's next action is: 'So he arose and went down with him to the king'. Even though Elijah's words have not been restricted by a specific authorized message (Elijah had already delivered that [vv. 3, 4]), Elijah carefully confines his words to those he had originally been given. Elijah does not take it upon himself to give the king a new message, as he does in ch. 21. He merely reiterates the message he had been given. While the order of the phrases is different, the actual wording is very close and Elijah neither adds anything to nor omits anything of substance from the contents of the original oracle. In view of the freedom with which Elijah treats Yahweh's words in 1 Kings 21, and earlier, this is quite surprising and implies a change in Elijah.

In this pericope Elijah shows no signs of excessive self-assertiveness, no signs of excessive concern with his own role or status, and no signs of being resistant to Yahweh's directives. He has become a model prophet. But the reader must still entertain some doubts about what appears on the surface to be the portrayal of an Elijah who is transformed since he still has not fulfilled Yahweh's commands in 19.19-21.

e. *Elijah's Submissiveness in 2 Kings 2.1-11*
The reader comes to recognize with this last of the Elijah stories that Elijah makes several attempts (or at least pretends to do so) to prevent

Elisha from receiving the divine blessing which he is to receive as witness to Elijah's translation. The prophetic mantle, infused with power (v. 8), is only given to Elisha because of his own persistence—not because Elijah is trying to comply with Yahweh's directives in 1 Kgs 19.15-18. Elijah demonstrates by his seemingly pointless circuitous[49] journey that he either wants to get rid of Elisha altogether and thus not comply with Yahweh's directive, or that he wants to test Elisha's determination to be his successor.[50] In either case, Elijah is not portrayed, as he is in 2 Kings 1, as being careful to obey Yahweh's directives strictly. Even if Elijah only intends to test Elisha's resolve, this still amounts to taking it upon himself to 'pre-qualify' a man whom Yahweh has already chosen to replace him. Yahweh gives Elijah no authority to make a determination as to whether Elisha is qualified to serve in his place or not, nor whether he is to be infused with the divine power which Elijah presumably only possessed himself because Yahweh had given it to him. Yahweh has already made the decision to use and empower Elisha. By attempting to escape from Elisha, even if only as a test of Elisha's determination, Elijah is portrayed either as attempting to avoid complying with Yahweh's directive altogether or, more likely in my opinion, as complying in such a way that his own role is given more importance than Yahweh originally gave it.

Elijah shows the same tendency to do things his own way at the end of his life as he has shown earlier at Mt Carmel and Mt Horeb. The way he makes the transference of his spirit onto Elisha dependent on himself strikes the reader as being reminiscent of the way he asserts himself and his own role in 18.36, 37 and in 17.1.

### f. *Conclusions on Elijah as the Compliant Servant*
While Elijah's first words (1 Kgs 17.1) contain an implicit claim that he is a submissive servant of Yahweh, Elijah's subsequent words and actions demonstrate that this is not always true. While Elijah does demonstrate an obedient attitude in 1 Kings 17, in 1 Kings 18 it seems likely that the reader should infer that Elijah invents the contest on Mt Carmel and during it demonstrates an excessive concern for highlighting his own

---

49. Auld (1986: 154) notes that Gilgal means 'circle' (of stones), but fails to see its relevance. Elijah is taking Elisha in a circle. This view of course does not preclude recognizing that Elijah and Elisha are re-enacting the conquest in reverse with all the parallels with Joshua and Moses which such a re-enactment implies.

50. Auld (1986: 154) opts for Elijah testing Elisha.

role as Yahweh's servant. In ch. 19, Elijah's failure to wait for Yahweh's word when faced with Jezebel's threat shows that he is not always willing to trust Yahweh to protect him. The incident at Horeb shows that sometimes Elijah actually resists obeying Yahweh's instructions both in his hesitance to stand before Yahweh on the mountain and his refusal to be shifted from his insistence that he is the only one left. The fact that he never obeys two-thirds of Yahweh's directive to anoint his successors leaves the second-time reader finally unable to affirm his submissiveness unambiguously. The ambiguity of whether he actually obeys Yahweh's command to anoint Elisha to be prophet in his place and the fact that he does not go to Damascus as directed, and never anoints Hazael or Jehu, casts a shadow over the reader's evaluation of any other acts of obedience. While 2 Kings 1 portrays Elijah as a changed man who has suddenly become a 'model' prophet, his failure to obey Yahweh's directives to him in 19.15-18 leads the second-time reader to the conclusion that his transformation is never totally complete. In his last act, the transference of his spirit to Elisha, he once again seems to put himself and his role to the fore in a way which leads the reader to question his seeming transformation in 2 Kings 1.

## 5. *Conclusions*

I have analyzed three aspects of the narrative portrayal of Elijah: his charisma and self-assurance; his reliability as Yahweh's representative; and his submissiveness as Yahweh's servant. In each case I have argued that the second-time reader is likely to qualify what the first-time reader is likely to assume about Elijah initially.

Elijah seems at first to be full of self-assurance and charisma, but these characteristics turn out to be somewhat hollow in ch. 19. His self-assurance is only displayed when he faces relatively weak figures and he shows no ability to influence, that is no charisma towards, strong figures. His failure to face Jezebel and his hesitance to stand before Yahweh lead the reader to infer that even the self-assurance he seems to display in 2 Kings 1 is not entirely convincing.

Elijah also seems at first to be a thoroughly reliable representative of Yahweh. But the second-time reader comes to suspect the reliability of prophets and prophecy in general, and this suspicion has its effect on the reader's evaluation of Elijah. Elijah sometimes freely modifies messages Yahweh sends him to deliver and claims Yahweh's authorization for messages and actions which seem to stem from Elijah's own mind and his desire to assert the importance of his personal role in Yahweh's accomplishing of his purposes. The second-time reader comes to have doubts over the divine origin of any message or the divine authorization of any action for which Elijah does not have explicit narratorial confirmation. Once again Elijah's seeming transformation in 2 Kings 1 is not completely convincing to the second-time reader.

Elijah also seems, at first, to be a submissive servant of Yahweh. But once again, for the second-time reader, Elijah turns out to be a person who is prone to obey Yahweh's directives in such a way as to make his own role take on added importance and may actually sometimes be positively resistant to obeying some of Yahweh's directives. Elijah is certainly on Yahweh's side in the battle with Baalism, but he is also on his own side. His weaknesses are displayed most clearly in ch. 19, but they are present throughout most of the story of his life and have not completely disappeared in the second-time reader's evaluation of him even after his transformation in 2 Kings 1.

While the reader admires Elijah for taking a stand against the corrupting influence of Baalism, and it only shows the reader's own self-righteousness if too much condemnation is heaped upon Elijah for his fear of Jezebel, he is ultimately a heroic but slightly flawed character. He is neither completely good nor bad, but human, in that he is full of strengths and weaknesses. He does display the ability to change dramatically (2 Kgs 1), but the second-time reader is unlikely to infer that the change is absolute. He receives the almost unparalleled honor of being allowed to bypass death itself, but by the way he treats the transference of his spirit and role to Elisha as being dependent on him at his translation, he shows his tendency to draw attention to his own role.

# Chapter 4

## THE RELIABILITY OF ELISHA

### 1. *Introduction*

This chapter is an analysis of the reader's evaluation of the reliability of Elisha in the Primary History. It is the thesis of this chapter that the reader is invited by a large number of textual hints and clues to compare and ultimately to contrast Elijah and Elisha as characters. The reader comes to evaluate Elisha in terms of how he measures up to or does not measure up to Elijah. When the reader has completed the process of comparison and contrast Elisha emerges as a character who is both more and less, better and worse than Elijah. Moreover, in terms of his reliability as a guide to what the narrator's point of view might be he is a decidedly less trustworthy character.

The first-time reader of the Elisha narratives is repeatedly struck by a sense of literary *déjà vu*. Time and again Elisha does or says things which recall the deeds and/or words of his predecessor Elijah. For example, in 2 Kgs 4.1-7 Elisha performs a miracle for a woman and her children in which cooking oil is miraculously reproduced. The story has several obvious parallels with the story of the never-ending supply of meal and oil in 1 Kgs 17.8-16. Another example is Elisha's miracle of raising the Shunemite woman's son in 2 Kgs 4.8-37 as compared to Elijah's similar miracle for the widow of Zarephath's son in 1 Kgs 17.17-24. Like Elijah (1 Kgs 17.1), Elisha proclaims a famine (2 Kgs 8.1); like his predecessor, he gives an answer to a king who sends to a god inquiring as to whether he would recover from serious illness (2 Kgs 1.2-18; 8.7-15).

There comes a point in a first-time reading at which the force of these parallels (and there are many more than I have mentioned above) leads the reader to infer that Elijah and Elisha are being compared at every turn. The second-time reader then systematically re-reads Elisha's words and deeds in the light of the work and deeds of Elijah and from these comparisons and contrasts, as well as from other aspects of the portrayal of Elisha, assembles a picture of Elisha and of his reliability or otherwise.

Three aspects of the portrayal of Elisha will be examined. First and foundational is the portrayal of him as Elijah's legitimate successor. As his successor, Elisha is to carry on Elijah's battle with Baalism. I will examine the reader's evaluation of the legitimacy of Elisha's succession and his success in carrying on the unfinished work of Elijah.

Since Elisha is to succeed Elijah as prophet (1 Kgs 19.16), I next examine the reader's evaluation of the reliability of Elisha as a prophet from two angles. First I examine that part of the prophet's work which concerns the delivery of Yahweh's word (the second of the three aspects). Finally I examine that part of the prophet's work which concerns his being a channel of Yahweh's supernatural power (the third aspect).

## 2. *Elisha as Successor to Elijah*

### a. *Introduction*

In 1 Kgs 19.15-17 Yahweh instructs Elijah to anoint Hazael and Jehu as kings of Syria and Israel respectively, and Elisha as 'prophet in place of' Elijah. While this passage has already received treatment in terms of the narrative portrayal of Elijah, here our interest lies in its significance for the reader's evaluation of Elisha. The first-time reader is informed of two things: Elisha is to replace or succeed Elijah as prophet (v. 16b), and Elisha is to be involved in the violent judgment upon Israel for its worship of Baal (vv. 17b, 18). The second-time reader recognizes that in addition to these two tasks Elisha will also be responsible for 'anointing'[1] Hazael (2 Kgs 8.7-15) and Jehu (2 Kgs 9.1-10), the other two human instruments of the predicted violent judgment—even though it is Elijah who is actually given that task. Elisha must accomplish these tasks because Elijah left them unfinished when he was taken up into heaven (2 Kgs 2.11). The reader's question thus becomes, 'In those passages which concern Elisha's succession to Elijah's role or office, and his completion of Elijah's work, how is Elisha to be evaluated?'

### b. *The Call of Elisha—1 Kings 19.19-21*

*Introduction.* This pericope is a tantalizing one in that its interest lies as much in what it does not tell the reader as in what it does. Two things

---

1.    Gray (1970: 411) suggests that because of its use here the verb משׁח can also mean simply 'designate'. But this view fails to recognize that Yahweh's command is not literally fulfilled in the case of Hazael.

are, however, relatively clear. At the end of this passage Elijah has neither anointed Elisha nor been replaced by him in his prophetic role as Yahweh had directed. The difficulties multiply when the reader asks why these two things are so. Why didn't Elijah 'anoint' Elisha? Why didn't Elisha replace Elijah? And what relevance, if any, for the reader's evaluation of the reliability of Elisha does this enigmatic passage have? Before an answer, insofar as there is *an* answer, to these questions can be attempted three crucial exegetical matters must be investigated.

*What happens to Elijah's mantle?* Having been commissioned to anoint Hazael, Jehu and Elisha, Elijah finds Elisha behind a yoke of oxen in a field. Passing by the other eleven yokes with their ploughmen Elijah throws his mantle *to* (אל) Elisha and walks off.[2] The reader is not informed whether Elisha caught the mantle, picked it up from the ground or left it lying at his feet. In any case the next time the reader hears of the mantle it is being worn by Elijah, not Elisha, and he uses it for the miracle of parting the waters of the Jordan (2 Kgs 2.8). Subsequently it falls from Elijah's shoulders when he is taken up into heaven (2.13) and Elisha picks it up and uses it to recross the Jordan miraculously (2.14).

The second-time reader of 1 Kgs 19.19-21 surmises that in throwing his mantle to Elisha Elijah is actually offering him the symbol of succession and thus the opportunity to replace him as prophet. Whether Elisha literally returned the mantle to Elijah, kept it for himself, or left it lying for Elijah to pick up is irrelevant. Even if he retained it literally he did not keep it metaphorically. Even if we assume that Elisha actually picked it up, he did not really retain the thing which it signified, that is succession to Elijah's role or office as prophet. In short, the first-time reader's expectation that 19.19-21 might be the occasion on which Elijah obeys Yahweh's directive at Horeb concerning Elisha is frustrated by the way the story turns out.

*Elisha's request to bid farewell to his parents—1 Kings 19.20.* For the reader Elisha's request to 'kiss' his father and mother (v. 20) is a complication or retardation of the plot. At issue is whether this request implies a resistance or hesitance on Elisha's part to make a clean break with the past (Fohrer 1968: 24; cf. Lk. 7.61, 62) or whether the request

---

2.    That Elijah walks off is inferred from the fact that Elisha has to run after him in order to catch up with him.

only demonstrates Elisha's familial loyalty (Coulot 1983: 89-90) or even his quite appropriate manners (Kittel 1900: 155). The 'kiss' which he requests turns into a fairly elaborate festive occasion (v. 21). This may at first appear to be evidence that Elisha is delaying Elijah. If he wants to hold a farewell feast for the entire community, why does he only ask Elijah for time to 'kiss' his father and mother? But, in fact, by destroying the instruments of his trade in order to provide meat for the feast, Elisha is making a clear and presumably irreversible break[3] with his previous way of life.

Coulot (1983: 90-92) convincingly suggests that Elisha's feast is more than just a farewell party (*festin d'adieux*) and has a religious character. It is paralleled by other narratives in the Primary History in which an offering is made in gratitude to God to mark a particularly significant occasion of divine blessing.[4] In addition the word used to describe the killing of the oxen, זבח, 'can refer to both what a butcher does (Deut. 12.15, 21; Ezek. 34.3) and what is done by someone who slaughters an animal as part of a religious ritual' (*TDOT*, IV: 11). Thus while the first-time reader may momentarily be suspicious of Elisha's motives in requesting permission to return to 'kiss' his family, Elisha's actions (v. 21) indicate that he makes a clear and decisive break with the past in order to follow Elijah.

But the reader is still not clear about whether Elisha has completely or only partially accepted Elijah's offer to replace him as prophet. At the end of the pericope, Elisha arises from the feast, goes after Elisha, and ministers to him; he does not replace him (v. 21b).

*Elijah's enigmatic question*. Elijah's reply to Elisha's request is, 'Go! Return! For what have I done to you?' The reader would like to know the answer to Elijah's question. What exactly *has* Elijah done to Elisha? If we retain the *BHS* text in v. 19b, 'and Elijah passed by him and threw his mantle *to* him', one thing is clear. Elijah offers Elisha the opportunity to become prophet in his place, but it is Elisha's responsibility to decide whether he would accept the offer by putting the mantle on or not. For some reason, Elisha ends up not replacing Elijah but going after him and 'ministering' to him as Joshua did to Moses. Is the fact that Elisha does not replace Elijah at this point in the story due to some deficiency in

3.    Great wealth on the part of Elisha is not necessarily implied by the narrative.
4.    1 Sam. 6.14, 15, the return of the ark; 1 Sam. 10.8, the anointing of Saul; Judg. 13.15-20, the announcement of the birth of Samson.

Elisha or only what the reader would expect of the successor of Yahweh's principal prophet?

Christa Schäfer-Lichtenberger (1989) has recently argued that this text sets up Elisha as an ideal type (in its Weberian sense) of the prophetic successor. Like Joshua the successor of Moses, Elisha must serve a sort of internship under his predecessor before his actual succession. This explains for Schäfer-Lichtenberger (1989: 211-13) why in 1 Kgs 19.19-21 Elisha does not immediately replace Elijah, as the throwing of the mantle would suggest, but merely follows him and serves as his personal assistant.

But despite the many helpful textual observations in her study, Schäfer-Lichtenberger operates with a form of circular reasoning which is endemic to her method. She assumes that whatever Elijah and Elisha say or do in the narratives which concern the transference of prophetic leadership (1 Kgs 19.19-20; 2 Kgs 2.1-18) must be taken as ideal speech or behavior since Elisha is being set up as the ideal type of the prophetic successor. The evidence, however, which establishes the contention that Elisha is in these passages being portrayed as an ideal type comes from a reading of the text which assumes that whatever Elisha says or does is ideal. Nevertheless her suggestion that Elisha, like Joshua, here begins a sort of preparatory training for the actual succession is worthy of consideration.

*Summary and conclusions.* There is nothing in this passage which clearly demonstrates that Elisha has done anything which would lead the reader to infer that he was somehow deficient in his response to Elijah's offer. In fact, Elisha is portrayed as being the means, deliberately or fortuitously, of the partial rehabilitation of Elijah's prophetic work.

Elijah, for all the reader knows, comes from the experience of Horeb an unchanged man. As noted previously, the repetition of his somewhat bitter complaint against Yahweh (1 Kgs 19.14), even after he has received a Moses-like revelation of Yahweh's presence, argues against the supposition of a change in him. Directed to travel to Damascus to anoint Hazael, Elijah instead finds Elisha and throws his mantle to him and walks away. Since this is the only direct action that Elijah ever takes to obey the Horeb commission even partially, and, given his apparently unyielding stance of complaint against Yahweh at the time, Elijah's action may imply that he is trying to be rid of the entire business of being Yahweh's prophet as quickly as possible by shifting the responsibility to Elisha.

But Elisha's response to having the mantle thrown to him and seeing Elijah walk off is not to put it on and quickly replace Elijah as prophet. Instead he runs after Elijah and promises to follow him. He does not promise to replace him. Elisha can only do this, that is follow Elijah and minister to him, if Elijah remains in his position as prophet. What Elisha offers is to become Elijah's successor-designate, not his successor. Whether Elisha does this deliberately or because of his own reticence, he in effect forces Elijah to retain his prophetic mantle and thus becomes the means of Elijah's partial rehabilitation.

While his request to kiss his parents might momentarily seem to be 'stalling', his subsequent actions show his determination to make a clean and decisive break with the past and begin his new life as the eventual inheritor of Elijah's prophetic work. Even if, with Schäfer-Lichtenberger, we assume that Elisha's time of service as successor-designate is only to be expected, it is Elisha, not Elijah, who initiates it. By throwing his mantle to Elisha and walking away Elijah does not offer Elisha the opportunity to become successor-designate but the opportunity to replace him as prophet. The second-time reader infers this because Elisha's taking up of the mantle in 2 Kgs 2.13 and the use of it to cross the Jordan magically (v. 14) is an essential part of the confirmation that Elisha has succeeded to Elijah's position as prophet. It is Elisha who suggests that he merely follow Elijah and it is he who either literally or metaphorically returns the mantle to Elijah.

The reader may harbor lingering doubts about Elisha's response to Elijah's offer but these cannot overrule the fact that Elisha does make a decisive, even if somewhat delayed, break with his past. Furthermore, by seeking to follow Elijah, and not replace him immediately, Elisha 'pushes' Elijah into continuing as prophet.[5] Since Elijah, as it turns out, still has important work to do as Yahweh's prophet (e.g. the denunciation of Ahab for the Naboth incident in 1 Kgs 21), Elisha's action, even if accidental, is viewed by the reader in a favorable light. There is nothing in this pericope to suggest that Elisha is anything but a completely legitimate and model successor-designate.

---

5. Even if we assume that this is due to an inappropriate amount of reticence (we could just as easily assume that such reticence is appropriate or that Elisha deliberately pressured Elijah into continuing as prophet) on Elisha's part, he still helps to rehabilitate Elijah's work as prophet.

c. *The Spirit of Elijah Rests on Elisha—2 Kings 1.2–2.25*
*Introduction.* As we have seen, in 1 Kgs 19.19-21 it turns out that Elisha is not anointed to take the place of Elisha but only called to be his assistant and successor-designate. The actual succession now takes place in narrative. Part of the narrative tension[6] which the first-time reader experiences in this passage concerns whether Elijah will in fact fulfill any part of the commission in 1 Kgs 19.15-18 to anoint Hazael and Jehu, and more specifically whether Elisha will finally be anointed or in some other way designated as successor to Elijah. By a series of carefully structured clues the narrator emphasizes the legitimacy of the succession of Elisha. Hobbs (1985: 17) in commenting on 2.11 has observed that chs. 1 and 2 of 2 Kings form a coherent whole which emphasizes this legitimacy:

> Chapters one and two are so structured that what precedes v 11 leads inevitably to it and what follows v 11 moves decisively away from it, while at the same time repeating in reverse order the stages leading to the ascension. In other words chapters one and two form an inverted narrative, an extended chiasmus.

The following observations on the symmetry of geography and content in these chapters are based on Hobbs's work. The implications which are drawn for the portrayal of Elisha are, however, my own.

*The Geographical Symmetry of 2 Kings 1.2–2.25.* The thematic center of this narrative towards which it flows and from which it ebbs is the translation of Elijah in 2.11. The symmetry between the locations of Elijah and Elisha as a pair leading up to the former's translation, and those of Elisha by himself following it serve to emphasize the central importance of that event for the narrative. This symmetry is displayed diagrammatically in the chart below.

---

6.    By informing the reader in advance that Elijah was about to be taken up into heaven by a whirlwind (2.1) the tension is shifted from the fate of Elijah to that of Elisha.

*Geographical Symmetry in 2 Kings 1.2–2.25*

A The Mountain 1.9-15a

B Samaria 1.15b, 16

C Gilgal[7] 2.1-2a

D Bethel 2.2b-4a

E Jericho 2.4b-6a

F Banks of Jordan 2.6b,7

G Crossing the Jordan 2.8

H Transjordan 2.9-13

G′ Crossing the Jordan 2.14

F′ Banks of Jordan 2.15-17

E′ Jericho 2.18-22

D′ Bethel[8] 2.23, 24

C′

A′ Mount Carmel 2.25a

B′ Samaria 2.25b

Several things may be noted concerning the effect of this pattern upon the reader's evaluation of Elisha. First of all and most obviously this pattern serves to reinforce the legitimacy of Elisha as Elijah's replacement. By taking Elijah's place geographically in retracing his journey Elisha also replaces Elijah in his role as prophet. This symmetry leads the reader to infer that Elisha has truly replaced Elijah in his position as prophet as well as in his topographical position.

But the geographical symmetry is not perfect. It contains slight variations and these variations may well be subtle indicators that while Elisha has truly and legitimately replaced Elijah as prophet, he differs from Elijah in at least two principal ways.

The first and perhaps most obvious variation from the symmetry of the pattern is Elijah's trip to Gilgal (2.1) which is not duplicated by Elisha when he is alone. The reader of course knows that Gilgal is very close to, if not identical with, the place where Elijah and Elisha eventu-

7.   Technically this happens on the way from Gilgal.
8.   Technically this happens on the road to Bethel.

ally cross the Jordan.[9] If the Gilgal trip is removed from Elijah's itinerary he follows a logical pattern, traveling in a generally southeasterly direction from Samaria to Bethel to Jordan to the banks of the Jordan near or at Gilgal and then into Transjordan. Elisha conversely travels in a generally northwesterly direction, crossing the Jordan to Gilgal, then Jericho, Bethel and ultimately Samaria. The point of this observation is that Elijah's first journey to and from Gilgal is rather pointless geographically speaking. In 1.16 Elijah ends up at Samaria. From 2.1 we learn that he had traveled to Gilgal. The reader is informed that Elijah is about to be taken up into heaven by a whirlwind, which the second-time reader knows is to occur in Transjordan. For Elijah to travel circuitously away from Gilgal to Bethel only to turn back to Jericho and from there return to Gilgal or very near it in order to cross the Jordan seems a wasted journey, geographically speaking.

But if this part of the journey seems pointless when viewed geographically, might it have significance when viewed from another perspective? As noted in the previous chapter, Elijah's intentions in asking Elisha to remain behind are unclear. Either Elijah genuinely wants Elisha to remain behind for some reason or he is merely testing the depth of Elisha's loyalty to him. As I will argue, Elisha knows that whatever Elijah's motives in asking him to stay behind might be, he must remain with his master if he is to be established as his legitimate successor. Therefore, what at first appears to be quite selfless loyalty on Elisha's part, in promising never to forsake his master as long as he lives and in keeping that promise, is intermingled with Elisha's more self-interested desire to have his own succession to Elijah's position as prophet established beyond all doubt.

As noted above, the narrative tension that the reader might have experienced about exactly what Elijah's circuitous journey is leading up to is precluded by 2.1 where the reader is informed of Elijah's approaching translation. But the reader is not the only one who knows in advance that Elijah is about to be translated. The sons of the prophets know (2.3a, 5a), Elisha knows (2.3b, 5b), and Elijah himself knows (2.9, 10).

The narrative is elusive, however, concerning one crucial piece of information. Do those who know of Elijah's impending translation know that the others know, and if so, do they think that the others know that they know? The significance of this information for the portrayal of

9. There is no reason to posit two Gilgals on the basis of this text. See Hobbs 1985: 18-19.

Elisha will become clear at the end of our analysis.

The sons of the prophets at both Bethel and Jericho seem to be unaware of the fact that Elisha knows of Elijah's imminent fate, hence their question, 'Do you know that today Yahweh will take your master from being over you?' (vv. 3, 5). It seems unlikely that they speak this question in Elijah's hearing since they first physically move near to Elisha (v. 3, ויצאו אל־אלישע; v. 5, אל־אלישע ויגשו), which would have been unnecessary if they were addressing Elisha openly without concern as to whether or not Elijah heard their conversation.

Elisha's response to their query on each occasion is, 'Of course I know it. Be quiet!' It is difficult to determine why Elisha tells them to be quiet. Nelson (1987: 159) suggests that by this command Elisha both 'silences the future and seems closed to it' and yet also 'grasps the need for silence' and thus passes one of the tests of his succession. To affirm both of these options simultaneously seems somewhat contradictory, although either of them is feasible on its own. Hobbs (1985: 20) suggests that the imperative 'reflects the very strong sense of urgency Elisha felt during this period'.

Another possibility is that Elisha did not want Elijah to know that he knew what lay in store for his master. If this is so, then the self-interested aspect of Elisha's promise to Elijah is highlighted. Since Elisha knows that Elijah's normal earthly existence as Yahweh's prophet is about to end, and that therefore as successor-designate he is about to be promoted to Elijah's vacated position, the reader assumes that Elisha's promise to remain with his master to the end could well be motivated by more than the purely selfless devotion of a loyal subordinate to a beloved superior. By staying with Elijah to the end Elisha seeks to ensure that his master will not leave him without his being established as his successor. If in addition the reader supposes that Elisha by telling the sons of the prophets to 'be quiet' is attempting to keep Elijah blissfully ignorant of the fact that he knows of Elijah's approaching ascension, Elisha is seen to be attempting to manipulate the situation for his own benefit all that much more clearly. On this reading he wants Elijah to think that his professions of loyalty are motivated solely by his selfless desire to serve his master to the end when in fact they are also motivated by his knowledge that if he remains with Elijah he will be promoted to Elijah's vacated position as prophet.

It is of course impossible for the reader to make a clear judgment from the details of this text alone concerning Elisha's motives in telling the sons of the prophets to be quiet. It is entirely possible that, as Hobbs (1985: 20) seems to suggest, Elisha wants to hurry up the process of succession and so the question of the two groups of the sons of the prophets is seen as a distraction from Elisha's determination to see the succession achieved. It is also possible to infer if we are only considering the details of this text that, as Nelson (1987: 159) suggests, Elisha doesn't want to be reminded of the personal loss that he is about to face (cf. his response of grief at the loss of Elijah in v. 12) or that Elisha feels that the solemnity of the moment must not be disturbed by the curiosity of the sons of the prophets.

But if this text is read in the context of the entire Elisha narratives the craftiness and manipulativeness that is a part of the portrayal of Elisha later on in his life (e.g. 2 Kgs 8.10) must have its influence on the second-time reader's perception of him here. While this is not absolutely conclusive it does add credence to what might otherwise seem to be an overly cynical or suspicious reading of Elisha's motives in telling the sons of the prophets to be quiet. In any case, whether he is trying to fool Elijah or not, Elisha's actions during the geographically unnecessary and circular trip of Elijah that starts at Gilgal show his determination to be established as Elijah's successor. So Elisha's solemn promises to remain with Elijah as long as he lives are not necessarily merely expressions of Elisha's obvious loyalty to Elijah. He also will benefit personally from sticking close to him. The reader infers from the Gilgal loop that Elisha is determined to be Elijah's successor by sticking with him no matter how illogical his path may be in arriving at the spot of his translation.

The second variation is the reversal of 'the mountain' and Samaria in Elisha's itinerary. As the chart above shows, Elijah began his journey from 'the mountain' and proceeded from there to Samaria, while conversely Elisha visited Mt Carmel and finished his journey in Samaria. While 'the mountain' upon which Elijah was sitting in 1.9-15 is not explicitly identified with Mt Carmel, the fact that fire from heaven comes down both at Carmel and at this mountain, partly to demonstrate to others Elijah's standing in Yahweh's eyes, makes the association between the two narratives and therefore the two mountains quite strong in the reader's eyes. The visiting of Mt Carmel by Elisha in 2.25 and his later residence there (4.25) show him to be a prophet who wants to be seen as associated with the place of Elijah's victory over the prophets of Baal. But Elisha ends up *dwelling* in Samaria, the capital of Israel and home of the line of Ahab whose wife Jezebel introduced a particularly vitriolic form of Baalism into the nation, rather than Mt Carmel.

This signals to the reader that Elisha's relationship to the kings of Israel is different from that of Elijah's. While it was not safe for Elijah to remain in the place of the royal residence because of the hostility of the royal family, Elisha is able to live in Samaria for the most part without fear of reprisal from Ahab's son Jehoram or Jezebel who is now queen mother in Israel. The reader must not make too much of this contrast for a good part of the relative lack of intense hostility on the part of the royal family against Elisha must be attributed to the fact that Jehoram at least partially rejected the campaigning Baalism of his mother (3.2) and was therefore more amenable to the prophets of Yahweh than were his parents. But the impression remains that things are easier for Elisha than they were for Elijah. Elijah felt he had to stand alone and while he made his isolation too much a virtue he nevertheless earns the reader's respect for his courageous independence.[10] While Elisha's task is by no means easy, and while he still has to battle continuously with the king of Israel, the threat which Elijah encountered in the time of Ahab and Jezebel has diminished. Although Elisha cannot be personally faulted for the fact that he lived in a less dangerous time than did Elijah, the courageous independence which is a prominent part of the reader's evaluation of Elijah as a character is missing in Elisha's case.

*The symmetry of contents in 2 Kings 1.2–2.25*
Hobbs has observed not only the geographical symmetry but the symmetry of themes, phraseology and content between the two halves of the extended chiasmus in 2 Kgs 1.2–2.25. The chart below is based upon Hobbs's (1985: 17-18) observations.

Clearly the remarkable symmetry between the two halves of this narrative identifies Elisha as the rightful successor to Elijah as prophet and this is the primary and most obvious purpose of this narrative. But Hobbs does not notice that this carefully structured narrative also gives subtle indications that the narrator is calling upon the reader to contrast as well as compare Elijah and Elisha. Elisha is not simply a second Elijah. The second-time reader, of course, knows this and sees the subtle anticipations in this narrative of what is to come in the later portrayal of Elisha.

---

10. The fact that this courage turns out to be somewhat hollow, as I have argued in Chapter 3, does not alter this.

A 2.11 The Translation of Elijah

| | |
|---|---|
| B 2.10 Elisha promised double portion of Elijah's spirit if he sees Elijah's ascension | B´ 2.12 Elisha sees Elijah being taken up |
| C 2.9 Elisha requests double portion of Elijah's spirit | C´ 2.13 Elisha picks up Elijah's mantle, the symbol of succession |
| D 2.8 Elijah uses mantle to cross the Jordan | D´ 2.13, 14 Elisha uses mantle to cross the Jordan |
| E 2.7 Sons of prophets witness the crossing of Elijah and Elisha | E´ 2.15 Sons of prophets witness the crossing of Elisha alone |
| F 2.2-6 Sons of prophets ask if Elisha knows of Elijah's departure | F´ 2.16-18 Sons of prophets ask Elisha to allow them to confirm Elijah's departure |
| G 1.1-8, 16, 17 Story in which a request for healing from a god is met by a word from God and a fulfillment formula. King dies without progeny | G´ 2.19-22 Story in which a request for healing from a repre-sentative of Yahweh is met by a word from God and a fulfillment formula. Miscarriages stop. |
| H 1.9-15 Challenge to the status of a prophet with a command, 'Come down' is met with word of judgment followed by the death of the challengers | H´ 2.23, 24 Challenge to the status of a prophet with a command, 'Go up' is met with a word of judg-ment followed by death of the challengers |

One such anticipation is the ambiguity of meaning in the phrase 'a double portion of your spirit' (2.9). Scholars (e.g. Jones 1984: 385) often correctly call attention to the fact that what Elisha requests is probably an allusion to Deut. 21.17 where the firstborn son is recognized as having a right to a double portion (Heb. פי שנים) of the possessions of his father when the inheritance is divided between the sons. Thus it is assumed that Elisha is not asking for twice the spirit or power of Elijah, but merely twice as much as anyone else receives and therefore the recognition as being rightful heir to Elijah, his 'father'. The logic of the allusion to Deut. 21.7 is that the reader is led to expect that Elisha will turn out to be less of a channel of divine power than his master Elijah was, though more of one than other prophets.[11]

11. If the parallel is to be taken seriously the 'double share' is given only when there are other sons who also have competing claims on the inheritance. If Elisha

But Elisha's request for a double portion can also be understood in its ordinary sense as a simple request to have twice the power of Elijah. In other words, Elisha wants to be a greater channel of Yahweh's power than was his predecessor. The second-time reader knows that in a sense Elisha turns out to be both a greater channel of Yahweh's power and less of a channel of that power. The miracles associated with Elisha's ministry outnumber those of Elijah and demonstrate an even more remarkable ability to channel Yahweh's power than do Elijah's. But as will be shown below, there are reasons to suspect that Elisha's use of the miraculous is not always entirely admirable nor reliable. The wording of Elisha's request can thus be read as having a sort of double entendre for the reader. On the one hand, Elisha is to be only the most significant of several of Elijah's heirs while on the other he is to have twice the power of Elijah. He is to be both more and less as a channel of divine power and, it turns out, more and less as a person.

While most standard translations of the account of the striking of the waters obscure the point, a literal translation of the Hebrew of 2.14 reads:

> Then Elisha took the mantle of Elijah which had fallen from him and struck the waters. And he said, 'Where is Yahweh the God of Elijah, yes, he?' Then he struck the waters and they parted, these (to one side) and those (to the other) and Elisha crossed over.

While I would not want to put too much weight on the point it seems clear that Elisha has to strike the water twice in order for the miracle to work.[12] Certainly it must be acknowledged with Hobbs (1985: 22) that, 'Since he [Elisha] is able to duplicate what Elijah had done, the true succession is confirmed'. But the miracle does not work the first time and it is only after he has asked, 'Where is Yahweh, the God of Elijah, yes he?', and has struck the waters a second time, that the waters are parted. The contrast with Elijah's earlier performance of the parallel miracle is clear. Elijah strikes the waters only once, enabling both himself and Elisha to cross safely. Elisha must strike it twice and, between the two blows, ask whether Yahweh the God of Elijah is still acting through his successor so that he alone can cross. Elijah performs the miracle effortlessly. Elisha has to work at it and plead with Yahweh on the basis of Yahweh's relationship with his predecessor not on the basis of his own relationship with Yahweh. Does Elisha possess less, more, or the

wanted to be the only heir, as his words are often taken, the allusion to Deut. 21.17 is inappropriate.

12. The Lucianic Greek text makes this explicit by adding ἐκ δευτερου.

same amount of power to work miracles relative to his master? From this narrative he has less, even if only slightly so.

Upon seeing Elisha recross the Jordan into Cisjordan in the same miraculous fashion that they had earlier witnessed Elijah and Elisha cross into Transjordan, the sons of the prophets conclude, 'The spirit of Elijah rests upon Elisha' (v. 15). But for some reason the sons of the prophets want to make sure that Elijah is truly gone and not lying helpless on some mountain or in some valley (v. 16). On the one hand they recognize that Elisha now has the power of Elijah. On the other hand they want to confirm for themselves that Elisha has replaced Elijah once and for all. Schäfer-Lichtenberger (1989: 213) suggests that confirmation by the prophetic schools was part of the understood legitimation process of succession. While this may well have been true this fails to account for the way in which the narrator leads the reader to distinguish the perceptive Elisha, who 'saw' Elijah taken up into heaven (v. 12), from the sons of the prophets who did not 'see' it. They therefore are less perceptive and so make an unnecessary trip to confirm what Elisha and the reader already know. Elisha does not need the confirmation of the sons of the prophets because he, unlike them, is able to perceive the real situation. This pericope thus establishes the legitimacy of Elisha's succession by affirming Elisha's perception in contrast to that of the sons of the prophets.[13]

But this pericope also makes clear that Elisha's succession to the position of prophet is not something which was obvious to everyone. While the sons of the prophets show a lack of perception when they query whether Elijah really has been permanently removed from the human scene, their skepticism does show that Elisha's status as prophet was not as obvious as that of Elijah's, whose status is never questioned by the sons of the prophets. Elisha and the reader do not need the testimony of the sons of the prophets in order to establish the legitimacy of his succession. The reader has the testimony of Yahweh himself (1 Kgs 19.16) as well as that of Elijah to confirm this. But the fact that Elisha's succession is questioned, even if it is by somewhat unperceptive sons of the prophets shows that he does not share the same self-legitimating status within the story world which Elijah had.

13. Nelson (1987: 159) remarks that,

> Elisha's growth to fit the mantle of Elijah is highlighted by a reverse process among the sons of the prophets. At first they predict what will happen (vv. 3, 5) and correctly interpret what has taken place (v. 15). However, their insistence on a search for Elijah shows that they are less perspicacious at the end of the story than they were at the start.

Within the structural symmetry of 2 Kgs 1.2–2.25 the story of the healing of Jericho's waters parallels Ahaziah's attempt to ask a foreign god, Baalzebub the god of Ekron, whether he would be healed of his injuries from a fall (1.2-8, 16, 17). By contrast in 2 Kgs 2.19-22 the men of Jericho ask Elisha, a representative of Yahweh the God of Israel, whether he could help in healing the bad waters and barren land of Jericho. In each situation a message that purports to be from God is given. In 1.1-8, 16, 17 Elijah delivers a message of judgment and death. In 2.19-22 Elisha delivers one of healing. In both cases the narrator gives confirmation that the prophetic word is accurately fulfilled. Obviously Ahaziah asked the wrong god for healing and Yahweh's representative Elijah, as usual, gives a message of judgment. The men of Jericho asked the representative of the right God and received the promise of healing.

In this narrative Elisha functions as a sort of positive alter ego to Elijah, whose work was mainly to warn of judgment against the family of Ahab. Elisha's work includes this negative aspect of Elijah's work but he goes beyond his predecessor in that much of his activity is devoted to the positive function of helping to solve the problems of the remnant of Yahwistic Israelites with whom he lived and worked. While the positive function is not entirely absent from the portrayal of Elijah (cf. 1 Kgs 17.8-24) it never involves Israelites and it is by comparison with Elisha a very small part of his activity.

This passage thus leads the reader to the inference that while Elisha has indeed replaced Elijah as his legitimate successor, Elisha's function goes beyond Elijah's largely negative one to one which includes the bringing of both blessing and curse, grace and judgment to the people of Israel depending on their presumed loyalty to Yahweh. In this sense Elisha is more and better than Elijah.

The positive aspects of Elisha's service to Yahweh are highlighted by noticing that this passage is not only the counterpart of 2 Kgs 1.1-8, 16, 17 within the chiastic structure of chs. 1 and 2 of 2 Kings. It is also a positive counterpart of 1 Kgs 16.34. As noted in the previous chapter, the fulfillment of Joshua's curse on Jericho as recorded in 1 Kgs 16.34 plays a part in creating in the reader the expectation of divine judgment on the house of Ahab. As anticipated, Elijah's ministry is largely composed of the deliverance of messages of divine judgment against the house of Ahab. But in 2 Kgs 2.19-22 some of the effects of the curse on Jericho seem to be undone. Instead of being a place whose rebuilding results in the death of the children of Hiel, the rebuilder, Elisha's miracle ensures that the barrenness or miscarriage, that is the absence or the death of children, caused by the water and land of Jericho is stopped. In a sense Elisha reverses the curse of Jericho. Instead of being a place of divine judgment it becomes, with the miracle of Elisha, a place where healthy children are born and a company of the sons of the prophets and others loyal to Yahweh can live, raise their families and thrive. Just as the curse on Jericho serves as a sort of introduction to and anticipation of the ministry of Elijah, Elisha's reverse of the curse of Jericho serves as an indicator that his work, in contrast to Elijah's, will be shifted in its emphasis more to the positive side.

The account of the mocking of Elisha (2 Kgs 2.23-24) is a very difficult text for modern readers who attempt to align themselves with a hypothetical ancient Hebrew reader. As Nelson (1987: 161) notes, 'The modern reader may wish that the narrator had chosen some story other than verses 23-25 to legitimize Elisha's power'. He continues:

> The ancient reader, untroubled by our post-industrial revolution apotheosis of childhood, doubtless found this a satisfying story. Those juvenile delinquents got exactly what they deserved! To insult God's prophet is to insult God.

Certainly Nelson has a point in that modern interpreters, if they are even to begin to comprehend a text like this, must suppress the moral horror at the abuse of children which so influences a modern reader's response to this text and attempt to read the text on its own terms.

But even when this has been taken into account Elisha's curse must be seen as an example of excess (Hobbs 1985: 24). Within the chiastic structure of the larger pericope 2 Kgs 1.2–2.25 this story parallels 2 Kgs 1.9-14 where Elijah calls down fire from heaven upon Ahaziah's first two captains of fifty along with their regiments. Elijah's status as a representative of Yahweh is directly challenged by the captains who, under royal directive, command Yahweh's prophet to 'come down' and face the wrath of the king (1.9, 11). The military might of the king is pitted against the divine power which Yahweh has given Elijah. Elijah's response in each case, 'If I am a man of God let fire come down from heaven and consume you and your fifty men', shows that Elijah's status as Yahweh's representative is at stake. As at Mt Carmel, where Elijah also put his credibility as Yahweh's representative on the line, Yahweh responds positively and the fire from heaven totally destroys the two companies of soldiers.

While even this story with its violent display causes many modern readers trouble, at least the victims were military men who were a genuine threat to the personal safety of Elijah. Elisha, by contrast, curses youths[14] who posed no apparent threat to his personal safety and whose only crime is to mock him with the words, 'Go up baldy, go up baldy'. The upshot of the curse is that two she-bears ripped open forty-two of them.[15]

It is difficult to know with precision the ages of the youths but it does seem likely that they were mocking more than just Elisha's natural baldness. A shaved head was a relatively common form of mourning for the dead or over other traumatic events in Israel[16] but it seems unlikely in this context to be the point of the youths' mocking. The law did legislate against artificially created baldness in the cult of the dead[17] but again in this context this seems improbable.

It is sometimes suggested (Gray 1970: 480) that the boys are mocking the artificially created bald spot or tonsure which it is alleged the early prophets maintained along with a distinctive garment and mark or stigma which identified them as prophets of Yahweh. By mocking Elisha's tonsure the youths were mocking the legitimacy of his prophetic office or role and thus setting themselves against one of Yahweh's primary chosen means of addressing Baalism in Israel.

While this view must not be excluded as a possibility,[18] a much more likely explanation seems nearer to hand. In 1.8 the reader is given a rare Old Testament example of the physical description of a person's appearance. Elijah is described as, 'a hairy man[19] with a leather girdle girded around him'. Elijah, the hairy man, is sitting on a mountain where he is commanded to 'come down'. Elisha, on the other hand, is a bald man who is commanded to 'go up'. The contrast between the two prophets is striking and no matter what motive is attributed to the youths' mocking of Elisha, the reader surmises that Elisha is being mocked for being different from and inferior to Elijah. Faced with the suggestion that he does not somehow measure up to his predecessor Elisha curses

---

14.  In v. 23 they are termed נערים קטנים. In v. 24 they are termed ילדים.

15.  While the text makes no explicit connection between Elisha's curse and the mauling of the she-bears, the juxtaposition of the two events makes this implicit.

16.  Lev. 19.26-28; 21.5; Deut. 14.1.

17.  Amos 8.10; Mic. 1.16; Isa. 3.24; 22.12; Jer. 16.6; Ezek. 7.18.

18.  Lindblom's (1962: 69) main arguments for this are questionable. His evidence is this text and fairly remote analogies from the history of religion.

19.  Heb. בעל שער.

the youths, who are now termed children (ילדים), in the name of Yahweh, whereupon two she-bears rip open forty-two of them.

Elisha's action can only be contrasted negatively with the parallel action of Elijah. Elijah's personal safety was threatened by adult military men who attempted to force the man of God to submit to the king's wrath. Elisha's personal dignity was mocked by 'youths', or 'children' whose crime was to compare him unfavorably with his master. When the two stories are compared the reader infers that Elisha is being portrayed as being morally inferior to Elijah.

d. *Hazael Becomes King of Syria—2 Kings 8.7-15*
*Introduction.* When Elijah was taken up into heaven in a whirlwind he left two of the three final tasks which Yahweh had given him at Horeb (1 Kgs 19.15-18) unfinished. While Elisha had been designated as and empowered to be his successor, Hazael and Jehu had not been anointed as the kings of Syria and Israel. At the end of 2 Kgs 8.7-15 Hazael has become king of Syria. The question then becomes, 'How did this come about?' Certainly Elisha is somehow involved in this but the text is once again allusive about exactly how and why. Two key exegetical questions must be asked and if possible answered before Elisha's involvement can be understood and evaluated.

*How did Benhadad die?—2 Kings 8.15.* According to some modern readers the narrative is not absolutely clear about the circumstances of Benhadad's death. Gray (1970: 532) suggests that the Hebrew word translated 'coverlet' in RSV refers to mosquito netting which was soaked with water to serve as a sort of air conditioner. Benhadad's death, which was fortuitous, was discovered the next day when servants (presumably) removed it to hang it up to dry.

But this strains the reader's credulity and is more a testimony to the ingenuity of an exegete who wants to exonerate Elisha from what he views as moral impropriety than to a consideration of the text on its own terms. There is no reason to doubt that the subject of לקח in v. 15 is Hazael.[20] It seems highly unlikely that Hazael, who is portrayed as Benhadad's chief assistant, would have ordinarily been the one to tend to the king's bodily needs. Furthermore, it seems curious that Hazael is said to have spread the wet mosquito netting only over Benhadad's face. Didn't the royal neck and arms need protection from flying pests? The

---

20. Contra Gray 1970: 529, 532.

rapid sequence of the verbs also argues against this view (he took, then he dipped, then he spread, then he died—then Hazael became king). It seems clear that Hazael assassinated Benhadad and that Elisha at least gave him the idea, even if he did not directly instruct him to kill his master.

*Did Elisha lie?—2 Kings 8.10.* The attempt of interpreters to exonerate Elisha from the charge of lying in this text[21] is at least as old as the transmitters of the Masoretic tradition who give as the Kethib of Elisha's first words to Hazael, 'Go! Say, "He will surely not live"', while retaining the Qere, 'Go! Say to him, "You will surely live"'. This is at least more credible than Labuschagne's (1965: 327-28) suggestion that 'You will certainly recover' is really indirect speech and refers to Hazael rather than Benhadad. Gray's (1970: 530) suggestion that לֹא or לֹו be repointed to לֻא or לֻו, the optative particle, and the resulting phrase be translated 'Life to the king!' is possible, but there is no evidence for it and the motivation seems to be the same as with the other view, that is to exonerate Elisha from the charge of lying. Montgomery and Gehman (1951: 393) suggest that in the first answer Elisha gives his, 'own spontaneous response which is followed and contradicted by a supervening affect of second sight'. They continue, 'the prophet does not always know at first or knows only in part'. Würthwein (1984: 319) cannot accept that the text as it stands would ever have been transmitted orally and then written down. While he prefers a source-critical solution to the riddle of the text, he recognizes that in the text as it stands Elisha either lies or acts deceptively, even if not deliberately so.

Others (Fricke 1972: 103; Skinner 1911: 315) separate the two halves of the answer. The first part answers the king's question. His illness is not terminal. The second part, however, refers to the king's death by another means. Jones (1984: 444), who assumes Hazael was already planning a coup, goes on in commenting on v. 13, 'The Lord has shown me that you are to be king over Syria', to absolve Elisha of any responsibility for Hazael's treachery:

> These words can hardly be interpreted as a sign of Elisha's involvement in
> the moves to take the throne from Benhadad; it may, however, be conceded
> that such a message from the prophet would have given Hazael confirmation
> in his resolve to take the throne.

21. Montgomery and Gehman 1951: 393: 'There is a large variety of ancient evasion of the text'. I would add that modern evasion is also common.

But surely these last three views are particularly obvious examples of just how entrenched idealistic readings of Elisha are in the traditional scholarship on these narratives. There is no evidence to suggest with Montgomery and Gehman that Elisha suddenly has a second revelation which contradicts the first spontaneous outburst. The second half of the message is dependent on, but in clear contrast to, the first both in grammatical structure (*waw* in a contrastive sense + perfect) and in the opposition between the antonyms חיה and מות which are both put in an emphatic form (*qal* infinitive absolute + imperfect). The contrast is between what Elisha tells Hazael to do, that is tell the king that he will certainly live, and what Elisha tells Hazael he knows but which Hazael is not to tell the king about, that is that he will certainly die.

Würthwein's view is problematic in that he claims on the one hand that in the text as it stands Elisha lies or acts deceptively, while on the other hand that it is wrong to view this lie or deception as deliberate. If it is not deliberate then Elisha must be incredibly stupid. While it is conceivable that he might have unintentionally encouraged Hazael's usurpation of the Syrian throne, it is hard to imagine how he could have directed Hazael to tell Benhadad one thing and then told him that in fact the opposite was to be the case without doing so intentionally.

Elisha's reply to Hazael seems to be perplexing to Hazael since he stares at Elisha until he is embarrassed.[22] Hazael's response suggests strongly that what Elisha has just said is self-contradictory. Is it really conceivable that Elisha did not know that he had given Hazael such a contradictory-sounding response? Not unless Elisha is much less intelligent than he appears in the rest of the narratives.

The suggestion by Jones and others that in the first half of Elisha's answer he gave Benhadad a true response to his real question, that is 'Will I recover from this illness?', while in the second he informed Hazael that Benhadad would die from other causes is possible, although I think unlikely. The motivation for this interpretation again seems to be to absolve Elisha from the charge of instructing Hazael to lie. While Elisha may on this reading be cleared of the charge of directing someone to lie for him on a technicality, he must surely be found guilty of using deception. To say as Jones does that Elisha is not involved in

---

22. That it is in all probability Hazael who does the staring is shown by the fact that the subject of the verbs is only identified explicitly when it is changed. Elisha is explicitly identified as the subject of the weeping which implies that he is probably not the subject of the previous actions.

Hazael's moves to usurp the throne seems incredible. Elisha tells Hazael to tell Benhadad what is at best a partial truth and informs Hazael that despite the message Benhadad will really die.

Hazael's response is to stare at Elisha over this perplexing message until Hazael becomes embarrassed. Elisha then breaks out in tears over the havoc Hazael will wreak upon Israel. When Hazael inquires how one of such low position[23] as himself could do such things, Elisha informs him that he will do so as king of Syria. To say that Elisha is not involved in Hazael's usurpation after such a conversation stretches credulity. It could be argued, I suppose, that Hazael, on the basis of Elisha's word, merely expected Benhadad to die of his illness, after which he would become king. But according to the wording of v. 13 Hazael does not think of himself as in a position to succeed to the throne. We could of course assume that Hazael only pretends to think of himself as a mere servant while in fact he was deviously plotting the overthrow of the king. The embarrassment of Hazael when Elisha asks him to tell the king only part of the truth, however, seems to me to indicate a certain naivety on Hazael's part. While this is not absolutely conclusive it certainly accounts for the evidence better than Jones's alternative.

1 Kgs 19.15 leads the first-time reader of 2 Kgs 8.7-15 to wonder whether Elisha might here complete one of Elijah's unfinished tasks. While he does not literally 'anoint' Hazael in this passage, the second-time reader knows that Elisha does here designate him as king. Yes, Hazael actually carries out the assassination and usurpation. Since Benhadad does not die of his illness as Hazael might have anticipated from Elisha's words, Hazael apparently takes matters into his own hands. True, Elisha did not explicitly instruct him to kill his master. But he did instruct him to tell a half-truth and he did assure him that Yahweh had decreed that he would be king. I see no way to avoid the inference that Elisha was very much involved in Hazael's usurpation of the throne. While Elisha may not have lied in some simplistic sense, he most certainly was involved in encouraging Hazael's deception and ultimately his usurpation of the Syrian throne.

*The evaluation of Elisha in 2 Kings 8.7-15.* This text relates how Elisha completed one of the two unfinished tasks which Yahweh had given Elijah in his final commission to him at Horeb (1 Kgs 19.17). As Elijah's successor Elisha is to carry on Elijah's work. By completing a task

23. On the use of the word 'dog' to denote servant see Margalith 1983 and 1984.

which Elijah had left undone Elisha shows himself to be Elijah's legitimate successor. While Elisha did not literally 'anoint' Hazael (Elijah did not literally anoint Elisha either) he did designate him to be king of Syria and set in motion a series of events which led to Hazael actually becoming king of Syria. In this regard Elisha is seen to be an effective successor to his master.

But the means which Elisha uses to accomplish this divinely commissioned task are less than admirable. The request of a king for divine guidance as to whether he or someone close to him would recover from a serious illness is paralleled in two other places in Kings. In 1 Kgs 14.1-17 Jeroboam sends his disguised wife to inquire of Ahijah the prophet as to whether their sick son would recover. Ahijah recognizes the disguise and not only announces the child's death but adds an oracle of dynastic doom against Jeroboam's line. In 2 Kgs 1.2-18 Ahaziah attempts to ask Baalzebub, the god of Ekron, as to whether he would recover from a serious fall. Elijah delivers a prophecy of doom announcing his death.

The reader cannot but compare Ahijah's and Elijah's response to a request for guidance about healing to Elisha's. Ahijah and Elijah confront the inquirer with the very unwelcome message that in fact the ill person would die. Elisha by way of contrast uses deception to encourage Hazael to lie to his master, and Hazael then makes sure that he never has a chance to recover by suffocating him. While Elisha's deception does lead to the fulfillment of part of Yahweh's purpose and it is directed at those on the 'other side' and is therefore against Yahweh's enemies, Elisha's chosen means of furthering Yahweh's purposes compares unfavorably with those of Elijah and Ahijah. Ahijah and Elijah were not afraid to deliver bad news to hostile kings (1 Kgs 14.1-16; 21.20-28). Elisha uses deception to accomplish Yahweh's purposes. In this narrative while Elisha completes one of Elijah's unfinished tasks and thereby demonstrates the legitimacy of his succession, he does so in a way that compares unfavorably with another prophet Ahijah and with his erstwhile master Elijah.

*e. The Anointing of Jehu—2 Kings 9.1-13*
In this passage Elisha, through an intermediary, anoints Jehu king over Israel. In so doing Elisha accomplishes, albeit indirectly, the last of the tasks which Elijah had left unfinished when he was translated into heaven. While the son of the prophets who was directed by Elisha to perform the anointing expands Elisha's brief message into a call for a

bloody coup against the entire house of Ahab (vv. 7-10), there is no reason to suspect that Elisha here does anything which might bring into question his reliability. That he performs the anointing through an intermediary is no more significant than the fact that in a sense Elijah was performing this task through his intermediary Elisha.

The text does round off the completeness of Elisha's succession of Elijah. After this text all three of the instruments of divine judgment of which Yahweh spoke are designated and functioning in the way in which Yahweh directed in 1 Kgs 19.15-18. Elisha goes beyond his master Elijah in the sense that he actually fulfills the work which Elijah had not completed.

### 3. *Elisha the Prophet*

a. *Introduction*
In 1 Kgs 19.16b Yahweh directs Elijah to anoint Elisha to be prophet in his place. In this passage 'prophet' is a sort of shorthand for a wide variety of tasks which Elijah performed, functions which he served, and roles which he filled. Elisha, according to Yahweh's directive, is to take over this variety of tasks, functions, and roles from Elijah.

Since Elisha does in fact succeed Elijah as prophet, and since prophets are involved in the reception or the claim of the reception of super-natural knowledge, the reader's question becomes, 'How does Elisha's reception and transmission of supernatural knowledge or his claims to do so, compare and contrast with those of Elijah?' When the reader asks this question of the relevant texts, Elisha is seen to be, as I will show, both more and less of a prophet. He displays a greater range of abilities to know the humanly unknowable and yet his 'knowledge' is sometimes incomplete (2 Kgs 4.27). Further, he can use his knowledge in a crafty way (2 Kgs 13.14-19). It is possible that he sometimes does not tell all he knows (2 Kgs 3.27) and on at least one occasion as we have already seen he is almost certainly deceptive (2 Kgs 8.10). On another occasion a prediction of his turns out to be clearly wrong (2 Kgs 3.16, 27).

b. *The Extent of Elisha's Knowledge*
*Introduction.* Elisha displays knowledge or claims to possess knowledge of persons and events which are: a) in the present time but a long distance away; b) in the near or distant future; and c) geographically near and in the present time but invisible to ordinary human perception. In

the extent of his knowledge he goes beyond that of even his predecessor Elijah.

*The spatial dimension of Elisha's knowledge.* Elisha is portrayed as possessing the remarkable ability to see the actions and hear the words of people who are too far away to be seen or heard by ordinary human means.

The first example of this ability is reported in 2 Kgs 5.26. Gehazi, resenting the fact that the Syrian Naaman had received healing from Elisha without having had to pay anything for it (v. 20), surreptitiously follows Naaman and after giving him an improbable story as to why Elisha had suddenly changed his mind about receiving payment, returns with two festal garments and two talents of silver which he hides in the house (vv. 21-24). Elisha's query, 'Where have you been, Gehazi?' (v. 25), attempts to elicit a self-confession from Gehazi, who denies that he has gone anywhere. Elisha replies, 'Didn't I travel with you in my mind when someone turned from his chariot to meet you?' (v. 26). While the 'someone' in Elisha's statement is somewhat vague, in its context this could be no one other than Naaman. The fact that Elisha's description of what Gehazi had received from Naaman differs markedly from what he had actually received probably indicates the large sum of money involved and what Gehazi could buy with it rather than the inexactitude of Elisha's knowledge.[24] Elisha here demonstrates the clairvoyant power to see and hear things which took place at a distance.

While Gehazi's furtive encounter with Naaman was only a 'short distance' away (5.19) 2 Kgs 6.8-12 informs us that Elisha can even hear the secret conversations of the military strategists of Syria in Damascus, which is about 150 kilometres away. The servants of the king express the view that Elisha even hears the words spoken in the king's bed chamber (v.12)! This remarkable ability of Elisha's goes far beyond anything which even Elijah is portrayed as possessing and Elisha puts it to good effect in defense of Israel.

In 2 Kgs 6.26-33 Elisha shows knowledge of the king of Israel's words which were spoken while the king was walking on the city walls (v. 26) and Elisha was sitting in his house (v. 33). The king having heard of the start of cannibalism as a result of the Syrian siege says:

---

24. Nelson (1987: 180) states that Elisha here, 'either exaggerat[es] his crime for effect or spin[s] out some of the things that could be bought with the money'.

> May the gods do the same to me and even worse if the head of Elisha son
> of Shaphat remains on his shoulders today (6.31).

Elisha has somehow come to know of the king's words since he asks
the elders who were sitting in his house with him, 'Do you see how this
murderer has sent to take off my head?' There is no indication that
Elisha has heard of the king's threatening oath by natural means and
therefore the reader infers that Elisha is once again being portrayed as
having the ability to overhear the words of people who are beyond the
reach of normal hearing.

*The temporal dimension of Elisha's knowledge.* Elisha not only has
knowledge of events from which he is spatially separated, he also has
knowledge of events from which he is temporally separated, that is he
knows the future.

In 2 Kgs 2.1-6 Elisha claims to know that Elijah is about to be taken
from being over him, but this knowledge of Yahweh's future actions is
no more than the sons of the prophets have. Elisha's knowledge of the
future, while quite remarkable to ordinary mortals who do not possess
such knowledge, is merely comparable to that of any other prophet at
the time. Elijah also knows of his impending translation. This passage
thus keeps the reader from assuming that knowledge of the future is a
gift unique to Elisha. In fact it seems as though all prophets have some
knowledge of the future and Elisha is no different from other prophets
in this regard.

In 2 Kgs 3.16-19 Elisha is called upon to inquire of Yahweh as to
whether the coalition of the kings of Israel, Judah and Edom gathered
against Moab is to be defeated by the lack of water in the wilderness of
Edom. Jehoram, the king of Israel, states the belief that Yahweh had
called them together in order to give them into the hands of the Moabites
(v. 10). Jehoshaphat, however, requests guidance from a prophet of
Yahweh (v. 11). When he is informed that Elisha is nearby, he expresses
his confidence in Elisha's reliability as a spokesman of Yahweh (v. 12).
Elisha's message promises that the water will be supplied and also that
in addition the Moabites will be defeated (vv. 16-19).

While the story takes a surprising turn at the end, Elisha's prognostica-
tions turn out, at least initially, to be quite accurate. In 3.16, 17 Elisha says:

> Thus says Yahweh, 'I will make this river bed full of pools'. For thus says
> Yahweh, 'You will not see wind and you will not see rain but the river will
> be full of water so that you, your cattle and your beasts might drink'.

The fulfillment of this prediction occurs the next morning at the time of offering the sacrifice.[25] The reader is told, 'Look! The water came from the direction of Edom and the land was filled with water' (v. 20). In 3.18, 19 Elisha continues his message, but this time it appears to be his words rather than a direct quotation of Yahweh's words.

> This is a simple matter in the eyes of Yahweh. He will also give Moab into your hands and you will defeat every fortified city and every chosen city. And every good tree you will fell and every spring of water you will stop and every good portion of ground you will spoil with stones.

In 3.21-25 we have the record of Moab being given militarily into the hand of Israel. Interestingly, Moab's defeat follows directly from the supply of water which, because of its reflection on the red earth, the Moabites confuse with blood (v. 23). In 3.25 Israel either unwittingly fulfills Elisha's prediction or deliberately obeys what they consider to be his directive even though this is technically in contravention of Moses' instructions in Deut. 20.19, 20. They overthrow the cities, cover the best pieces of land with stones, stop the springs and fell the best of the trees.

Thus both parts of Elisha's prediction initially prove accurate. The water is supplied and Moab is soundly defeated in battle. Elisha thus clearly demonstrates his ability to know the future. But as noted above, Elisha does not merely deliver Yahweh's oracle. He also speaks in his own voice about future events. His knowledge of the future is thus not limited to the specific messages which Yahweh gives him to speak. He also predicts the future in a much more direct way without having to quote Yahweh.

In 2 Kgs 4.8-17 Elisha predicts something further into the future than events which occur the next day. He predicts that a wealthy woman of Shunem, who had generously provided food and lodging for Elisha and his servant Gehazi, would have a son during the following spring (v. 16). His prediction again proves accurate (v. 17). Interestingly Elisha does not consult Yahweh about this matter or deliver an oracle to the woman with the divine promise of a child. He merely predicts it.

In 2 Kgs 6.32, 33, the king of Israel blames Elisha for the desperation which the Syrian king Benhadad's siege of Samaria had brought upon the people of Israel (6.28-31). This is understandable from the king's point of view since Elisha had just previously used his miraculous power

---

25. Cf. 1 Kgs 18.36, a propitious time for a miracle which authenticates a prophet to occur.

to defeat the Syrians almost singlehandedly (6.8-23). Elisha's failure to use his power in this instance seems incomprehensible to the king given that the Israelites had been turning to cannibalism in their desperation (6.28-31). Like Jezebel before him, the king makes an oath to kill the uncooperative prophet (v. 31).[26] Elisha's knowledge of the future is shown by the fact that he is able to warn the elders in advance that the messenger and following him the king himself are coming with the intention of decapitating Elisha (v. 32). Although there is only a short period of time between Elisha's prediction and its fulfillment, he does demonstrate a knowledge of the future which is not explainable by ordinary means. Elisha is able to see the messenger and hear the footsteps of the king before the messenger and the king arrive.

In 7.1-28 Elisha predicts the incredibly low cost of foodstuffs that the besieged, famine-stricken city with its hyper-inflated prices (6.25) would experience the next day (7.1). He also predicts that the king's personal adjutant would see the prediction come true but not be able to eat the suddenly plentiful and inexpensive food (7.2). Both of these incredible predictions prove accurate (7.16, 20). The miraculous way in which Yahweh has to act in order to bring this incredible series of events to pass (7.6, 7) demonstrates that Elisha could only have obtained this information by supernatural means.

In 2 Kgs 13.14-25 the dying Elisha predicts that Joash will strike down Syria in battle, but only three times (v. 19). While it is not clear exactly how far into the future this prediction reaches we are told that after Hazael's death Joash defeated Hazael's son Benhadad in battle three times (v. 25). A period of perhaps several years into the future is implied.

The above passages portray Elisha as being able accurately to predict the future, whether that future be a few minutes away (6.32, 33), the next day (3.16-19; 7.1-20), the next year (4.8-17) or even further into the future (13.14-25). Elijah was also able to predict the future accurately (e.g. 1 Kgs 17.1) so in this respect Elisha is similar to his master. There are, however, more examples of Elisha's ability given than of Elijah's and so Elisha's ability is somewhat more prominent than Elijah's. In other words Elisha's ability accurately to predict the future is only quantitatively not qualitatively different from his master's.

---

26. Unlike the case of Jezebel whose threat in 1 Kgs 19.2 seems somewhat hollow, in this instance the king follows right behind his messenger in order to see that his oath is fulfilled.

*Elisha's ability to see the invisible.* On two occasions Elisha explicitly displays the ability to see the invisible. Since Elijah is present on the first of the two occasions the reader surmises that he also has the ability to see the invisible. Elisha cannot, therefore, be said to differ from his master in this regard. On both occasions what Elisha is able to see are the invisible chariots and horses of fire which at least sometimes accompanied Elijah and later Elisha.

In 2 Kgs 2.1-18 Elijah promises that Elisha will be given a double portion of his spirit on condition that Elisha 'sees' (ראה) Elijah being taken from him (v. 10). Elisha does in fact 'see' (ראה) this event and it is subsequently confirmed, initially to the satisfaction of the reader and later to the satisfaction of the sons of the prophets, that Elijah's spirit does in fact come to rest upon Elisha (2.15-18).

The doubt expressed by the sons of the prophets as to whether Elijah has actually been permanently taken from Elisha (v. 16) shows that they had not seen the translation as Elisha had. The most obvious reason for this is that they had remained on the other side of the Jordan (v. 7) and were therefore physically prevented from seeing the event because of the distance. Elisha had a better vantage point.

But as has been noted previously, the 'seeing' in view in this passage is more than mere physical sight. The sons of the prophets lacked the insight or perception which Elisha possessed. Even though they know that Elijah is to be taken away by Yahweh that very day (vv. 3, 5), when they see the obvious evidence of this fact—Elisha returning without Elijah, wearing Elijah's mantle and then using it to perform a miracle (vv. 14, 15)—they question whether the translation has really occurred. They are portrayed as lacking insight in that on the one hand they recognize that Elijah's spirit was now resting on Elisha (v. 15), but on the other they cannot accept that Yahweh has taken him up into heaven as they had earlier been anticipating (vv. 3, 5).

Elisha is able to see what even the sons of the prophets, who had a premonition or revelation of the translation, could not see. He sees the chariots and horses of fire separating him from his master as a prelude to Elijah being taken up into heaven in a whirlwind. He knows that Elijah's conditions for his receiving a double portion of his spirit have been fulfilled. He also knows that Elijah has been taken up into heaven by a whirlwind and is not lying helpless on some mountain or in some valley as the sons of the prophets were assuming. He sees the chariot and horses of fire for himself and has the insight to recognize their significance.

The second occasion is described in 2 Kgs 6.8-23. In this passage the king of Syria is informed that his recent military reverses have not been caused by a disloyal spy who had infiltrated the ranks of his senior officers as he suspected, but by Elisha's clairvoyant ability to hear his private conversations all the way from Israel (vv. 8-13). He travels by night with a great army, which includes horses and chariots, to Dothan where Elisha is staying, and he surrounds the city (v. 14). When Elisha's assistant rises early the next morning he sees the army and expresses his quite understandable fear to his master (v. 15). Elisha reassures him by informing him that despite all appearances an army superior to the one threatening them is protecting them. He then prays that Yahweh would enable his assistant to see what Elisha could already see, the invisible horses and chariots of fire which surrounded and protected Elisha (v. 17). By contrast he prays that the Syrian forces will be incapacitated by temporary blindness, so enabling him to lead them to Samaria as virtual prisoners of war (vv. 18-20). The horses and chariots of fire which Elisha is able to see at the translation of Elijah are now Elisha's protective force. They are invisible to others, except by special dispensation, but not to Elisha or presumably to Elijah.

In conclusion we can say that Elisha and presumably Elijah have invisible supernatural powers which aid them in their struggles. Whether they were present at all times or only in special circumstances is unclear. Their visibility to Elisha and presumably Elijah shows that, in contrast to ordinary human beings such as Elisha's assistant and even the sons of the prophets, Elisha and Elijah could, at least in some circumstances, see the invisible.

### c. *Problems with Elisha's Prophetic Knowledge*
*Introduction.* While Elisha's supernatural knowledge equals that of Elijah and in the variety of its scope and the frequency with which it is displayed even surpasses it, there are problems associated with it which lead the reader to question just how trustworthy Elisha is as a channel of supernatural knowledge. That he has remarkable clairvoyant gifts is indisputable. The way in which he uses these gifts is, however, not always laudable, and not always consistent. The real, likely, or possible deficiencies which the reader sees in Elisha's reception and delivery or use of knowledge derived supernaturally run the gamut of the problems connected with prophecy. On at least one occasion the supernatural knowledge which Elisha deems necessary to deal with a situation is

withheld from him (2 Kgs 4.27). On another Elisha receives the information but in delivering it seems to mix his own words in with the message (2 Kgs 3.16-19). On that same occasion he claims to have received knowledge of the future, but subsequent events indicate that his prediction turns out to be inaccurate or false. Elisha also seems on one occasion to suppress the hidden conditions in a commanded symbolic action with a deceptive effect (2 Kgs 13.14-19; 24, 25). On still another Elisha encourages Hazael to deliver a false or radically misleading message (2 Kgs 8.7-15).

Thus, while Elisha's access to supernatural power is truly astounding, he is not portrayed as a completely reliable receiver and sender of that knowledge.

*Deception or suspicion of deception in Elisha's prophetic work.* I have already commented on the deception in which Elisha is involved in encouraging Hazael to give a false or misleading message to his master, and by implication prompting him to seize the throne by force (2 Kgs 8.10). But this is not the only occasion when the reader suspects that Elisha may be acting in a wily or crafty manner. While the recipients of Elisha's chicanery are in each case his and the narrator's ideological enemies these texts help to undermine the reader's confidence in the reliability of Elisha as a channel of supernatural knowledge. When Elisha is compared with Elijah in this respect, he is seen to be a decidedly less trustworthy prophet since Elijah confronted his ideological adversaries head-on and thus had no need to use morally questionable methods in order to deliver words of divine judgment against them.

2 Kgs 13.14-25 is the last narrative in the story of Elisha. Joash the king of Israel visits Elisha as Elisha is about to die. In tears he cries, 'My father, my father! The chariots of Israel and its horsemen!' (v.14). While Joash was like all of the other kings of Israel in continuing in the sin of Jeroboam son of Nebat, in this passage he at least tries to make it appear that he has great respect for Elisha. The visit itself shows this. The use of the phraseology of self-subordination in referring to Elisha (my father) and the weeping also indicate it. Furthermore, Joash's words are an exact repetition of Elisha's own words at the translation of his master Elijah and as such are an attempt to express to Elisha the same sort of loyalty and respect which Elisha had for his master. Joash's words are perhaps also intended to express the same sort of fear for the future which Elisha also felt at the loss of his master. Thus the reader infers that

while Joash was certainly an ideological foe of Elisha's, he must have at least partially recognized the reality of Elisha's divine power and its legitimacy.

Undoubtedly the reader will infer that Joash is acting at least partially out of fear. Elisha had used his remarkable powers to deliver the nation from foreign oppression on more than one occasion (2 Kgs 5.6-8; 6.8-10; 6.24–7.20). For the nation to lose that sort of protection would be a very great loss from the king's point of view. The reader could assume that Joash is cynically trying to see what benefits he could gain from Elisha. But even if it is assumed that Joash's motives are entirely selfish and his display of grief and loyalty affected, he still has some respect for Elisha's power. Furthermore there is, as far as I can see, no indication in the narrative that Joash is acting other than genuinely.

Elisha, however, deals with Joash in a disingenuous fashion. Elisha involves Joash in two symbolic actions: shooting an arrow and then striking the ground with the remaining arrows. It is unclear whether these are purely symbolic actions or also involve sympathetic magic (Fohrer 1966). In any case, Elisha begins with the first symbolic action by leading Joash to believe that he would 'defeat the Syrians in Aphek until [he made] an end of them' (RSV 13.17). He then asks Joash to take the remaining arrows and strike the ground with them (v. 18). Joash complies by striking the ground three times. Elisha then with inexplicable anger says a remarkable thing:

> If you had struck the ground five or six times you would have struck the Syrians until you made an end of them. But now you will (only) strike the Syrians three times (v. 19).

The Hebrew for 'to make an end of them' (עד-כלה) is identical in both vv. 17 and 19. When Joash fires the arrow he is promised he would completely defeat (עד-כלה) the Syrians. When, however, he obeys Elisha's order to strike the ground with arrows, Elisha suddenly informs him of some very important new rules. Elisha gives Joash no indication as to how many times he should strike the ground, and even more importantly he does not inform him just how important his response would be for his nation's future. Furthermore, by first guaranteeing that Joash would be enabled to obliterate the Syrian military threat and then rescinding that guarantee because Joash had unwittingly not hit the ground two or three more times, Elisha acts in an arbitrary and deceptive fashion. Assured of victory Joash has it snatched from his grasp because the small print was not even there for him to read.

Commentators often try to avoid concluding that Elisha is acting arbitrarily by assuming, with no textual warrant, that Joash is somehow lacking in the manner of his response to Elisha's directive to strike the ground with arrows. According to Auld (1986: 200) Joash is 'half-hearted'. According to Jones (1984: 504) 'determination' and 'spirit and energy' are lacking. For Nelson (1987: 218) Joash fails a 'test of aggressiveness' while Skinner (1911) sees a 'lack of grit and determination' and Hobbs (1984: 170) infers that 'he has a tendency to think small'. For Gray (1970: 599) he acts 'perfunctorily, humoring the dying man rather than sharing his conviction'. Kittel (1900: 259) argues that a lack of confidence in both God and in himself led to Joash unconsciously striking the ground with timidity. According to Robinson (1976: 125):

> He must have known that the striking was symbolic and showed that he had not the will or the character to be God's instrument for the task that was being laid upon him.

While such unanimity among commentators over an inference is rare and not easily swept aside, all these interpreters fail to give adequate consideration to the fact that Joash had already been given the assurance of complete victory over Syria. The second symbolic action is ordered without any explanation as to its specific significance and certainly without any indication that the first reassurance could be reversed if Joash did not strike the ground five or six times. Indeed on the analogy of the first symbolic action it would not be out of character for Joash to have struck the ground only once. After all he only had to shoot one arrow. Elisha has already been involved in the deception of an ideological adversary (2 Kgs 8.10), so it would not be surprising, even to the first-time reader, if Elisha used deception again. It is only the presumption of an idealistic portrayal for Elisha which can account for the failure of most interpreters to recognize the arbitrary way in which Elisha treats Joash and thereby the fortunes of the nation as a whole.

A further deception occurs in the account of the three kings' campaign against Moab (2 Kgs 3.16-27). It is not clear in this passage just who is responsible for the deception. It is clear, however, that Elisha leads the three kings to believe that they will be victorious in their campaign against Moab (3.16-19). They are in fact initially successful and their success seems to the first-time reader to be confirmation of the accuracy of Elisha's prophecy (3.20-26). But then inexplicably, by means of an abominable act of child sacrifice by the king of Moab, 'great wrath' comes upon Israel and they return to their land without obtaining the victory they sought and were led to believe was coming (3.27).

The first-time reader is given some clues which warn that trouble may lie ahead for the alliance. For the second-time reader these hints are even more important for the evaluation of the reliability of Elisha in this narrative. By a series of hints the reader is led to see the analogy between this passage and 1 Kings 22 (Auld 1986: 157-58). In both passages the king of Israel initiates a military campaign to retake territory which he once controlled but which has been lost to him. In both cases he invites Jehoshaphat to accompany him in battle. In each passage Jehoshaphat accepts the invitation, using in each acceptance statement the identical sentence, 'I am as you are, my people are your people, my horses as your horses' (1 Kgs 22.4; 2 Kgs 3.7). In both passages Jehoshaphat requests that guidance be sought from Yahweh through one of his trustworthy prophets. In both passages Israel ends up losing the battle and the prophetic guidance which they receive is closely tied up with the issue of prophetic deception. In 1 Kings 22, Micaiah claims that the positive messages that the other Yahweh prophets were giving were prompted by a lying spirit which Yahweh sent to those prophets with the aim of deceiving Ahab. In 2 Kings 3 Elisha's prophecy has a deceptive effect if not a deceptive intention. Given the underhanded way in which Elisha treats his ideological adversaries in 2 Kgs 8.7-15 and 13.14-19, the deceptive effect of his prophecy in this passage, and the analogies noted between this chapter and the deception perpetrated by either Micaiah or the 400 prophets in 1 Kings 22, the second-time reader of this pericope is bound to ask, 'What role, if any, does Elisha play in the deceptive effect of his prophecy in 2 Kings 3?' If he is deceptive on other occasions and the narrative ties Elisha's role by analogy to the deception of the prophet(s) of 1 Kings 22 it is quite natural for the second-time reader to ask whether he is being deceptive here. The difficulty for the reader in coming to a clear-cut answer to this question is tied up with two difficult interpretive problems in the text.

The anticlimax or surprise plot reversal which occurs in v. 27 is difficult to understand.[27] The source of 'great wrath' which comes upon Israel following the sacrificing by the king of Moab of his eldest son and heir apparent is difficult to determine. The noun translated 'wrath' (קֶצֶף) is usually used of divine wrath although the related verb is fairly evenly

---

27. Brueggemann (1982: 16) candidly comments, 'I am at a loss to understand v. 27'.

divided between having divine and human subjects.[28] If a human subject is assumed in this case the obvious candidates are the Moabites, or Israel's other alliance partners from Judah and Edom, perhaps including Israel itself. If a divine subject is assumed the candidates are Yahweh or Chemosh, the Moabite god. Gray (1970: 490) argues:

> This can hardly refer to the indignation of the Moabites, since there is no mention of their further action against the Israelites and their allies, and the only explanation is that it might refer to the anger of God or the anger of Chemosh, which was inferred from the apparently panic reaction and sudden withdrawal of the allies.

But this seems too categorical. It is just as easy for the reader to infer the renewed vigor of the Moabites in battle having witnessed the desperation of their king as it is to infer the panic reaction of Israel and its allies.

There may, however, be some significance in the fact that the wrath only comes upon 'Israel' and not Judah and Edom. It seems unlikely that if it were the wrath of the Moabites it would only be directed at Israel since the Moabite king had just attempted to break through to his neighbor the king of Edom, whose alliance with Israel and Judah was, from his point of view, especially traitorous (v. 26). It also seems unlikely, though not impossible, that the great wrath which came upon Israel came from inside Israel itself. But the reader would in such a case expect different wording.

That the reader would infer that Judah and possibly also Edom[29] turned upon their ally Israel in disgust that Israel's campaign had resulted in child sacrifice is possible, and this view does explain the wrath coming upon Israel rather than the entire alliance. The use of this noun of human anger is, however, rare.[30] While this must not be excluded as a possibility it seems more likely that divine anger is in view here. But if so, is the divine anger that of Yahweh or Chemosh?

Certainly the reader must assume that the king of Moab intended to stir his god Chemosh into action and not Yahweh. Montgomery and Gehman (1951: 363) among others note that the use of child sacrifice in private and political emergencies is found both in Israel and elsewhere. Alternatively, by offering his firstborn son, the king may be assumed to be making up for a deficiency in his prior obedience to his god by now

---

28. See BDB, p. 893.
29. Gray's (1970: 484) conjectural emendation to 'Aram' is unnecessary.
30. Only in Est. 1.18 and Eccl. 5.16.

offering up his firstborn as was demanded by the dictates of his religion. But this does not necessarily mean that the narrator would have the reader infer that Chemosh is the source of the wrath which comes upon Israel. It may be that the king's intention to arouse Chemosh to action is in the narrator's view a futile gesture since Chemosh, unlike Yahweh, was only the figment of the king's imagination. But the text does leave open the possibility that for the narrator Chemosh does exist and is the source of the great wrath that came upon Israel. Nelson (1987: 169-70) helpfully recognizes the openness or ambiguity of the text at this point:

> As though suggesting that certain questions are better left unanswered, the narrator lets us decide. In a sense, whether this was Yahweh's wrath or the wrath of Chemosh does not ultimately matter. Perhaps gods other than Yahweh do exist (cf. Deut. 32.8-9; Dan. 12.13, 20), but the question of who is really God was decided and disposed of by 1 Kings 18. The plot of Kings as a whole makes it clear that Yahweh controls events inside and outside Palestine and that alien armies and foreign kings perform Yahweh's will for good or ill. Perhaps this text is hinting that even foreign gods like Chemosh do so as well.

Ultimately Yahweh is in control of this situation whether or not Chemosh is an intermediary in causing Israel's defeat. So the reader must assume that whether or not Yahweh is the direct source of the wrath, Yahweh did control the outcome of the battle and could have revealed that information in advance through his prophet Elisha had he so desired. The question then becomes whether Yahweh was himself responsible for withholding this information from the kings, and if so, did he act deceptively.

While the reader must assume that Yahweh could have revealed the outcome of the battle to the three kings, it should not be missed that the three kings' original problem and the point of their query to Yahweh was the lack of water (vv. 9, 10). In the part of Elisha's message in which he claims to quote Yahweh (3.16, 17) and does not speak in his own voice the problem of the water is addressed and in its fulfillment resolved in a fairly straightforward manner (v. 20). According to Elisha Yahweh had said:

> [I will] make this dry stream-bed full of pools. For thus says Yahweh, 'You shall not see wind or rain, but this stream-bed shall be filled with water, so that you, your cattle and your beasts may drink' (3.16, 17).

In v. 20 we are informed of the fulfillment:

> And in the morning, when the sacrifice is offered, Look! Water coming from the way of Edom! And it filled the land with water.

If anything Yahweh 'over-fulfilled' Elisha's word for it was not only the dry stream bed (נחל) which was filled with water but the entire land (ארץ).

But the second half of Elisha's message seems to be Elisha's own words and is not fulfilled in such a clear fashion:

> This is a trifling thing in the eyes of Yahweh. He will also give the Moabites into your hands and you will strike every fortified city and every choice city, and every good tree you shall fell; and you will stop every spring of water, and you will mar every good piece of land with stones (3.18, 19).

Elisha's words appear to be his own message added on to the end of what he had received from Yahweh (v. 15).[31] This seems clear not only from the change in person but also from the fact that Elisha directs the military men to violate the Mosaic legislation about only cutting down non-fruit-bearing trees when building siege works (Deut. 20.19, 20). For Elisha to predict or recommend that Moses' rule be broken may make it unlikely that Elisha received that part of his message from Yahweh. Elisha adds to Yahweh's word his own message which promises victory over the Moabites—a victory whose comprehensiveness is indicated in v. 19.

Elisha's message in v. 18 and 19 seems at first to find fulfillment in a fairly straightforward fashion. The red appearance of the water (v. 22) is interpreted by the Moabites as being the blood of the three allied armies who are assumed to have turned on one another (v. 23). This enables the allied forces to trap and defeat the Moabites in a most one-sided fashion. In v. 25 Elisha's prediction in v. 19 is fulfilled. Elisha had predicted that they would: 1) strike *every* fortified and every choice city; 2) cut down *every* good tree; 3) stop up all springs of water; and 4) mar *every* good piece of land. The last three of these four are recorded as being fulfilled in the reverse order in which Elisha mentioned them in a quite precise fashion (v. 25). The inclusive words 'all' and 'every' are used both in the prediction and in the fulfillment.

But the first of Elisha's predictions in v. 19 does not fare so well. He predicted that the allied military forces would 'strike *every* fortified city and *every* choice city' (v. 19). In the fulfillment we are told simply, 'They overthrew *the* cities' (v. 25). The first-time reader might assume that *all* the cities are intended even after Kir-hareseth becomes a temporary plot-complicating exception (v. 25b). But then the city upon whose

---

31. Nelson (1987: 167) refers to vv. 18 and 19 as Elisha's 'interpretation of the oracle'.

wall the king of Moab offers up his son becomes a permanent exception and leads to the undoing of the entire prophecy (v. 27). Elisha's prophecy about the cities is initially fulfilled, even if imprecisely so. But ultimately the prophecy about the cities is wrong and the initial giving of the Moabites into the hand of the three kings (vv. 18, 24) is ultimately reversed. I do not see how the implication that this turns out to be a false or at least misleading prophecy can be avoided. Elisha predicts victory (v. 18), but Israel ends up returning home without that victory (v. 27).

Further, it is precisely that portion of Elisha's message which is given in his own voice (vv. 18, 19) that turns out to be false or misleading. Yahweh promised only water (vv. 16, 17). It is Elisha's supplemental prophecy, given in his own voice, which gives the kings and perhaps the first-time reader the false impression that Israel and its allies will win the battle against Moab.

What does this lead the reader to infer about Elisha? Either he is at least on this occasion an inept prophet who unwittingly gives an inaccurate, incomplete, and misleading prediction; or he is a deceptive prophet who does not give all of the message Yahweh had given him including the most important part—the ultimate outcome of the battle; or he is a reliable prophet, but Yahweh chose on this occasion to withhold the most important information from him so that the three kings end up being deceived into thinking that Yahweh has promised them ultimate victory. In other words either Elisha is inept or deceptive or Yahweh is deceptive.[32]

The narrative does not make clear which of these alternatives is being put forward for the reader. Each of them has its attractions. If Micaiah is to be believed (1 Kgs 22.19-23), Yahweh is not above putting lies in the mouths of those who are at least ostensibly his prophets. If this is the narrator's point of view it would not be surprising if Yahweh only revealed part of the future to Elisha in order to deceive the king of Israel into overconfidence and consequently defeat in battle. While we have already seen reason to treat Micaiah's words with caution at this point,[33] this option should not necessarily be ruled out completely in this instance.

In 2 Kgs 4.27 Elisha claims that Yahweh had hidden the cause of the Shunemite woman's distress from him. If Yahweh did not tell all in that instance it is not out of the question that he has withheld part of the

---

32. That Yahweh might be inept is possible, but I have excluded such a possibility from my analysis by the assumption of the reliability of the narrator and Yahweh.

33. See Chapter 3.

information about the future from Elisha in 2 Kings 3.

The inference that Elisha is somewhat inept as a prophet has in its favor two considerations. The first is that the very part of Elisha's message which turns out to be untrue is given in his own words, which may well imply that he is speaking on his own authority and not merely rewording a revelation received from Yahweh. Also in its favor is the fact to be demonstrated below that as a miracle-worker Elisha does not always perform with complete efficiency. If he is less than completely reliable as a channel of supernatural power perhaps he is less than completely reliable as a prophet.

The inference that Elisha might be acting in a deceptive fashion and deliberately withholding a crucial portion of the message which Yahweh gave him in order to lure the king of Israel into a false sense of security and an unwitting defeat is also possible. The second-time reader knows that Elisha has a track record of using deception when revealing Yahweh's knowledge of the future against his ideological foes (2 Kgs 8.10; 13.14-19). It is quite possible for the second-time reader to infer that this is another instance of this character trait being displayed.

It is not possible to come to a definite conclusion about the reliability of Elisha in this passage. He could be inept. He could be deceptive. He could be reliably relaying Yahweh's word, a word which has a deceptive effect and presumably intention.

*Possible inaccuracy in Elisha's predictions.* We have already seen the inaccuracy in Elisha's prediction of how the armies of the three kings would fare against the cities of Moab (2 Kgs 3.19a, 25-27). There are also other *possible* inaccuracies in Elisha's predictions.

The story in 2 Kgs 8.1-6 is a text in which Elisha could be suspected of inaccuracy, although this is far from certain or likely and only just possible. Two matters could cause disquiet in the reader. The first is the presence of Gehazi having a personal conversation with the king of Israel. In 5.27 after the incident involving the accepting of gifts from Naaman, Elisha says to Gehazi, 'Therefore the leprosy of Naaman will cling to you and your descendants forever'. In 8.1-6, however, Gehazi seems to be perfectly healthy, able to engage freely in ordinary social intercourse, even with the king of Israel.

It is possible, however, that the 'leprosy' which Gehazi contracts from Naaman rendered him only ceremonially unclean and did not place limitations on his social contacts (Hobbs 1985: 68). Another possibility is that these events in 8.1-6 occurred before the events of ch. 5 and the reader is expected to infer this. The reader must assume both that 2 Kgs 8.1-6 is in chronological order and that Gehazi has not already had leprosy in 8.1-6 in order to infer that Elisha's prophecy proved inaccurate. Even if both of these assumptions are accepted it must further be assumed that Elisha's prophecy was never rescinded. It seems more plausible to assume that either Gehazi's leprosy was of a type which did not limit his social interaction with others[34] and its contagious nature was unknown or that the narrative in 8.1-6 records events prior to the cursing of Gehazi in 5.27.

A second potential problem in 2 Kgs 8.1-6 is the length of the predicted famine (seven years). The prediction is never said to be fulfilled and there is no indication that the king of Israel is in the least affected by the famine. In fact when the woman returns from her refuge in the land of the Philistines the king not only restores her land and possessions, he also gives to her the yield of her fields for the seven years while she was gone. The reader might wonder how the fields could yield anything in a seven-year famine.

In addition, the parallels between this passage and Elijah's announcing a drought (1 Kgs 17.1) could be used to infer that Elisha's prediction does not come true. Elisha's famine purportedly lasts seven years while Elijah's drought only lasts one full year and parts of two others (18.1), but in terms of its effectiveness in putting pressure on the king of Israel, Elijah's is far more effective (1 Kgs 18.2, 5-7). At the end of a drought which lasted less than three years, the king of Israel is reduced to scouring the countryside personally to find pasture for his dying horses and seeking to harm Elijah (18.10). By contrast, at the end of seven years[35] of famine which Elisha announces, the king of Israel is sitting at his court asking Gehazi to recount the great deeds of Elisha (2 Kgs 8.4). Furthermore, the accuracy of Elijah's announcement is confirmed in the clearest terms (1 Kgs 17.2-16; 18.1-6), while Elisha's famine is not said to have actually occurred.

The parallels at least show that Elisha's famine, even though promising to be even greater than Elijah's drought (seven years to one year and parts of two others), turns out to be by comparison a rather timid

---

34. A strong presumption that this is so comes from the fact that Naaman's leprosy does not seem to have limited his social activities to any great extent (5.1-5).

35. Joseph's seven lean years, which could only be overcome by careful advance planning, show the potential effect of a seven-year famine (Gen. 41.46-57; 47.13-26).

and ineffectual affair which does not prod the king into repentance or even disturb him into hostility towards Elisha. The only person who seems to suffer from the affair is the Shunemite woman and her family who spend seven years living in an alien environment.

But there are other considerations which make the second-time reader wary of assuming that Elisha's prophecy is being portrayed as being inaccurate. To begin with, a famine even for seven years is not necessarily as severe an ecological crisis as a total lack of moisture for parts of three years. The king may well not have been prodded into repentance or even hostility towards Elisha because the phenomenon was not serious enough. The restoration of the woman's yield may well have been a quite modest gesture.[36] All things considered, there is certainly no necessity or even strong presumption in favor of the reader accusing Elisha of wrongly predicting a seven-year famine.

*The incompleteness of Elisha's prophetic knowledge.* In 2 Kgs 4.27 Elisha complains that Yahweh had hidden the cause of the Shunemite woman's distress. Elisha feels that this is a very important piece of information in the circumstances. This indicates that Elisha could not turn his prophetic knowledge on and off like a tap. Sometimes Yahweh chooses not to reveal everything that is of relevance to a situation. In this sense Elisha's knowledge is incomplete, although there is no reason to believe that this is due to some deficiency on his part.

*Conclusions on problems with Elisha's prophetic knowledge.* We have seen that Elisha is on two or perhaps three occasions personally implicated in the deception of those who were to receive his prophecies. While Elisha is involved in deceiving his ideological foes, not his friends, the second-time reader must compare him unfavorably with Elijah in this regard.

On one occasion part of Elisha's prediction proves inaccurate (3.18, 19). It is also possible that his predictions about Gehazi's and his descendants' leprosy (5.27) and about the seven-year famine (8.1) prove inaccurate, although this is improbable. Elijah's predictions never proved to be inaccurate although one of his predictions was put off to a later generation (1 Kgs 21.20-29). On one occasion Elisha's prophetic knowl-

36. Auld 1986: 178, 179: 'The king even back-dated her restitution of income, in hollow or absent-minded magnanimity—the produce of seven famine-torn years had been small enough!'

edge is incomplete, although this is not something of which the reader would necessarily be critical.

It may be that in 2 Kgs 3.18, 19 Elisha mixes his own words in with the genuine revelation he has received, although again this is uncertain. Elijah also seems to mix his own words in with Yahweh's words (1 Kgs 21.17-26), so even if this was certain, Elisha would not compare unfavorably with Elijah in this regard.

### d. *Conclusions on Elisha the Prophet*

We have seen that Elisha displays a range of supernaturally obtained knowledge which certainly equals and in some respects exceeds that of Elijah. Elisha has knowledge of events and conversations which are spatially removed from him which Elijah does not display. Elisha's predictive ability is more pronounced than Elijah's while both can evidently see the invisible horses and chariots of fire which at least sometimes protected them.

But, as we have seen, there are more problems associated with Elisha's clairvoyant gifts than with Elijah's and these lead the reader to question his complete reliability as a channel of Yahweh's word.

Elisha is thus more and less than Elijah as a prophet, better and worse. His powers exceed those of Elijah, but his personal reliability as a prophet and the moral rectitude in the manner in which he expresses these remarkable gifts is suspect.

### 4. *Elisha the Wonder-Worker*

### a. *Introduction*

Perhaps the most striking and obvious thing about the Elisha narratives is the way in which Elisha performs miracles which parallel incidents in the life of Elijah. And yet the miraculous element is much more prominent in the Elisha narratives. Commenting on 2 Kings 4 Auld (1986: 162) remarks:

> In this chapter we find further examples of Elisha stories very reminiscent of tales told of Elijah. Miracles in fact bulk much larger in the traditions concerning Elisha than in the Elijah material. They are a common enough element in religious story-telling. And I have already suggested that part of their purpose is to heighten the importance of Elisha, and claim for him a stature like that of Elijah. Many may share my suspicion that the more claims are made the less they are to be heeded, and that Elijah continues to shine through as the more important and significant figure of the two.

While Auld is adopting a different methodology from mine I share his suspicion. Elisha performs more miracles and demonstrates a greater range of powers than does Elijah, but the way in which he uses that power and the purposes for which he uses it show him to be an unreliable figure and to an extent an undesirable one.

b. *The Range of Elisha's Miraculous Power*
*Introduction.* The miracles which Elisha performs are greater in number, in the variety of kinds of miracles and in the means used, and in the sheer magnitude of the power which they demonstrate compared with the miracles which Elijah performed.

*The number of Elisha's miracles.* The miracles or apparent miracles[37] which Elijah performed are: 1) the reproducing jar of meal and cruse of oil (1 Kgs 17.8-16); 2) the healing (raising) of the widow of Zarephath's son (1 Kgs 17.17-24); 3) the calling down of fire at Carmel in the contest with the prophets of Baal (1 Kgs 18.20-40); 4) calling down fire on two military men and their regiments (2 Kgs 1.9-12); and 5) crossing the Jordan by means of his mantle (2 Kgs 2.8).

Elisha's miracles are more impressive. The miracles which Elisha performs are: 1) recrossing the Jordan with Elijah's mantle (2 Kgs 2.13, 14); 2) healing the waters of Jericho (2 Kgs 2.19-22); 3) using a curse to manipulate the actions of wild animals (2 Kgs 2.23-25); 4) the never-ending jar of oil (2 Kgs 4.1-7); 5) the giving of a son by a prophetic word (2 Kgs 4.11-17); 6) the raising of that son from the dead (2 Kgs 4.18-37); 7) the removal of death from the pot (2 Kgs 4.38-41); 8) the reproduction of the bread of the first fruits (2 Kgs 4.42-44); 9) the healing of Naaman (2 Kgs 5.1-14); 10) the transference of leprosy from Naaman to Gehazi (2 Kgs 5.19b-27); 11) causing an iron implement to float (2 Kgs 6.1-7); and 12) the striking of the Syrians with temporary blindness (2 Kgs 6.18-23).

It should be remembered that Elijah is also the beneficiary of Yahweh's miraculous deeds. He is fed by ravens for a period of time (1 Kgs 17.2-6) and twice by an angel of Yahweh (1 Kgs 19.4-8). He witnesses the theophanic phenomena of earthquake, wind, fire and still small voice (1 Kgs 19.11, 12) and is enabled by Yahweh to run faster than a chariot over some distance (1 Kgs 18.46). Perhaps most significantly he ends his earthly existence without experiencing death by being taken up into

37. As noted in Chapter 3 some of these may be only apparent miracles.

heaven in a whirlwind (2 Kgs 2.11). But while these instances show the special relationship which Yahweh had with Elijah and his concern for his needs, they do not contribute to the reader's sense of Elijah being a great miracle-worker himself. The miracles which Elisha performed are far greater in number than those which Elijah performed.

*The variety of Elisha's miracles.* Elisha's miracles show a breadth in the variety of materials and persons affected and means used which is greater than that displayed in the miracles of Elijah. Elijah's miracles affect: 1) oil and meal (1 Kgs 17.8-16); 2) a comatose or dead boy (1 Kgs 17.17-24); 3) a drenched altar with a bull on it (1 Kgs 18.38); 4) two captains and their regiments (2 Kgs 1.10, 12); and 5) the Jordan (2 Kgs 2.8). The means he uses to perform the miracles are: 1) his prophetic word (1 Kgs 17.14); 2) bodily contact, with prayer (1 Kgs 17.19-21); 3) prayer by itself (1 Kgs 18.36, 37); 4) his own words (2 Kgs 1.10, 12); and 5) his mantle (2 Kgs 2.8).

Elisha's miracles affect: 1) the Jordan river (2 Kgs 2.14); 2) the water of Jericho (2 Kgs 2.19-22); 3) forty-two youths who mocked him (2 Kgs 2.23-25); 4) oil (2 Kgs 4.1-7); 5) the reproductive processes of a childless woman with an old husband (2 Kgs 4.11-17); 6) the dead son of that woman (2 Kgs 4.18-37); 7) the stew in the famine-stricken sons of the prophets' pot (2 Kgs 4.38-41); 8) the bread of the first fruits (2 Kgs 4.42-44); 9) the body of Naaman (2 Kgs 5.1-14); 10) the body of Gehazi (2 Kgs 5.27); 11) an iron implement at the bottom of the Jordan (2 Kgs 6.1-7); and 12) the eyesight of the Syrians (2 Kgs 6.18-23). Clearly Elisha's miracles affect a greater variety of different objects and persons than do Elijah's.

Elisha also uses a greater variety of means in performing his miracles. Like Elijah, Elisha uses the former's mantle (2 Kgs 2.14). He uses the power of his curse which is carried out by two she-bears (2 Kgs 2.23-25). He uses salt in a new bowl along with a prophetic word (2 Kgs 2.19-21). He uses an entire neighborhood's household vessels (2 Kgs 4.1-7). He uses his own words alone (2 Kgs 4.16) and his prophetic word (2 Kgs 4.42-44). He uses prayer and bodily contact to raise a dead boy (2 Kgs 4.18-37). He uses meal to neutralize a poisoned stew (2 Kgs 4.38-41). He heals Naaman of leprosy by telling him to wash himself in the Jordan seven times (2 Kgs 5.8-14) and gives Naaman's leprosy to Gehazi by mere statement (2 Kgs 5.27). In 2 Kgs 6.1-7 he makes an iron implement float by throwing in a stick at the spot at which it fell into the Jordan and he uses prayer to strike the Syrian army with blindness and to remove that blindness (2 Kgs 6.18-20).

*The magnitude of Elisha's miracles.* In addition to the above the reader comes to the conclusion that Elisha is portrayed as a greater wonder-worker by the cumulative affect of seeing all of Elisha's miracles and his prophetic powers demonstrated.

It seems as though Elisha can do virtually anything. He can do something as difficult as raising the dead (2 Kgs 4.18-37) or something as comparatively simple as making an iron implement float (2 Kgs 6.1-7). He can heal the bad waters of Jericho (2 Kgs 2.19-22) or use the dirty water of the Jordan to heal a leper (2 Kgs 5.1-14). He evidently has power over inanimate objects (2 Kgs 6.1-7), over animals (2 Kgs 2.24) and the bodies of people (2 Kgs 4.18-37; 5.1-14, 27). He can make existing food edible (2 Kgs 4.38-41) and cause an inadequate amount of food to stretch miraculously so that there is a surplus (2 Kgs 4.42-44). He can heal bodily maladies (2 Kgs 5.1-14; 6.20) or cause them (2 Kgs 5.27; 6.18). He can bring about a miracle by quoting a message revealed to him by Yahweh (2 Kgs 2.21); by prayer to Yahweh (2 Kgs 6.18-20); or by simply declaring that a miracle will occur without reference to Yahweh at all (2 Kgs 4.16). By his word he can bring about the birth of a child (2 Kgs 4.17) or cause the death of forty-two boys (2 Kgs 2.24). In fact even after his death his rotting bones can perform miracles (2 Kgs 13.20, 21)! Actually Elisha is very much like Yahweh in that he has the power 'to kill and make alive; to wound and to heal' (Deut. 32.39).

In addition, the miracles of Elisha which most closely parallel the miracles of Elijah seem to be done efficiently by Elisha. In 2 Kings 4 Elisha performs three miracles which have very close and striking parallels to Elijah's miracles. In 2 Kgs 4.1-7, 42-44 in two separate miracles Elisha causes oil and meal to reproduce miraculously as in Elijah's miracle in 1 Kgs 17.8-16.[38] In 1 Kgs 17.17-24 Elijah's healing or perhaps raising the son of the widow of Zarephath is related. In 2 Kgs 4.8-37 Elisha first announces the birth of and then raises from the dead the child of the Shunemite woman. 2 Kings 4 thus forms a direct parallel to 1 Kgs 17.8-24.

When the reader compares the two sections and the roles of Elijah

---

38. Some of the similarities are: 1) oil miraculously reproduces itself; 2) meal; 3) bread or its constituent ingredients is reproduced; and 4) a widow is helped.

and Elisha in them as miracle-workers, the reader concludes that Elisha is portrayed as the more powerful of the two. As we have seen in the analysis of Elijah, Elijah's 'miracle' of the never-ending oil and meal may be only an apparent miracle. Elisha's miracle of the reproducing oil, the closest parallel, is within the story world clearly a genuine miracle.[39] The reader is in no doubt that Elisha performed his miracle while there is some doubt about Elijah's. Additionally Elijah's miracle produced only enough meal and oil barely to keep the woman, her son, and Elijah alive. Conversely Elisha's miracle produced an abundance of oil, as much as the woman and her neighbors could possibly hold in all of the available vessels. The meal and oil in Elijah's miracle were used to make bread. Even if we assume that the miracle was genuine there was only ever just enough to make one more meal. By contrast when Elisha received the bread of the firstfruits and caused it to multiply there was an abundance of food so that there was some left over. The precious meal (קמח) is paralleled by the meal (קמח) which Elisha threw into the pot of poisoned stew (2 Kgs 4.41) in order to remove any harm from the stew. The fact that Elisha could throw away meal while every last crumb was needed by Elijah's widow is perhaps best explained by the difference in the relative desperation of the two situations. In the drought Elijah and the widow were so desperate they needed the last handful, while in the famine (2 Kgs 4.38) food was more plentiful and the meal could be spared.

But it is possible that the juxtaposition of the stories of the poisoned stew (2 Kgs 4.38-41) and the bread of the firstfruits (2 Kgs 4.42-44) offers the reader another possibility. Perhaps Elisha is such a wonder-worker that he can supply a surplus of bread at a moment's notice. In such circumstances throwing away the meal in order to perform a miracle on stew is hardly extravagant.

The wonder-working power of Elisha as over against that of Elijah is also emphasized by comparing the two stories of the healing or raising of the widow of Zarephath's son (1 Kgs 17.17-24) and the raising of the Shunemite's son (2 Kgs 4.8-37). In the first story it is not entirely clear that the boy had died.[40] We are only told that his illness was so severe

39. Auld 1986: 162: 'We noticed as we dealt with [the Elijah miracle stories] that several were open to a miraculous reading although they did not require it. Yet, where Elijah's actions were more ambiguous, Elisha's are quite manifestly those of a wonder worker.'
40. Auld 1986: 111: 'It is true that Hebrew even more than English talks of people reviving without implying that they had been actually physically dead'.

that there was no breath left in him (v. 17a). In the second story we are told in no uncertain terms that he died (v. 20). The ambiguity of the first story makes it unclear whether Elijah has really raised the boy from the dead or merely healed him by a less remarkable miracle. The second story is quite straightforward. The child had died and Elisha raised him from the dead.

The uncertainty which clouds the Elijah stories in 1 Kings 17 casts doubt in the reader's mind as to whether his miracles are actually genuine. While the reader may well conclude that they are, the very raising of the question by the vagueness of the stories creates uncertainty in the reader. By contrast the Elisha stories make it unambiguously clear that his miracles were genuine. If Elijah can raise a boy who has no breath in him but may or may not be dead, Elisha can definitely raise a dead boy. If Elijah can cause enough oil and meal to be miraculously reproduced in order to feed a widow, her son, and himself, Elisha can cause enough bread to be miraculously reproduced to feed 100 men with some left over and enough oil in one day to fill all the vessels in an entire neighborhood. Elisha's miracles are at least as good and probably superior to Elijah's and this leads the reader to infer that Elisha is the greater wonder-worker of the two.

c. *Problems in Elisha's Use of Miraculous Power*
*Introduction*. While Elisha is a greater wonder-worker than Elijah, the way in which he performs certain miracles creates doubt in the reader about his moral reliability and his competence. Elisha sometimes uses his power for morally dubious ends and on a few occasions he appears to have difficulty in getting a miracle to work as he intends.

*The morality of Elisha as a miracle-worker*. We have already seen that in the story of Elisha cursing the youths (2 Kgs 2.23-25) he makes use of his miraculous power for a morally questionable purpose. While the reader does not excuse the behavior of the youths, the curse of Elisha is brought down on children who mock the bald Elisha's personal dignity for being inferior to his hairy master. This contrasts sharply with the parallel Elijah narrative (2 Kgs 1.9-11) and shows that in moral terms Elisha is second best.

*Miracles which do not work the first time*. On two occasions Elisha seems to have a slight difficulty in getting a miracle to work. First, as already noted, the Hebrew text of 2 Kgs 2.14 makes clear that Elisha, in contrast to Elijah, has to strike the water a second time with Elijah's mantle before the Jordan is parted so that he can cross on dry ground.

Secondly, in 2 Kgs 4.8-37 Elisha eventually raises the son which he had originally promised to a wealthy woman of Shunem. While the narrative tension eventually finds its resolution things do not progress in the way in which Elisha and the reader expect. To begin with, the death of the child seems odd since he was born as a result of Elisha's promise. Surely Elisha could not be so heartless as to give a childless woman with an aged husband a son only for that child to die at a very young age. Secondly, Elisha, who promised the birth of the child, knows nothing about his death because 'Yahweh hid it from [him]' (v. 27). Thirdly, Elisha expects that he can heal the child by sending Gehazi merely to lay Elisha's staff upon the face of the dead child but in fact this does not work (vv. 29-31). Finally even Elisha praying and laying his own body upon the child's, much as Elijah had done in the parallel miracle (1 Kgs 17.20, 21), does not work initially (vv. 32-34). After this initial unsuccessful attempt Elisha walks back and forth in the house as though worried that the miracle will not work.[41] Only at the second attempt does the miracle work.

While Elijah stretches himself upon the widow of Zarephath's son three times as opposed to Elisha's two times, there is no indication in 1 Kings 17 that Elijah had any difficulty in accomplishing the miracle. Elisha by contrast is first perplexed that he was not given prescience of the boy's death. He then attempts and fails to raise him with his staff. Next he prays and stretches himself upon the child and when this is unsuccessful he walks about worriedly. Finally he is successful at the second attempt at stretching himself upon the body of the child. The plot complications not only make a more interesting story. They also create the impression in the reader that Elisha has trouble with the miracle. This seems unusual when the second-time reader remembers that the mere touch of Elisha's bones causes a resurrection after his death. Elisha's initial confidence in the power inherent in his staff is shown to be misplaced. Unlike Elijah's mantle or Moses' rod, Elisha's staff has no extraordinary power attached to it. Unlike Elijah, Elisha may show his lack of confidence in his own ability to perform the miracle by walking back and forth.

---

41. Hobbs (1985: 52, 53) says, '"And he walked...back and forth" reflects a sense of agitation on the part of the prophet at the failure to wake up the dead boy'.

While this is a subtle point and should not be stressed too much, Elisha appears to be less in control of the miraculous power than he initially thinks he is and less in control in this narrative than Elijah is in the parallel. On the one hand Elisha possibly performs a more difficult miracle than Elijah (raising a dead boy as compared with healing a child who is perhaps only comatose). But on the other hand more things seem to go wrong for him. He seems to require more effort than Elijah in performing similar miracles. He seems less confident. It is as though he has greater power but less ability to predict the exact effects of that power.

*Elisha's last miracle—2 Kings 13.20, 21.* Most modern Western readers have great trouble with the miracles of Elisha even beyond what I have mentioned for our reader. This is because of the difficulty we have in believing the reports of miracles in general. To me as a modern Western reader I must admit frankly that one of Elisha's miracles seems incredible even if I do my best to suppress the doubts I have as a post-Enlightenment person about the miraculous. The story of the revival of a dead man whose corpse touches the bones of the dead Elisha (2 Kgs 13.20, 21) seems to many modern readers almost farcical.

This story implies that Elisha's miraculous power is of such a magnitude that even his dead body is still infused with power several months or perhaps even years after his death.[42] Elisha could evidently raise the dead not only when he was alive but even after he had died. My difficulty as a modern reader with this story is shared by others. Hobbs (1985: 170) asserts that, 'Such color is hardly historical'. Brueggemann (1982: 49) comments, 'Even at death, he is not finished. Albeit perhaps with unbridled imagination, here Elisha is seen to have power even in death.' Nelson (1982: 218) hints that perhaps the text is not to be taken literally:

> The last story about Elisha (vv. 20-21) is told with his whole career in view
> and again reflects on Israel's situation. The chariots of Israel are gone;
> raiders invade without opposition. Yet the prophet whose career was
> characterized by the gift of life (8.4-5) still gives life even from his bones.

42. The narrative is ambiguous about just how long after Elisha's death this story is supposed to have taken place. The fact that it is specifically Elisha's bones and not just his corpse implies a considerable period of time. For the textual problem see Hobbs 1985: 162.

> The story is told with some humor. Read in context, the impact seems to be that there is hope for Israel yet (cf. vv. 4-5, 23), even though the glory days of Elijah and Elisha are dead and gone.

The possibility that even a hypothetical ancient reader might see some humor in this story cannot be absolutely discounted. Just because the reader is assumed to accept the miraculous in a matter-of-fact way does not mean that we should assume that the reader necessarily reads every miracle story as though it actually happened.

But the danger with this line of reasoning is obvious. As modern scholarly readers we generally distrust miracle reports. But we cannot impute this distrust to our reader, who is a Yahwistic Hebrew living in the post-exilic period. Our suspicions should probably be transferred to the reliability of the narrator.

Even on its own terms, however, this text does lead the reader to infer something about Elisha. Elijah had such stature in Yahweh's eyes that he received the honor of foregoing physical death and was swept up to heaven in a whirlwind. When Elisha's death, marvelous though its sequel may have been, is compared with Elijah's translation, Elisha comes off second best. Elijah forgoes death and transfers at least part of his power to his successor. Elisha dies an ordinary physical death and has no successor, even though his corpse did raise one dead person. With Elisha's death 'the glory days' as Nelson puts it, are over. Elisha did not pass on to others what Elijah had passed on to him.

### d. *Conclusions on Elisha the Wonder-Worker*
Even though Elisha displays greater miraculous power than Elijah, whether that power is measured in terms of the number, variety, or awe-inspiring nature of his miracles, he still does not measure up to the stature of Elijah. Elisha repeats Elijah's miracles by doing them better. But still the reader is not impressed. Elisha's morality in channeling miraculous power is suspect. Even his raw ability is suspect since he has to try two or three times to get some of his miracles to work. When compared to Elijah's, his competence in knowing when not to use his awesome power is doubtful as is his consistency in getting his miracles to happen.

### 5. *Conclusions*

We have seen that Elisha can only be properly evaluated as a character when he is compared to and contrasted with Elijah. The three major aspects of his characterization which we have analyzed each give two different but complementary pictures of Elisha. On the one hand he measures up to and in some respects even surpasses Elijah, but on the other he is decidedly inferior. When the question of reliability is raised he is a decidedly less trustworthy character than Elijah.

On the positive side Elisha is shown to be a fully legitimate successor to Elijah. By retracing his steps and paralleling his actions Elisha takes the place of Elijah. He even surpasses Elijah in that he finishes the work which Elijah had left uncompleted by having Jehu anointed as king of Israel and designating Hazael to be the king of Syria. As a foreteller of the future he certainly equals Elijah in the ability to predict the future accurately and surpasses him in the number of times he displays this ability. He displays the clairvoyant gift of being able to overhear conversations which take place a great distance away, in contrast to Elijah. He, like Elijah, can see the invisible horses and chariots of fire which sometimes protect them. As a miracle-worker he clearly outshines Elijah. He performs more miracles, which are more varied, and which have a greater degree of difficulty than the miracles of Elijah.

But there is a quite noticeable negative element in the portrayal of Elisha and this negative element leads the reader to question his reliability in a way that Elijah's is never questioned. While Elisha retraces Elijah's steps and thus takes his place there are subtle suggestions in the narrative that he differs from Elijah in a negative way. His seemingly selfless loyalty on the Gilgal loop may have a touch of self-interest in it. His miraculous power takes a little extra effort and he uses it to bring about the death of youths who present no real threat to him personally. He is involved in deception in the very act of completing Elijah's work of designating Hazael as king of Syria. His predictions of the future may on occasion be deliberately deceptive or inaccurate in a way that Elijah's predictions never were. His miracles do not always work smoothly, a fact which leads the reader to question his competence. These negative aspects of the portrayal of Elisha lead the reader to cast some doubt on his reliability both in terms of his ability and his morality.

Elisha is thus both more and less, better and worse than Elijah and in terms of the reader's confidence in him as a reliable conveyor of the narrator's point of view is a decidedly less trustworthy character than Elijah.

The type of analysis undertaken in this work, although relatively new to biblical scholarship, has proven its fruitfulness. I have demonstrated that there is plenty of evidence to suggest that given the parameters of my analysis three of the four characters are portrayed as having some significant element of unreliability in them.

In the case of Joshua I have argued that he is portrayed as developing into a thoroughly reliable figure. The reader should not fault him for having to go through the process of maturing as a leader since the narrator gives no indication that he is deficient at any point during the process of development. At the end of his life he is an entirely reliable character whose speech and actions have the narrator's moral and ideological approval.

The reader infers that the deuteronomic Moses is also portrayed as being a fairly reliable character, although we have seen that he may be being portrayed as also having some significant faults.

In the case of Elijah, I have made less definite claims. I have presented an analysis which I find convincing but which is admittedly not the only way of reading the evidence. I have suggested that the reader could well infer that Elijah is portrayed as never really recovering from the experiences at Jezreel and Horeb (1 Kgs 19) and that the issues which caused his downfall there (his fear of Jezebel and his distrust of other Yahwists) never receive resolution. I have also argued that the reader would probably infer that the seemingly idealistic portrayal of Elijah in 1 Kings 17 and 18 is undermined in ch. 19. The second-time reader infers, therefore, that there never really was an idealistic Elijah, only an Elijah who at first appeared to be so. It is possible, although I think unlikely, for the reader to infer that Elijah is portrayed as starting well (1 Kgs 17, 18), stumbling (1 Kgs 19), and then gradually regaining his stature to become once again, at the end of his life, a very reliable character (1 Kgs 21; 2 Kgs 1).

My claims for the reader's likely evaluation of the reliability of Elisha are more definite. I have argued that the reader would and should infer that Elisha is portrayed as a character with serious flaws and weaknesses.

Taken as a whole this work provides a credible argument for suggesting that the 'good guy or bad guy' way of reading biblical characters is inadequate. Three of the four characters analyzed, all of whom are usually assumed to be portrayed as very idealistic characters, have been shown to be portrayed as being unreliable to one degree or another. Here is a further argument for interpreters being open to the possibility of great complexity of characterization and of subtlety in the means used to accomplish that characterization in these narratives.

# BIBLIOGRAPHY

Alter, R.
1981        *The Art of Biblical Narrative* (New York: Basic Books).
Auerbach, E.
1975        *Moses* (trans. R.A. Barclay and I.O. Lehman; Detroit: Wayne State University Press).
Auld, A.G.
1986        *Kings* (DSB[OT]; Edinburgh: St Andrews Press).
Bar-Efrat, S.
1989        *Narrative Art in the Bible* (JSOTSup, 70; Sheffield: JSOT Press).
Barzel, H.
1974        'Moses: Tragedy and Sublimity', in K.R.R. Gros-Louis (ed.), *Literary Interpretations of Biblical Narratives* (Nashville: Abingdon): 120-40.
Beegle, D.M.
1972        *Moses, The Servant of Yahweh* (Grand Rapids: Eerdmans).
Berlin, A.
1983        *Poetics and Interpretation of Biblical Narrative* (Bible and Literature Series, 9; Sheffield: Almond Press).
Bertholet, A.
1899        *Deuteronomium Erklärt* (KHAT; Tübingen: Mohr).
Boling, R.G. and G.E. Wright
1982        *Joshua* (AB, 6; Garden City, NY: Doubleday).
Bronner, L.
1968        *The Stories of Elijah and Elisha as Polemics against Baal Worship* (Pretoria Oriental Series, 6; Leiden: Brill).
Brueggemann, W.
1982        *2 Kings* (Knox Preaching Guides; Atlanta: John Knox Press).
1987        'The Embarassing Footnote', *TTod* 44: 5-14.
Buber, M.
1958        *Moses. The Revelation and the Covenant* (Harper Torchbooks, 77; New York: Harper & Row).
Budd, P.J.
1984        *Numbers* (WBC, 4; Waco, TX: Word Books).
Buis, P. and J. Leclercq
1963        *Le Deutéronome* (Paris: Librairie LeCoffre).
Butler, T.C.
1983        *Joshua* (WBC, 7; Waco, TX: Word Books).
Campbell, J.
1949        *The Hero with a Thousand Faces* (Balligen Series, 17; Princeton: Princeton University Press).

Carroll, R.P.
1969        'The Elijah-Elisha Sagas: Some Remarks on Prophetic Succession in
            Ancient Israel', *VT* 19: 402-15.

Chaney, M.L.
1986        'Systemic Study of the Israelite Monarchy', *Semeia* 37: 53-76.

Chatman, S.
1978        *Story and Discourse. Narrative Structure in Fiction and Film* (Ithaca,
            NY: Cornell University Press).

Childs, B.S.
1979        *Introduction to the Old Testament as Scripture* (London: SCM Press).
1980        'On Reading the Elijah Narratives', *Int* 34: 128-37.
1985        *Old Testament Theology in a Canonical Context* (London: SCM
            Press).

Clines, D.J.A.
1978        *The Theme of the Pentateuch* (JSOTSup, 10; Sheffield: JSOT Press).
1990        *What does Eve do to Help? And Other Readerly Questions to the Old
            Testament* (JSOTSup, 94; Sheffield: JSOT Press)

Coats, G.W.
1988        *Moses. Heroic Man, Man of God* (JSOTSup, 57; Sheffield: JSOT
            Press).

Cohen, S.
1962        'Tishbe', *IDB* 2: 653-54.

Cohn, R.L.
1982        'The Literary Logic of 1 Kings 17-19', *JBL* 101: 333-50.

Coogan, M.D.
1978        *Stories from Ancient Canaan* (Philadelphia: Westminster Press).

Coulot, C.
1983        'L'investiture d'Elisée par Elie (1 R 19,19-21)', *RSR* 57: 81-92.

Craigie, P.C.
1976        *The Book of Deuteronomy* (NICOT; Grand Rapids: Eerdmans).

Cross, F.M.
1973        'The Themes of the Book of Kings and the Structure of the
            Deuteronomistic History', in F.M. Cross, *Canaanite Myth and Hebrew
            Epic. Essays in the History of the Religion of Israel* (Cambridge, MA:
            Harvard University Press): 274-89.

Culler, J.
1975        *Structuralist Poetics. Structuralism, Linguistics and the Study of
            Literature* (London: Routledge & Kegan Paul).

De Vries, S.J.
1985        *1 Kings* (WBC, 12; Waco, TX: Word Books).

Driver, S.R.
1902        *Deuteronomy* (ICC; Edinburgh: T. & T. Clark, 3rd edn).

Driver, G.R.
1961        'Abbreviations in the Massoretic Text', *Textus* 1: 112-31.

Eissfeldt, O.
1965        *The Old Testament. An Introduction* (trans. P.R. Ackroyd; Oxford:
            Basil Blackwell).

Eslinger, L.
    1989        *Into the Hands of the Living God* (Bible and Literature Series, 24; Sheffield: Almond Press).
Fohrer, G.
    1966        'Prophetie und Magic', *ZAW* 78: 25-47.
    1968        *Elia* (ATANT, 53; Zurich: Zwingli-Verlag, 2nd edn).
Fokkelman, J.P.
    1981        *Narrative Art and Poetry: Full Investigation Based on Style and Structural Analysis* (Assen: Van Gorcum).
Forster, E.M.
    1963        *Aspects of the Novel* (ed. O. Stallybrass; Harmondsworth: Penguin Books).
Freedman, D.N.
    1976        'Deuteronomic History', *IDBSup*: 226-28.
Fricke, K.D.
    1972        *Das Zweite Buch den Königen* (BAT; Stuttgart: Calwer Verlag).
Friedman, R.E.
    1981        *The Exile and Biblical Narrative* (Chico, CA: Scholars Press).
Gemser, B.
    1952        'Beeber Hajjarden: In Jordan's Borderland', *VT* 2: 349-55.
Gerbrandt, G.E.
    1986        *Kingship according to the Deuteronomistic History* (SBLDS, 87; Atlanta: Scholars Press).
Gray, J.
    1970        *I & II Kings* (OTL; London: SCM Press, 2nd edn).
    1986        *Joshua, Judges, Ruth* (NCBC; Grand Rapids: Eerdmans).
Gregory, R.I.
    1990        'Irony and the Unmasking of Elijah', in *idem, From Carmel to Horeb. Elijah in Crisis* (JSOTSup, 85; Sheffield: JSOT Press).
Gros-Louis, K.R.R.
    1974        'Elijah and Elisha', in K.R.R. Gros-Louis (ed.), *Literary Interpretations of Biblical Narratives* (Nashville: Abingdon Press): 177-89.
Groves, J.W.
    1987        *Actualization and Interpretation in the Old Testament* (SBLDS, 86; Atlanta: Scholars Press).
Gunkel, H.
    1930        'Mose', in *RGG*.
Gunn, D.M.
    1978        *The Story of King David. Genre and Interpretation* (JSOTSup, 6; Sheffield: JSOT Press).
    1980        *The Fate of King Saul. An Interpretation of a Biblical Story* (JSOTSup, 14; Sheffield: JSOT Press).
    1990        'Reading Right. Reliable and Omniscient Narrator, Omniscient God, and Foolproof Composition in the Hebrew Bible', in D.J.A. Clines, S.E. Fowl, and S.E. Porter (eds.), *The Bible in Three Dimensions. Essays in Celebration of Forty Years of Biblical Studies in the University of Sheffield* (JSOTSup, 87; Sheffield: JSOT Press).

Gutbrod, K.
1951        *Das Buch vom Lande Gottes* (BAT, 10; Stuttgart: Calwer Verlag).
Hamlin, E.J.
1983        *Inheriting the Land. A Commentary on the Book of Joshua* (ITC; Grand Rapids: Eerdmans).
Hobbs, T.R.
1985        *2 Kings* (WBC, 13; Waco, TX: Word Books).
James, H.
1963        *Selected Literary Criticism* (ed. M. Shapira; Harmondsworth: Penguin Books).
Jobling, D.
1986        *The Sense of Biblical Narrative. II. Structural Analysis in the Hebrew Bible* (JSOTSup, 39; Sheffield: JSOT Press).
Jones, G.H.
1984        *1 and 2 Kings* (2 vols.; NCBC; London: Marshall, Morgan & Scott).
Kittel, R.
1900        *Die Bücher der Könige übersetzt und erklärt* (HKAT; Göttingen: Vandenhoeck & Ruprecht).
1929        *Great Men and Movements in Israel* (trans. C.D. Wright and C.A. Knoch; New York: MacMillan).
Kline, M.G.
1963        *Treaty of the Great King* (Grand Rapids: Eerdmans).
LaBarbera, R.
1984        'The Man of War and the Man of God: Satire in 2 Kings 6.8–7.20', *CBQ* 46: 637-51.
Labuschagne, C.J.
1965        'Did Elisha Deliberately Lie?—A Note on II Kings 8.10', *ZAW* 77: 327-28.
Lilley, J.P.U.
1978        'By the River Side', *VT* 2: 164-71.
Lindblom, J.
1962        *Prophecy in Ancient Israel* (Oxford: Basil Blackwell).
Lohfink, N.
1960        'Wie stellt das Problem Individuum-Gemeinschaft in Deuteronomium 1.6-3.29?', *Scholastik* 35: 403-407.
1962        'Die deuteronomische Darstellung des Übergangs der Führung Israels von Moses auf Josue', *Scholastik* 37: 32-44.
1963        *Das Hauptgebot. Eine Untersuchung literarischer Einleitungsfragen zu Dtn 5-11* (AnBib, 20; Rome: Pontificial Biblical Institutute).
Mann, T.W.
1979        'Theological Reflections on the Denial of Moses', *JBL* 98: 481-94.
Margalith, O.
1983        'KELEB: Homophone or Metaphor?', *VT* 33: 491-95.
1984        'The *Kelābîm* of Ahab', *VT* 34: 228-32.
Mayes, A.D.H.
1979        *Deuteronomy* (NCBC; London: Marshall, Morgan & Scott).
1983        *The Story of Israel Between Settlement and Exile. A Redactional Study of the Deuteronomistic History* (London: SCM Press).

McConville, J.G.
1984        *Law and Theology in Deuteronomy* (JSOTSup, 33; Sheffield: JSOT Press).
1989        'Narrative and Meaning in the Books of Kings', *Bib* 70: 31-49.
Milgrom, J.
1983        'Magic, Monotheism and the Sin of Moses', in H.B. Hoffman *et al.* (eds.), *The Quest for the Kingdom of God: Studies in Honour of G.E. Mendenhall* (Winona Lake, IN: Eisenbrauns): 251-65.
Miller, P.D.
1988        'Moses My Servant. The Deuteronomic Portrait of Moses', *Int* 42: 345-55.
1989        *Deuteronomy* (IntBC; Atlanta: John Knox Press).
Miscall, P.D.
1986        *1 Samuel. A Literary Reading* (ISBL; Bloomington, IN: Indiana University Press).
Montgomery, J.A. and H.S. Gehman
1951        *A Critical and Exegetical Commentary on the Books of Kings* (ICC; Edinburgh: T. & T. Clark).
Moore, R.D.
1990        *God Saves: The Elisha Stories* (JSOTSup, 95; Sheffield: JSOT Press).
Moore, S.D.
1988        'Stories of Reading: Doing Gospel Criticism as/with a Reader', in *SBL Seminar Papers* (Atlanta: Scholars Press): 141-59.
Mowinckel, S.
1964        *Tetrateuch-Pentateuch-Hexateuch* (BZAW, 90; Berlin: Töpelmann).
Nelson, R.D.
1981        *The Double Redaction of the Deuteronomistic History* (JSOTSup, 18; Sheffield: JSOT Press).
1987        *First and Second Kings* (IntBC; Atlanta: John Knox Press).
1988        'The Anatomy of the Book of Kings', *JSOT* 40: 39-48.
Newing, E.G.
1988        'The Moses-Yahweh Dialogues and the Confucian Loyal Advisor', *AJT* 2: 413-25.
Noth, M.
1966        *Die israelitischen Personennamen in Rahmen der gemeinsemitischen Namengebung* (Hildesheim: Georg Olms).
1968        *Numbers* (trans. J.D. Martin; OTL; London: SCM Press).
1981        *The Deuteronomistic History* (JSOTSup, 15; Sheffield: JSOT Press).
Ong, W.J.
1982        *Orality and Literacy. The Technologizing of the Word* (London: Methuen).
Peckham, B.
1985        *The Composition of the Deuteronomistic History* (Atlanta: Scholars Press).
Perelman, C.H. and L. Olbrechts-Tyteca
1969        *The New Rhetoric. A Treatise on Argumentation* (trans. J. Wilkinson and P. Weaver; Notre Dame, IN: University of Notre Dame Press).

Phillips, A.
1973        *Deuteronomy* (CBC; Cambridge: Cambridge University Press).
Polzin, R.M.
1980        *Moses and the Deuteronomist* (New York: Seabury Press).
1989        *Samuel and the Deuteronomist* (San Francisco: Harper & Row).
Porter, J.R.
1963        *Moses and the Monarchy. A Study in the Biblical Tradition of Moses*
            (Oxford: Basil Blackwell).
Rad, G. von
1960        *Moses* (World Christian Books, 32; London: Lutterworth).
1962        *Old Testament Theology* (trans. D. Stalker; Edinburgh: T. & T. Clark).
1966a       'The Deuteronomic Theology of I and II Kings', in *The Problem of
            the Hexateuch and Other Essays* (trans. E.W. Trueman Dicken;
            London: Oliver & Boyd): 205-21.
1966b       *Deuteronomy* (trans. D. Barton; OTL; London: SCM Press).
Rendsburg, G.A.
1988        'The Mocking of Baal in I Kings 18.27', *CBQ* 50: 414-17.
Rendtorff, R.
1983        *Das Alte Testament. Eine Einführung* (Neukirchen–Vluyn:
            Neukirchener Verlag).
1990        *The Problem of the Process of Transmission in the Pentateuch* (trans.
            J.J. Scullion; JSOTSup, 89; Sheffield: JSOT Press).
Rimmon-Kenan, S.
1983        *Narrative Fiction: Contemporary Poetics* (New York: Methuen).
Robinson, J.
1976        *The First Book of Kings* (CBC; Cambridge: Cambridge University Press).
Rofé, A.
1970        'The Classification of the Prophetical Stories', *JBL* 87: 427-40.
1974        'Classes in the Prophetical Stories: Didactic Legenda and Parable'
            (VTSup, 26; Leiden: Brill): 143-64.
1988        *The Prophetical Stories* (Jerusalem: Magnes Press).
Salinger, J.D.
1951        *The Catcher in the Rye* (Harmondsworth: Penguin Books).
Savran, G.
1987        '1 and 2 Kings', in R. Alter and F. Kermode (eds.), *The Literary
            Guide to the Bible* (London: Collins): 146-64.
1988        *Telling and Retelling. Quotation in Biblical Narrative* (ISBL;
            Bloomington, IN: Indiana University Press).
Schäfer-Lichtenberger, C.
1989        ' "Josua und Elisha"—eine biblische Argumentation zur Begründung
            der Autorität und Legitimität des Nachfolgers', *ZAW* 101: 198-222.
Schmid, H.
1968        *Mose. Uberlieferung und Geschichte* (BZAW, 110; Berlin: Töpelmann).
1976        *Der sogenannte Jahwist. Beobachturgen und Fragen zur
            Pentateuchforschung* (Zürich: Theologischer Verlag).
Seters, J. van
1975        *Abraham in History and Tradition* (New Haven, CT: Yale University
            Press).

Skinner, J.
1911        *Kings* (Century Bible; Edinburgh: T.C. and E.C. Jack).
Slotki, I.W.
1950        *Kings: Hebrew Text and English Translation with an Introduction and Commentary* (London: Soncino Press).
Smend, R.
1975        'Der biblische und der historische Elia' (VTSup, 28; Leiden: Brill): 167-84.
Sockman, R.W.
1954        'I Kings, Exposition', *IB*: 18-186.
Soggin, J.A.
1972        *Joshua. A Commentary* (trans. R.A. Wilson; OTL; London: SCM Press).
Staley, J.L.
1988        *The Print's First Kiss: A Rhetorical Investigation of the Implied Reader in the Fourth Gospel* (SBLDS 82, Atlanta: Scholars Press).
Sternberg, M.
1987        *The Poetics of Biblical Narrative* (ISBL; Bloomington, IN: Indiana University Press).
Steuernagel, C.
1900        *Das Deuteronomium und Joshua* (HKAT; Göttingen: Vandenhoeck & Ruprecht).
Sumner, W.A.
1968        'Israel's Encounters with Edom, Moab, Ammon, Sihon and Og According to the Deuteronomist', *VT* 18: 216-28.
Thompson, J.A.
1974        *Deuteronomy* (TOTC; Leicester: Inter-Varsity Press).
Tigay, J.H.
1982        *The Evolution of the Gilgamesh Epic* (Philadelphia: University of Pennsylvania Press).
Todorov, T.
1977        *The Poetics of Prose* (trans. R. Howard; Oxford: Basil Blackwell).
Tompkins, J.P. (ed.)
1980        *Reader-Response Criticism. From Formalism to Post-Structuralism* (Baltimore, MD: Johns Hopkins University Press).
Trible, P.
1995        'Exegesis for Storytellers and Other Strangers', *JBL* 114: 3-19.
Turner, L.A.
1990        *Announcements of Plot in Genesis* (JSOTSup, 96; Sheffield: JSOT Press).
1983        *In Search of History* (New Haven, CT: Yale University Press).
Vater, A.W.
1980        'Narrative Patterns for the Story of Commissioned Communication in the Old Testament', *JBL* 99: 365-82.
Walsh, J.T.
1982        'The Elijah Cycle, a Synchronic Approach' (unpublished PhD thesis, University of Michigan).

Weinfeld, M.
1972        *Deuteronomy and the Deuteronomic School* (Oxford: Oxford University Press).
Wenham, G.A.
1981        *Numbers* (TOTC; Downer's Grove, IL: IVP).
Whybray, R.N.
1987        *The Making of the Pentatuech. A Methodological Study* (JSOTSup, 53; Sheffield: JSOT Press).
Wiener, A.
1978        *The Prophet Elijah in the Development of Judaism. A Depth-Psychological Study* (Littman Library of Jewish Civilization; London: Routledge & Kegan Paul).
Woudstra, M.H.
1981        *The Book of Joshua* (NICOT; Grand Rapids: Eerdmans).
Wright, G.E.
1953        'Deuteronomy', *IB*: 311-37.
Würthwein, E.
1984        *Die Bücher der Könige. 1 Kön. 17—2. Kön. 25* (ATD; Göttingen: Vandenhoeck & Ruprecht).
Zimmerli, W. and J. Jeremias
1952        *The Servant of God* (SBT, 20; London: SCM Press).

# INDEXES

## INDEX OF REFERENCES

### OLD TESTAMENT

| Reference | Pages |
|---|---|
| 10.9 | 74, 75 |
| 10.10 | 74 |
| 10.11 | 74, 77 |
| 10.12-14 | 74 |
| 10.12 | 74 |
| 10.13 | 74 |
| 10.14 | 74, 77 |
| 10.15 | 74 |
| 10.16-43 | 74, 77 |
| 10.19 | 77 |
| 10.25 | 76, 77, 83, 85, 87 |
| 10.26 | 85 |
| 10.28-43 | 85, 92 |
| 10.28 | 92 |
| 10.29 | 76, 85 |
| 10.30 | 77, 92 |
| 10.31 | 76, 85 |
| 10.32 | 77, 92 |
| 10.33 | 76 |
| 10.34 | 76, 85 |
| 10.35 | 92 |
| 10.36 | 76, 85 |
| 10.37 | 92 |
| 10.38 | 76, 85 |
| 10.39 | 92 |
| 10.42 | 77 |
| 10.43 | 74, 85 |
| 11.1-20 | 77 |
| 11.1-15 | 75, 92 |
| 11.1-5 | 76 |
| 11.4 | 75, 77, 84, 85 |
| 11.6 | 83, 85, 87 |
| 11.7 | 75 |
| 11.8-15 | 75 |
| 11.8 | 77, 92 |
| 11.10 | 92 |
| 11.11 | 92 |
| 11.12 | 92 |
| 11.13 | 92 |
| 11.14 | 92 |
| 11.15 | 87 |
| 11.16-43 | 75 |
| 11.16 | 75 |
| 11.17 | 75 |
| 11.18 | 75 |
| 11.19 | 75 |
| 11.20 | 80 |
| 11.21-27 | 75 |
| 11.22 | 26 |
| 11.23 | 81 |
| 11.42 | 75 |
| 13.8-33 | 81 |
| 13.13 | 26 |
| 14.6-12 | 81 |
| 14.12 | 81, 84 |
| 14.24 | 81 |
| 15.63 | 26 |
| 16.10 | 26 |
| 17.3 | 81 |
| 17.4 | 81 |
| 17.12 | 26 |
| 17.13 | 26 |
| 17.14-18 | 26, 87 |
| 17.14 | 86 |
| 17.15 | 86 |
| 17.16 | 84, 87 |
| 17.17 | 87 |
| 17.18 | 87 |
| 18.1 | 87 |
| 18.3 | 87 |
| 20.1-9 | 81, 89, 90 |
| 20.2 | 87 |
| 20.7-9 | 90 |
| 21.1 | 82 |
| 21.2 | 82 |
| 21.3 | 82 |
| 21.41 | 82 |
| 21.42 | 82 |
| 21.43-45 | 26 |
| 22.5 | 93 |
| 23.5 | 86 |
| 23.6 | 86, 87, 93 |
| 24.25 | 89, 93, 94 |
| 24.26 | 89, 93, 94 |
| 24.29 | 78, 82 |
| 27.1-11 | 81 |
| 35.1-8 | 81 |

*Judges*

| Reference | Pages |
|---|---|
| 13.15-20 | 152 |
| 20.10 | 71 |

*1 Samuel*

| Reference | Pages |
|---|---|
| 6.14 | 152 |
| 6.15 | 152 |
| 10.8 | 152 |
| 13.8 | 19 |
| 13.13 | 19 |
| 13.14 | 19 |
| 22.10 | 71 |

*1 Kings*

| Reference | Pages |
|---|---|
| 1.2-18 | 135 |
| 2.39 | 106 |
| 2.40 | 106 |
| 4.8-37 | 194 |
| 4.17 | 195 |
| 4.20 | 195 |
| 9.1-13 | 171 |
| 9.7-10 | 172 |
| 12.26–13.6 | 114 |
| 13 | 114, 126, 127, 132, 138, 141 |
| 13.1-32 | 15 |
| 13.9 | 126 |
| 13.11-32 | 129, 132 |
| 13.17 | 126 |
| 13.18 | 126 |
| 13.24 | 126 |
| 13.32–14.20 | 114 |
| 14.1-17 | 171 |
| 14.1-16 | 171 |
| 14.7-11 | 131 |
| 14.10 | 128 |
| 14.11 | 128 |
| 14.21-28 | 114 |
| 15.29-30 | 114 |
| 15.32–16.13 | 114 |
| 16.1-4 | 131 |
| 16.3 | 128 |
| 16.4 | 128 |
| 16.28 | 96 |
| 16.30-33 | 114 |
| 16.31 | 98, 117, 133 |
| 16.34 | 13, 114, 115, 164 |
| 17 | 96, 97, 100, 103, 106, 110, 112, 114, 135, 142, 146, |

# INDEX OF AUTHORS

# JOURNAL FOR THE STUDY OF THE OLD TESTAMENT
## SUPPLEMENT SERIES